MONGOLIAN BUDDHISM
THE RISE AND FALL OF THE SANGHA

MONGOLIAN BUDDHISM

THE RISE AND FALL OF THE SANGHA

by

Michael K. Jerryson

Silkworm Books

ISBN 978-974-9511-26-8

First published in 2007 by
Silkworm Books
6 Sukkasem Road, Suthep, Chiang Mai 50200, Thailand
info@silkwormbooks.com
www.silkwormbooks.com

FRONT COVER: "The Lama Pillager," Political Repression Museum of Ulaanbaatar. Artist and date of painting unknown. Michael Jerryson, 1999

Typeset by Silk Type in 11 pt. Adobe Garamond Pro.

CONTENTS

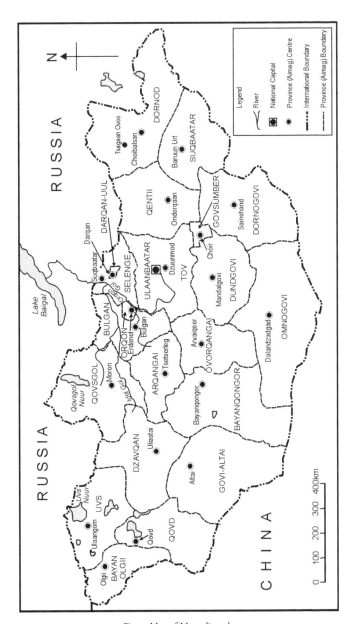

Fig. 1. Map of Mongolia today

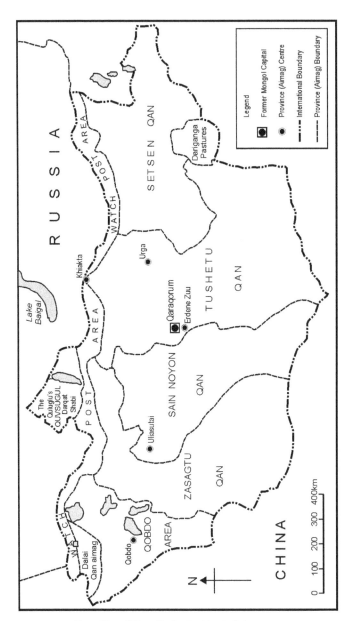

Fig. 2. Map of Mongolia showing historical place-names

1

INTRODUCTION

This work traces the evolution of Mongolian Buddhism as the institutional religion of Outer Mongolia, focusing particularly on its rise and fall from national identification. As a scholar of religious studies, an interdisciplinary field, I draw upon multiple disciplines in this work, in particular, sociology, cultural anthropology, and history.

The term *Mongolian Buddhism* has been debated throughout the Western socioreligious scholarship on Mongolia. The linguistic construction of the word *Buddhism* came into existence through the merging of the Sanskritic verbal stem *buddh-* with the Greek suffix *-ism*, and became a designation for members of a religious community. This referential treatment of Buddhism surfaced in nineteenth-century Europe alongside other religious designations such as Hinduism and Sikhism.[1]

Buddhism was further classified according to the doctrine of its two main schools: Mahayana (the Great Vehicle) and Theravada (the Path of the Elders).[2] These two doctrinal divides, with their inseparable ritual traditions, have spawned numerous subgroups, Zen and Tibetan Buddhism being among the most prominent in the West. Tibetan Buddhism is classified under the umbrella of Mahayana and further demarcated within the tradition of Vajrayana (the Diamond Vehicle). However, this binary categorization has come under close scrutiny due to the fact that the differences between Mahayana and Theravada Buddhism seem comparable to the ones between Mahayana and Vajrayana.[3] Yet among the different taxonomies and a multitude of appellations, one seldom encounters the term *Mongolian Buddhism* in reference to Buddhism in Mongolia. The Buddhist tradition of Mongolia is most often classified as a Vajrayana tradition within the subgroup of Tibetan Buddhism. At other times, Mongolia's Buddhist tradition comes under the umbrella of *lamaism*, another term used to describe Tibetan Buddhism.

Although popular among both historians and anthropologists, the term *lamaism* is problematic. Donald Lopez traces the use of the term to the Manchu empire in 1775 when the Chinese used the term *lama jiao* (lit., a lama or Buddhist teacher) at court.[4] European scholars appropriated the Chinese term and soon *lamaism* became the coined reference for any religion originating from Tibet. However, as Lopez notes, an examination of the term reveals that aside from relegating a Mongolian religion to a subgroup of a Tibetan religion, lamaism lacks relevance to the Tibetans themselves:

> As stated at the outset, there is no term in the Tibetan language for "Lamaism"; Tibetans refer to their religion as the "Buddhist religion" (*sangs rgyas pa'i chos*) or, more commonly, "the religion of the insiders" (*nang pa'i chos*). The use of the term "Lamaism" has been condemned by the spokesman for Tibetan culture. . . .[5]

Due to the various problems associated with the term, *lamaism* is not used in this work; I have used *Mongolian Buddhism* instead, a term invoked by contemporary Mongolian scholars such as Christopher Atwood and Bulcsu Siklos.[6] The use of this term acknowledges Mongolia's religious specificity as evidenced in the work of scholars such as Trevor Ling, who say that Buddhist traditions are differentiated by country.[7]

One other nuanced term in this work is the word *Sangha*, the name denoting Mongolia's Buddhist institution. Mongolian and Tibetan Buddhism generally apply the term Sangha when invoking the three Buddhist refuges, namely, the Buddha, the Dharma, and the Sangha, which in this context represents religious purity. However, the term *Sangha* can be applied outside the strictly theological context to connote a sociological meaning of "a clerical community, congregation, [or a] church."[8] Due to this latter meaning, the term *Sangha* is commonly used to refer to Buddhist monastic institutions in different countries.[9]

Although Buddhism is widely unknown in Mongolia, the region has become a popular tourist destination for travelers who wish to visit the so-called undiscovered Asia. One of the most prevalent guide-books for Western tourists is *Lonely Planet*, which describes Mongolia as a place that stirs up "visions of the untamed." On their website they claim that "even today, outside of Ulaan Baatar you may get the feel-ing you've stepped into another century rather than another country."[10] Yet despite these descriptions, the dominant focal point for current interest in orientalism has been ascribed, almost monopolistically, to its neighbor Tibet.

In the Western mind, Tibetan Buddhism overshadows Mongolian Buddhism. By offering a variety of pop-culture examples, Lopez demon-strates how Tibetan Buddhism has been a part of Western imagination, proclaiming that Tibetan Buddhism "has been *in* for some time."[11] Whereas Tibetan Buddhism has enjoyed continual support by various Western celebrities, groups, and associations, Mongolian Buddhism has found a very different reception. Rudiger Busto, in his examination of Kalmyk Mongols in the United States, finds that the US Mongol com-munity is marginalized due to a more "palatable identity" offered by Tibetan culture. To illustrate his point, he offers the example of the Diluv Gegeen Qotagt, a Mongolian lama who came to the United States in 1931 when religious tensions were escalating in Mongolia. After pos-ing in a picture for the University of California alumni magazine, the Diluv Qotagt was described as a Tibetan in a caption that read, "Dilowa Hutukhu / Grand Lama, Living Buddha, *Tibet*":

> While we cannot fault Bishop for the error—the Dilowa was, after all, in Berkeley to help produce a Tibetan-English dictionary—the slip from Mongol to Tibetan is just one example of how the Mongolian community in the US has been eclipsed by Tibetan identity, religion, and politics.[12]

Although Busto's example was from a magazine over fifty years ago, little has changed in the way that Mongols or Mongolian Buddhism have been portrayed.

Fortunately, this has not deterred academics from advancing Mon-golian scholarship or creating Mongolian organizations such as the Mongolian Society. Within the field of Mongolian studies, academic scholarship has uniformly and rightfully acknowledged the importance of Buddhism in the sociopolitical process. In the early 1900s, the Mongolian Sangha was the most dominant political influence in Outer Mongolia, having influenced cultural and social arenas for over a thousand years. However, after the Mongolian revolution of 1921, the Mongolian Sangha met its nemesis in socialism.

Early socialist efforts to eradicate the Mongolian Sangha were so thorough that as late as 2004 many reopened monasteries are without teachers, history, and books. A dramatic demonstration of how influential Buddhism was to Mongolia's culture and history is seen in its revival. One of the leaders of the new Mongolian Buddhist movement, Bakula Rinpoche, is not a Mongol. He is, in fact, a Ladakhi who served as India's ambassador to Mongolia. This cultural distinction highlights the crucial absence of Buddhism in recent generations and, in turn, offers a simple answer to the question of why the eradication of Buddhism was not fully recognized previously. During the socialist period, critical evidence surrounding Mongolian Buddhism's demise was completely inaccessible to scholars outside Mongolia.

Until 1990, Western scholars had no substantive means of gauging the magnitude of the socialist revolution and its impact on Mongol government statistics. This data was located exclusively in the socialist regime's archives.[13] Mongol scholars during this period were not permitted to discuss the devastation of the Mongolian Sangha in their work unless their premises were consistent with socialist propaganda. Therefore, any information that made its way out of the country failed to provide a complete account of the devastation of Mongolian Buddhism and the means that was used to efface Buddhism socially, politically, and economically.

Historians continue to debate why certain events occurred in Mongolia. While it is evident that the socialist regime, the Mongolian People's Republic, implemented orders to eradicate the Buddhist presence in Mongolia, it is unclear who promulgated them. Some assert that a segment of the Mongol government, the Dotood Yaam (Ministry of Internal Affairs, the "Green Hats"), was the force behind the orders. Others implicate Stalin and the Soviet intelligentsia for instituting this outright war on the Mongolian Sangha.

Many scholars have documented the transformation of Mongolia from a Buddhist society to a socialist entity, but none have focused exclusively on the changing role of Buddhism in Mongolian forms of governance and power. One is left, then, to rely on general works documenting Mongolian history and culture. George G. S. Murphy's *Soviet Mongolia* (1966) and Robert Rupen's *How Mongolia Is Really Ruled* (1979) and *The Mongolian People's Republic* (1966) have focused on Mongolia's political history and its relationship to the Mongolian Sangha. These writings largely discuss the political history of the twentieth century prior to Mongolia's democracy. For example, D. Dashpurev's *Reign of Terror* (1992) offers an updated account of the acts and effects on Mongolian Buddhism during the socialist period, but because it follows the same political historical timeline of Murphy and Rupen, it fails to provide a comprehensive measure for the evolution of the Mongolian Sangha.

Other attempts to chronicle the Mongolian Sangha have been impeded by the limited data available during the socialist era. Sechin Jagchid and Paul Hyer's *Mongolia's Culture and Society* (1979) has a remarkable amount of information pertaining to early Mongol life and culture, but has relatively little to say on the socialist repercussions on Mongol identity. Another work is Larry Moses's *The Political Role of Mongol Buddhism* (1977) , which reviews the political climate of the Mongolian Sangha in a comprehensive historical framework. Unfortunately, this work betrays a reactionary perspective that is at times both inaccurate and incomplete.[14]

Many contributions to the understanding of Mongolian history and culture have been made in recent years. Bat-Erdene Batbayer's (Baabar) *Twentieth Century Mongolia* (1999), edited with Christopher Kaplonski, is a historical and political account of Mongolia from the thirteenth century until the socialist period.[15] Uradyn E. Bulag's *Nationalism and Hybridity in Mongolia* (1998) and Christopher Kaplonski's *Truth, History and Politics in Mongolia* (2004) discuss the development of Mongolian nationalism and identity, focusing on the evolving Mongol identity amid political transformations.

C. R. Bawden's work has been a bountiful source of information for historians, sociologists, anthropologists, and religious scholars alike. In

The Modern History of Mongolia, Bawden begins his historical review in the sixteenth century and concludes it in the twentieth century, offering some data concerning the religious purges of the 1930s. Much of Bawden's work addresses the Mongolian Sangha during this time period, and his analyses are still applicable to any current study of the Mongolian Sangha.

In the examination of the history of the Mongolian Sangha and its interaction with politics, the works mentioned above provide general historical and cultural information necessary in tracing the Sangha's evolution. Additionally, scholarship by socialists, albeit restricted and at times heavily influenced by propagandist claims concerning the Mongolian Sangha, nevertheless provides important information on the economic sphere as it relates to the Sangha and politics.

In the present volume, chapter 2 places Mongolian Buddhism in its historical context and classifies the various waves of Buddhist influence thereafter. Chapter 3 documents the emergence of the Mongolian Sangha during the second wave of Buddhist influence.

Chapter 4 traces the historical placement and development of Mongolian socialism and its impact on the Mongolian Sangha. Chapters 5 and 6 describe the metamorphosis of the Mongol polity from Buddhism to socialism, paralleling the fall of the Mongolian Sangha with the corresponding rise of the Mongolian People's Revolutionary Party.

Chapter 7 presents a juxtaposition of the various eras—the demise of socialism, the introduction of democracy, and the reemergence of the Mongolian Sangha. Portions of this work concerning the socialist and postsocialist periods draw upon translations and fieldwork by the author in 1997 and 1999. Much of the fieldwork is reflected in the personal narratives found in the appendix, many of them recounting events that occurred during the socialist period. These narratives, while subjective, shed light on otherwise ambiguous or unknown details during this period. Postmodernist critique at times has questioned the use of personal narratives in history; however, as Richard Evans states, they are quite applicable to historical truth.[16]

Currently, new evidence is being gathered on the socialist and postsocialist periods of Mongolia. Ole Bruun's *Precious Steppe: Mongolian*

Nomadic Pastoralists in the Age of the Market focuses on the new forms Buddhism has taken in Mongolia's political climate since the socialist period. Christopher Kaplonski, a cultural anthropologist of Mongolia, who has extensively researched the political repression during the socialist period, has written another pertinent work, *Mongolia: Democracy on the Steppe: Post-communist States and Nations*. Finally, Prime Minister Q. Choibalsan's administrative aide, P. Shadgarsren, has published a work entitled *Minii Medeq: Marshall Q. Choibalsan,* which offers an inside account of Prime Minister Choibalsan's role during the decimation of the Mongolian Sangha.

This new scholarship comes at a crucial time as the Mongols face an important juncture in the reconstruction of their cultural identity. Some Mongols are curious about the past, but others are unwilling to look back upon the devastation. Unfortunately, Mongolia may not have the time to wait for a resolution of this ambivalence. Mongol youth, disadvantaged by a lack of recognized heritage, seem more interested in capitalism and Christianity. Because of the eradication of historical records and relics previously stored in monasteries, Mongolia now faces a void of information, just as it begins to delve into its own past. In many ways, contemporary academic studies of Mongolian politics and religion serve as a critical bridge in rediscovering Mongolia's cultural heritage.

Despite these obstacles, Mongolia is beginning in its own way to reflect upon its past. Mongolian newspapers are beginning to print personal accounts from the socialist period. An organization established by a Tibetan lama, Preservation of Mahayana Buddhism, hopes to reacquaint Mongolian youth with their history and promotes a national television series devoted to the history and viability of Mongolian Buddhism.[17]

By comparison, the focus of this book is perhaps more secular. It is my objective to trace historically the development and metamorphoses of the Mongolian Sangha, from the origins of Mongolian Buddhism during the thirteenth century until its deconstruction and later revival in the twentieth century. The unfolding of Mongolia's history reveals not only the diversified elements of the religious institution, such as its impact on the arts, medicine, and education, but also and more particularly its convergence with Mongolian culture and identity.

NOTE ON MONGOLIAN WORDS

The following chapters use a slightly different style for transliterating the Mongolian Cyrillic alphabet from the one normally used in European and US scholarship. Instead of transliterating the Cyrillic letter *x* as *kh*, this book uses the letter *q*, because this sound in English is closer to the Mongolian pronunciation. Thus, words such as *khan, Karakorum,* and *Khubilai* will appear as *qaan, Qaraqorum,* and *Qubilai,* respectively.

In general, I use the Cyrillic Mongolian instead of the Classical Mongolian alphabet for English transliterations throughout this book. In the past, some scholarship generated on Mongolia contained transliterated contemporary names based on Classical Mongolian spellings. For example, the Classical Mongolian letter for *n* has an "ng" sound and can be transliterated as such. However, because the Classical Mongolian pronunciation is not relevant to twentieth-century Mongolia, I use the Cyrillic Mongolian alphabet for contemporary names, as in *Choibalsan,* but Classical Mongolian for names and titles for people prior to the 1900s, such as *Chinggis Qaan.*

Regional specialists will detect a few other different transliteration styles for Cyrillic names in this text. The Mongolian word *baatar* (hero) is found in personal names and place-names throughout Mongolia, such as Suq*baatar* (The Axe-Hero) and the capital, Ulaan*baatar* (The Red-Hero). Although this latter is often written Ulan Bator by dropping or changing vowels and dividing words, I write it according to the Mongolian spelling.

My decision to use Cyrillic spellings corresponds with the current linguistic climate in Mongolia. Since March 25, 1941, the Mongolian government has based the Mongolian script on the Cyrillic alphabet.[18] Most of the definitions and Cyrillic spelling in this book are based on Gombojab Hangin's *Mongolian-English Dictionary.* Some words, such as *khutukhtu,* are not contemporary and are spelled in accordance with Lessing's Classical dictionary.

There are some Classical Mongolian words commonly found in the English language that do not reflect their true spelling. For example, *khutukhtu* when transliterated from the Classical alphabet should be spelled *qotagt*, *Jebtsundamba* is spelled *Jabzandamba*, and *Genghis* should be spelled *Chinggis*. I have chosen to to be true to the Mongolian spellings from the Classical language period. One other common word in the English language, *lama*, is spelled in Mongolian as *lam*; to ensure clarity for a Western audience it will be written as *lama*.

Lastly, in some of my interviews, personal names appear without a surname, since Mongolian surnames are only a twentieth-century phenomenon, usually a result of inserting a parent's name.[19] Some names appearing throughout the autonomous and socialist periods in Mongolia (1911–1990) are extremely common. It is, therefore, unclear from the limited interviews whether, for example, the Losol in the appendix is the same Losol as the revolutionary hero.

2

EARLY MONGOLIAN BUDDHISM (1246–1691)

In order to pinpoint an exact date for the origin of Mongolian Buddhism, one must first choose from among a myriad of proposed dates, and then carefully delineate Mongolian Buddhism from shamanism. When tracing the development of Mongolian Buddhism, it is important to remember that, although Mongolian Buddhism traces its roots to Tibet and shares an intimate history and ideology with Tibetan Buddhism, it is in its own right distinctly Mongolian. One of the many traits attributed to Buddhism's success within Asia has been its ability to absorb local deities into its own pantheon, resulting in a new Buddhism.

MONGOLIAN BUDDHISM

The indigenous religion of Mongolia prior to the coming of Buddhism is referred to as *shamanism*.[1] Shamanism in Mongolia is not routinized in the same way as Buddhism. If we were to examine the entirety of Mongolian shamanism, we would find that shamanism is found in rituals with no institutional structure beyond its specific locality, although scholars such as Caroline Humphrey maintain that shamanism has this potential when it plays a role in state politics.[2] In contrast, Buddhism's comprehensive metaphysical and ethical textual doctrines developed alongside the institution of the Sangha. This difference between shamanism and Buddhism is a self-conscious one among the traditions. Christopher Atwood writes, "This difference was recognized by the shamans themselves, who opposed their 'scriptureless faith' to the written doctrines of the Buddhist clergy."[3]

The two religions seem to converge at times in the study of Central Asian religions. The term *shamanic Buddhism* arises when investigating Tibetan Buddhism and its relationship with Bön, the indigenous religion of Tibet. In his anthropological work on Tibet, Geoffrey Samuel stresses the distinction between the clerical and shamanic forms of Buddhism, delineating them through a comparative metaphysical model and highlighting their separate worldviews. Yet the variation within Buddhisms alters such parameters, impacting upon the variables of comparison.[4] Whereas orthodoxic exploration was part of the daily life of a Tibetan lama, Mongolian Buddhism for the lamas was more orthopraxic.[5]

Mongolian doctrine was of no concern to the Buddhist missionaries from Chinese, Tibetan, and Mongolian monastic centers; rather, like Mongolian Buddhism itself, the missionaries focused on ritual. Throughout Mongolia lamas promoted Buddhist apotropaic rituals during the nineteenth century in an effort to reform the laity's so called evil ways.[6] Ritual, according to J. Z. Smith, is not a reaction to the sacred or an explanation of the sacred, but rather is a process by which something or someone is *made* sacred.[7] Therefore, because of the significance of ritual in the Mongolian context, it is perhaps more useful to distinguish shamanism and Buddhism through the instigators of the ritual, that is, the religious actors who implement the rituals and perform them according to authoritative or traditional patterns.[8] For Mongolian Buddhism, religious authority rests in the lamas, whereas for shamanism it lies with the *böö* (the Mongolian shamans).[9]

The contest for authority between Buddhist and other religious actors was present during the development of the Mongolian Sangha. Many Mongolian deities were so revered by the Mongol laity that the Mongolian Sangha found it nearly impossible to force the laity to decide between traditional beliefs and Buddhism. Deities from Mongolian practice and rituals were reclassified and absorbed into the Buddhist pantheon. One well-known example is the White Old Man, an exclusively Mongolian deity who was gradually introduced into Mongolian *tsam* (sacred ritual dance).[10] In the early twentieth century the thirteenth Dalai Lama, Thubten Gyatso, included this Mongol deity in a *tsam* (*cham* in Tibetan), thereby recognizing the legitimatization of the

White Old Man in Mongolian Buddhism.[11] Rituals, which are at the core of Mongolian Buddhism, became the locus for reinterpretation.

Another example of this can be found in cosmology. Although the Mongols readily adopted Buddhist soteriological notions of karma and reincarnation, they stood steadfast in their veneration of the local *tenggeri* (heaven), prompting Buddhism to incorporate this sacred locale within its cosmology.[12] Atwood believes that the development of Mongolian Buddhism springs largely from a linguistic and environmental reformation of ritual: "[M]any of the pioneer missionaries felt the need to adapt Buddhism to the Mongolian environment. Neichi Noin, who converted the East Mongols, emphasized the importance of giving rituals in Mongolian, not Tibetan, as well as modifying the music to suit Mongolian tastes."[13]

In his examination of the Mongolian fire cult, Atwood notes its full integration into the Buddhist pantheon.[14] These encounters with Mongol rituals and shamanism have helped to delineate Mongolian Buddhism from other forms of Buddhism in Asia.

Although Larry Moses speculates that Buddhism was not politically effective in Mongolia prior to Chinggis Qaan, there is now sufficient information to prompt reconsideration of this thesis.[15] There is evidence to indicate that Buddhism was present in Inner Mongolia and the southern regions of what is now Outer Mongolia. Why or how Buddhism was introduced prior to the thirteenth century remains uncertain. Mongolian ecclesiastical scholars offer the earliest dates as around the first century CE, but these dates remain largely unsubstantiated.[16] N. Tsultem cites Soviet archaeologist records, which place Buddhist schools in Mongolia as early as the ninth century CE.[17] Bawden posits similar dates, citing other archaeological finds.[18] For the present, it seems most accurate to say that Mongolia's conversion to Buddhism was gradual and stemmed from nearly seven hundred years of Buddhist influence.[19]

This conversion can be traced through well-documented insurgences, which emerged either by political means or through a Mongol figurehead. Although the primary focus is political, there are important social factors that relate to Mongolian Buddhism as well. Mongolian Buddhism provided a venue for art, paintings, sculpture, medicine, astrology, and most important, education. Chronicling the growth of Mongolian Buddhism and its Sangha serves as a window for understanding the cultural history of Mongolia. Each new surge of Buddhism was followed by some kind of recession. The formation of the Mongolian Sangha occurred in four distinct surges or waves, with each wave represented by a key political figure.

The first wave occurred in the thirteenth century, the second in the sixteenth century, a third in the eighteenth century, and a fourth wave that began in the early 1990s is still in progress.[20] Insufficient evidence at this time prevents the assertion of a fifth wave, which may have occurred prior to the other four. Hegemonic Buddhism dates to the rule of Gödan Qaan, the second son of Ögedei, so questionable claims concerning the origins of Mongolian Buddhism prior to this time must be put aside for now. Thus the first wave (Gödan's rule) in the thirteenth century was not extensive and served more as an introduction for the Buddhism to come.[21] I call the period of Gödan's rule the first wave.

In 1246 CE the leading representative from Sa-skya-pa Tibetan Buddhism, Sa-skya-Pandi-ta-Kun-dga'-rGyal-mTshan (Sakya Pandita), and his two nephews were summoned to the court of Gödan Qaan. Gödan Qaan, the grandson of the late Chinggis Qaan, was in charge of the empire's invasions into Central Asia and northern Tibet. When Sakya Pandita and his two nephews, Phyag-na-rdo-rje' and 'Phags-pa-blo-gros-rdo-rje ('Phags-pa), arrived at Gödan's court, they officially surrendered Tibet to Gödan. Their presence at court also served to pique Gödan's interest in Buddhism.[22]

In a number of ways, this meeting was as much a political maneuver as it was a religious encounter.[23] In Mongolia, the Mongol court was unquestionably strong, but it lacked a correspondingly strong religious authority. A religious endorsement would tip the balance in favor of Gödan as he attempted to expand his rule within the Mongol empire.[24] Similarly, as the Mongols had recently conquered Tibet, it was to the advantage of Sa-skya-pa to win the Mongols' patronage. In Tibet there was no unified political front, but the country was replete with religious authorities. A political endorsement would serve to distinguish Sakya Pandita's Sa-skya-pa religious school from the competing Nying-ma, bKa'-rgud and Bön schools. In short, each side needed the other's strength. In order to rule their countries, a religio-political connection was formed between the two leaders. This established connection by no means put a stop to other Tibetan schools' solicitation of Mongol favors. Tibetan ecclesiastical politicians often played a role in the Mongol court, as they vied for positions within it. Lamas from the bKa'-rgud school, specifically from the Karma-pa sect and the Sa-skya-pa school, traveled to the Mongol courts by invitation from Mongol heads of state.[25]

In 1249 Gödan was initiated into and became a protector of Tibetan Buddhism. Once again he summoned Sakya Pandita and this time appointed him vice regent of Tibet.[26] Not long afterward, in 1251, a nephew of Ögedei's, Möngke Qaan, who was leading renewed invasions into Tibet like his predecessors,[27] was in the midst of choosing a state-sponsored religion. Möngke Qaan had been exposed to different religions since his youth (his mother was a Nestorian),[28] and his decision proved pivotal, not only because of Möngke's stature but also because his city, Qaraqorum, had been the capital of the Mongol dynasty since the reign of Ögedei. Like other Mongol rulers, Möngke had the power to enforce religious edicts that affected his nomadic area, and as a result he was courted by many different religious groups.

For several years Möngke had allowed different faiths to practice and proselytize in the capital. There were, according to the European monk Rubruck, "a Christian Church, two Muslim mosques, and twelve temples of 'idolaters' (i.e., Buddhists)."[29] Finally, in 1254 Möngke mandated that several religious debates take place, the first between the polytheists (Taoists and Buddhists) and the monotheists (Muslims and Christians). At the end of the first debate, Rubruck and his Islamic counterpart were asked to leave Qaraqorum. Two years later, Buddhist arguments were advanced by 'Phags-pa and the purported insubordination by the Taoists led Möngke to give his support to Buddhism.[30]

After Sakya Pandita's journey to the Mongol court, one of his nephews, the young 'Phags-pa, was raised in Gödan's court. In 1253 Qubilai, soon to be the next *qaan* of the Mongol empire, met 'Phags-pa while visiting Gödan. It could be inferred that the presence of 'Phags-pa at the court of Gödan demonstrated Gödan's political might. During this period, after the death of Ögedei, Ogedei's sons were vying for control. Thus, Qubilai was very conscious of any disparities between himself and his political contenders.[31] It was necessary for Qubilai to distinguish himself and establish his credibility among the Mongols. He saw in 'Phags-pa someone who could be either a threat to his supremacy, or a means of acquiring it. Qubilai seized 'Phags-pa from Gödan and installed the Tibetan lama in his own imperial court. Through the years an older and more diplomatically versed 'Phags-pa continued to influence the Mongols, and this constituted the final element of the first wave of Buddhism into Mongolia.

Qubilai was converted to Buddhism by the Chinese monk Hai-yün in 1242 CE, approximately ten years prior to meeting 'Phags-pa.[32] It is possible that Qubilai, himself a shrewd political strategist, may have chosen to promote 'Phags-pa and his Buddhism for reasons other than his personal theological interests. Qubilai, founder of the Yüan dynasty, had moved the political capital of the Mongols from Qaraqorum to Peking. Under these circumstances, Qubilai needed to have his political role socially recognized, and that was made possible through Buddhism. Through Buddhist edicts, now it was possible for a simple nomad to be transformed into a *cakravartin*, a preordained ruler.[33] At this time, traditional Chinese philosophies were inflexible and presented Qubilai with political and social obstacles. It was Buddhism that enabled Qubilai and others who were viewed as outsiders to breach those dogmatic political and social boundaries. Moses claims that "the alternative of Buddhism offered an acceptable solution for dissidents within China, despite its barbarian support. Qubilai understood these prerequisites for barbarian rule perhaps better than any other barbarian ruler until the Manchus in the sixteenth century."[34]

'Phags-pa played an important role in this political endeavor by religiously legitimating the transformation. It was to Tibet's advantage to keep the Mongol empire Buddhist. Furthermore, he could secure the Sa-skya-pa legitimacy in Tibet through its ties to the Mongol court.[35] In this way, Buddhism became tied inextricably to the Mongol polity very early on. While Buddhism prospered in China proper, circumstances were different in Mongolia. Moving the capital from Qaraqorum to

Peking and the decline of the Mongol polity after the reign of Qubilai led to Buddhism's eventual decline in Mongolia.[36]

Reasons for this decline are numerous. However, it must be pointed out that within the Mongol empire at this time, Outer Mongolia experienced a drastic reduction in trade. Monasteries that formerly had thrived during Qubilai's rule were now dependent on the wealth of cities, visitors, and merchants, as it was the large laity who primarily sustained the lamas through meritorious contributions. The loss of trade in Mongolia dramatically reduced urban activity, which, in turn, reduced support of the monasteries.

Another reason for the brevity of the first wave not directly related to imperial designs was the social stature of Buddhist converts, because the conversions that occurred during this phase appear to have affected primarily the wealthy and political figures.[37] With the loss of their political power and the consequent loss of wealth, those who were most influenced by the first wave were either disenchanted with the economic conditions of the region or with Buddhism. Not surprisingly, by 1374 the extent of Buddhism had dwindled in the western region of Mongolia, the region closest to Tibet, and in the east where indigenous shamanism had regained its foothold.[38] As Bira notes, this fractious environment continued well into the fifteenth century:

> Mongolia, still not recovered from the ruinous consequences of the long years of wars of conquest, entered onto a lengthy period of political disintegration and of internecine wars, which were prolonged until the end of the 16th century.[39]

Yet Buddhism had not disappeared entirely. According to Moses, the Qalq Mongols, mostly situated in the central region of what is now Outer Mongolia, retained some Buddhist influences and continued to practice Karma-pa into the early fifteenth century. Some Mongolian nobility maintained their veneration of Buddhism until the advent of the second wave.[40]

THE BIRTH OF AN INSTITUTION

The second wave brought with it many changes, among them the development of a cohesive and organized institution, the Mongolian Sangha. Buddhist monasteries and lamas were present in Mongolia prior to 1264 CE; however, with Qubilai's move of the capital from Qaraqorum to Peking, the religious institutional structure of the first wave formed its roots primarily within China. Jagchid and Hyer posit that "landed institutions did not arise until the latter part of the sixteenth century, with the establishment of Buddhist temples."[41] This second coming of Tibetan Buddhism and its institutional thrust became entrenched in Mongolian culture.[42] The second wave was catalyzed by Altan Qaan[43] of the *tumet* (court), who had a significantly greater impact on Mongolian culture in terms of its surviving religious structures and influence upon the lay community.[44]

Since the first wave, the educational system had changed with gradual trends toward learning Tibetan and lama pedagogy.[45] George Cheney credits much of this trend to the dGe-lugs-pa and their focus on pedagogy among the Mongols, and states that "lamas who entered the [dGe-lugs-pa] type of monasteries received their early education by individual study or by attending school-type monasteries in their early years."[46] As Buddhism became more institutionalized, the educational sphere was dramatically affected. Educational institutions that were modeled on schools in Tibet and the Tibetan language threatened to eclipse the traditional study of the Mongolian language.[47] Mongol historians who emerged during this period reframed history against a Buddhist backdrop. Like most historians from this period, Guoshi Chorji was also a lama and was considered the most prominent Mongol historian of his time.[48] Bira, who was well aware of the Sangha's impact on the historical writings of this era, interprets that "Guoshi Chorji regards the history of Mongolia as an inseparable part of the history of the Buddhist world."[49]

Buddhist medicine, which had gained popularity during the first wave, rose in stature during the coming of the second wave, as did its institutional structures. Jagchid and Hyer note that "at the end of the sixteenth century, Tibetan Buddhism became almost universally adopted in Mongolia, and the lama *emchi* or doctor came to hold a prominent position."[50] Even though Jagchid and Hyer characterize the Buddhist medicinal practices as Tibetan, they also give evidence to the changes it underwent in Mongolia.[51]

During this period Mongol polity lacked cohesion. It was perhaps due to this lack of unified political structure that the nascent Mongolian Sangha prospered.[52] Just like the political structure prior to Chinggis Qaan, there were multiple feudal factions that fought over demarcations and social status rather than a single governing body.[53] In the midst of this relative anarchy, Altan Qaan, a powerful Mongolian prince, recaptured Qaraqorum from the Oirats, a western Mongol ethnic group, in order to extend his rule throughout Mongolia. Legitimacy for his rule required the possession of Qaraqorum, the traditional capital of Mongol rulers.[54] Thus, Altan's next step was to receive recognition from the religious community in a process strikingly similar to that of Gödan and Qubilai. Just as Qubilai had conquered the Chinese by moving into the Chinese capital of Peking, and legitimizing his rule through Buddhism, Altan attempted to do the same with the Mongols. In 1570, the Chinese approached the sixty-three-year-old Altan and offered him the title of Shun-iwang, the Rightful Prince.[55]

Altan had led campaigns into Tibet and was aware of the religious status of a particular Tibetan lama, bSod-nams-rgya-mtsho, from the dGe-lugs-pa school. He developed a respect for this religious leader during the raids against the Uighur in which he had taken two Tibetan lamas as prisoners. Much like Gödan, he was impressed by the lamas' faith, although Baabar portrays Altan's dGe-lugs-pa preference in strictly political terms.[56] In 1576 Altan invited bSod-nams-rgya-mtsho, the leader of the Tibetan dGe-lugs-pa sect, to his court. Once there, bSod-nams-rgya-mtsho bestowed teachings upon Altan Qaan, and the two exchanged promises of mutual support.[57] According to bSod-nams-rgya-mtsho's biography, there were eleven distinct events that produced concessions or alterations in Mongol and Tibetan politics. The events listed included the following:

d) The Mongolian laws were reformed.
e) Altan Khan identifies himself as Khubilai Khagan and bSod-nams rGya-mTsho as the 'Phags-pa Lama; and asked bSod-nams rGya-mTsho about their separate lives since then. . . .
j) bSod-nams rGya-mTsho ordains [Altan Khan].
k) Exchange of titles and gifts between bSod-nams rGya-mTsho and Altan Khan. Altan Khan gives bSod-nams rGya-mTsho the title of Dalai Lama Vajradhara. bSod-nams rGya-mTsho or the (third) Dalai Lama gives Altan Khan the title of Chos-kyi rGyal-po, lHa'i Tshans-pa Chen-po (The King-according-to-the-Faith, the Divine Maha-Brahman).[58]

This dialectical legitimization was effective for both men. The surrounding princes regarded the meeting between Altan and bSod-nams-rgya-mtsho as auspicious. This religious efficacy empowered Altan with more political leverage. Altan Qaan's alliance with the bSod-nams-rgya-mtsho was the beginning of the dGe-lugs-pa supremacy within Mongolian Buddhist politics. In turn, Altan attempted to impart a strong Buddhist influence on the Mongol populace by imposing restrictive laws on his subjects' oblations.[59] For Altan Qaan, this was one more step toward becoming a *cakravartin*, and political leverage may have been his motivation for his continual efforts to spread Buddhism. During the rest of his reign, Altan strove to bring the sacred and the secular closer together by promoting the ranks of lamas and the translation of religious texts.[60] Unfortunately, his death in 1582 prevented him from further uniting the Mongol factions. Although Altan's descendants were unable to attain his political might, they still profited from the Tibetan-Mongol alliance. Seven years after Altan's death, his family became part of the dGe-lugs-pa heritage, and the fourth incarnation of the Dalai Lama was reincarnated into the Altan Qaan's family.[61] The next eleven reincarnations of bSod-nams-rgya-mtsho retained the title of Dalai Lama, the fourteenth of whom is currently active in Dharmasala, India.[62]

Before Altan Qaan's death, another *qaan*, Abadai, was greatly influenced by Altan's political maneuvering. Abadai was converted by an impressive Tibetan lama from the lineage of the Karma-pa at a time which Moses estimates to be around 1577.[63] However, at this time the dGe-lugs-pa sect was enjoying great political strength in Tibet. Abadai thus recognized the considerable advantages of being anointed by bSod-nams-mtsho. Abadai journeyed to Altan's city, Köke Qota, where he met bSod-nams-mtsho and received a title.[64] Later, the Dalai Lama bestowed the title of Sain Noyon Qaan on Abadai's brother, Tumenkin.[65]

At this point in history, it can be said that Buddhism was finally beginning to take root in Mongolia. In an effort to centralize authority and eliminate the presence of shamanism, Mongol authorities assisted the dGe-lugs-pa in assimilating shamanistic rituals. Tibetan lamas were being sent into Mongolia to teach and Tibetan religious texts were translated for the masses.[66] Sa-skya-pa and Karma-pa lamas continued to teach and lay Buddhism continued to rise in popularity, albeit partly due to incessant political pressure. Monasteries began to change the physical landscape. According to Mongol scholars, two monasteries were built at the same time as Abadai's Erdene Zuu in order to engender auspiciousness, even though historians and Mongols alike assert that Erdene Zuu was the first monastery built in Outer Mongolia.[67] Of course, this assertion is based on the assumption that there was no earlier wave as noted above.

Today, Erdene Zuu enjoys indisputable historical prestige as the oldest surviving Buddhist monastery in Mongolia, an illustration of Abadai's lasting influence. Indeed, contemporary Mongols consider Abadai's role to be highly significant in the development of Mongolian Buddhism. In fact, his influence was still apparent in the nineteenth century when the Russian traveler Przhevalskii acknowledged the lasting legacy of Abadai in his observations of Urga, the capital of Mongolia.[68]

Altan and Abadai's advocacy of Tibetan Buddhism created, in effect, an optimal environment for a future Mongol leader to emerge. The third wave thus began with one of Abadai's descendants, Gombo-dorji, who managed to unite the Qalqa Mongols, an ethnic group of central Mongolia, by promoting his son, Zanabazar, as a dGe-lugs-pa incarnation. It is at this point in Mongolian history that Mongolian religious authority and Mongolian political authority converge under Zanabazar, a direct descendent of Chinggis Qaan and an incarnation of the dGe-lugs-pa. Christopher Kaplonski provides a comprehensive account of

Zanabazar and his impact on Mongolian history and nationalism in his work *Truth, History, and Politics in Mongolia*. Kaplonski notes, "It was perhaps in Zanabazar, although he never held an official political title, that the wedding of Church and state came to its peak."[69]

In 1639, when Zanabazar was still very young, the larger feudal princes recognized him as the religious leader of Mongolian Buddhism.[70] The recognition concerned a popular Mongol myth. Following the Tibetan tradition of mysticizing the birth of gurus and school progenitors, Zanabazar was depicted as a mystical and auspiciously heralded child. The myth presents Zanabazar as a baby who was paid respects by three Indian mendicants who mysteriously appeared at his *ger* (yurt) in the middle of the night.[71] Although myths are influential, Zanabazar's gene-alogy was probably of greater significance for the politicized princes.

Following Altan and Abadai's strategy, Gombo-dorji sent Zanaba-zar to Tibet at the age of fourteen to receive schooling from the Dalai and Panchen Lamas and, more important, their confirmation.[72] In this way, he was tied inextricably to the Tibetan polity by his allegiance to the Dalai Lama, receiving from the Tibetan leader the title of Jabzand-amba Qotagt, an honor still conferred upon his reincarnations.[73] When Zanazabar returned, the Setsen Qaan Sholoi bestowed on him the title of Bogd Gegeen (Brilliant Light), another title that was handed down to Zanabazar's future incarnations, and one that demonstrates Zanabazar's high status in Mongol society. It must be remembered that the first and particularly the second waves of Buddhism generated a profound social respect for Tibetan Buddhism in Mongolia. In turn, this provided a far-reaching political blanket upon which Mongol political leaders could spread their control.

However, it was not only Zanabazar's religious stature, but also his political and cultural skills, that left a lasting impact on Mongol society. Today, if one were to enter a Buddhist monastery in Mongolia, one would likely find a *thangka* (religious scroll painting) of Zanabazar in one of the many art galleries. The first Bogd Gegeen is considered by many to have been a skilled artisan.[74] The Mongolian art historian N. Tsultem views Zanabazar as an artist with exceptional talent who significantly influenced the evolution of classical religious art:

In Zanabazar's works the canons of Buddhist iconography are formally unchanged, but the sculpture assimilated them creatively and was used to produce living images of real people. . . . Zanabazar's talent gave life to Tibetan canons on Mongolian soil, and he is rightly held in esteem as the founder of the Mongolian classical religious art. His pupils, whose names are mostly unknown, continued his artistic principles for 300 years.[75]

Among Zanabazar's other accomplishments is his creation of the Mongolian Buddhist alphabet, the Soyombol, which appears on the Mongolian national flag. Only the leaders of the Mongol dynasty come close to matching Zanabazar's relevance in Mongol history.[76]

It is interesting to note that after returning from Tibet Zanabazar retained the services of a number of Tibetans and, henceforth, the Jabzandamba Qotagt would foster a legion of *shabinar* (religious disciples).[77] The institution of the *shabi*[78] became a crucial development during the third wave of Mongolian Buddhism. These Tibetans were initially religious disciples who were donated to Zanabazar as a symbol of loyalty and respect. Later, however, the *shabinar* played a critical role in the conversion of the laity, as their positions crossed social boundaries and entitled the *shabi* to some economic advantage. *Shabi* were exempt from most taxes and duties except for an amount paid directly to their Jabzandamba, an economic privilege enjoyed by the elite members of the Sangha.[79] Even Soviet historians note the significance of the *shabinar*, who altered the economic and political structure of Outer Mongolia for the next three centuries: "The Mongolian lama priesthood produced quite a large contingent of clerical-feudal intellectuals who devotedly served the interest of Mongolian feudalism . . . they included Undur-gegen Zanabazar."[80]

The increasing numbers of ordinations of lamas and the growing class of *shabi* incurred a greater economic burden on the laity. These sociopolitical evolutions could not have come at a more precarious time for the Mongols, for the Manchus were gaining momentum under the guidance of K'ang-Hsi.

3

MONGOLIAN BUDDHISM UNDER
THE CH'ING DYNASTY
(1691–1911)

Under the Manchu administration, the Mongol political system changed dramatically as a direct result of altercations with the Mongolian Sangha. During this period the tie between Mongolia and Tibet remained constant. While there were no further waves of Buddhist influence, the conflict with shamanism continued to escalate. This was the time of the Manchus, who manipulated the established Mongolian Sangha in an effort to control Outer Mongolia. Unfortunately, Chinese interaction with Mongolian Buddhism during this period has often been overlooked in the assessment of the modern Mongolian Sangha.

In an effort to prevent any insurrections, the Manchus used a traditional Chinese ploy that would demarcate new boundaries and divide the Mongolian *aimag* (provinces). Baabar refers to this ploy, underscoring the political importance of such geographic restructuring:

> Dividing Mongolia into numerous small units was sure to aggravate [Mongolian divisions'] tendency toward individualism and independence and thereby prevent them from organizing themselves and conspiring against "The Heavenly Dragon."[1]

However, at the same time, the Manchus were keenly aware of the waves of Buddhist influence in Outer Mongolia as well as the political metamorphoses that followed each respective surge. They understood the significance of Tibetan Buddhism in Mongol polity, particularly the importance of the Dalai Lama. Manchu policies focused on weakening the "horizontal" ties between Mongol factions while strengthening the "vertical" ones to China, the latter accomplished primarily through the Sangha.[2] Political and religious affairs were further linked together by the Manchus, who encouraged the collapsing of religious and political status by bestowing noble rank and title on high-ranking lamas.[3] By now the Mongolian Sangha was responsible not only for Mongolia's religious sphere, but also medicine, education, and even the sciences.[4] Prince Dorgon, the regent of the Ch'ing empire, invited the Dalai Lama to Peking and thereupon made concessions in order to gain the Dalai Lama's political support for the Manchu expansion into Outer Mongolia:

> The [Fifth] Dalai Lama stayed in Peking from September, 1652 to January, 1653, holding discussions with the Manchus about conditions in Outer Mongolia. . . . The Dalai Lama willingly consented to do all he could in this regard, but as a price for his backing he expected the Peking court's solid support and patronage for his sect of Buddhism. . . . By these means the Manchus persuaded the Mongolian Buddhist church to assist their cause.[5]

Prince Dorgon served as regent until the rightful emperor, K'ang Hsi, was old enough to rule. Like his predecessors, K'ang Hsi viewed Outer Mongolia more as a buffer region than as an area for possible expansion of the Ch'ing dynasty: "Manchu policy was essentially a conservative and reactionary one. In theory, it was the antithesis of a colonial policy in the currently accepted meaning of the term, since it aimed to prevent the economic penetration and exploitation of Mongolia from the homeland."[6]

The Manchu's entreaty of the Dalai Lama was merely the beginning of a repetitious pattern of subtle and, in later years, more direct manipulations. When the Manchus conquered Mongolia in 1691, they knew that in order to retain their control they needed the acquiescence of the Mongolian Sangha.[7] Realizing its potential leverage, the Manchus allowed the proliferation of Tibetan Buddhism in Mongolia as well as the translation and printing of the Tibetan Buddhist Tanjur (the commandments of the Buddha) and numerous volumes of the Kanjur (Buddhist doctrine).[8]

The population of *shabinar,* or religious disciples, grew significantly during Zanabazar's reign. The *shabinar,* comprised of both lama disciples and lay devotees, remained an economic privilege for the high-ranking lamas in the Mongolian Sangha.[9] These high-ranking lamas, according to Bat-Ochir Bold, were "as a rule community members of aristocratic background. . . . Apart from their differing degrees of holiness, these high-ranking dignitaries as a rule held the office and honours of chief monks of monasteries which, in the majority of cases, they had founded."[10]

Many of these high-ranking lamas noted the economic benefits contributed by Zanabazar's *shabinar* and began to use their own *shabinar.* This significant increase in the number of *shabi* had a considerable impact on the Mongolian economy. For one thing, the *shabinar* were exempt from state tax. Consequently, taxes imposed on the laity rose substantially. The Mongolian Sangha also profited from the establishment of the *jas* (monastery treasure or property), a treasury developed through the regular donations of land and animals, offerings made largely by the nobility.[11] The first established *jas,* founded in the capital Urga in 1656, set an example for every other monastery to follow.[12]

In 1809, the Gandan monastery was constructed in the city of Urga, the capital of Mongolia.[13] At the time of the completion of Gandan, the capital city of Qaraqorum effectively lost its former political and religious focus for the monastic community and, with the integration of the *shabinar* into Mongol culture, potent changes began to affect the empire. As the Manchus tightened their hold on the Mongolian Sangha, the function of the *shabinar* was deliberately circumvented.

All classes of *shabi* who were initiated as religious disciples, were now treated as servants who were to perform menial tasks. This change was evidenced by the duties the Sangha selected for them to fulfill. Whereas during the time of Zanabazar the Tibetan *shabinar* were considered disciples undertaking religious training who also performed menial tasks, by the 1800s the *shabinar* were viewed as nothing more than servants whose sole purpose was to serve the *qotagt* (the clergy). The *shabinar* were assigned so many tasks that they had no time to pursue their religious studies. Moses records that, "Beyond paying taxes, the *Shabi* performed the manual labor tasks required to maintain the temples and monasteries. Work that involved 'tending the monastery cattle herds, grinding grain, cultivating, transporting goods, repair and build buildings, kindling bricks, and preparing *argal* [dung] fuel.'"[14]

It is evident that the *shabi,* in effect, were downgraded from the role of a religious disciple to the role of peasant, a process which, coupled with aggressive proselytizing, enabled the monasteries to amass considerable wealth. Beginning in the eighteenth century, this change in Mongolian Buddhism reconfigured the infrastructure of the Mongolian Sangha into a feudal system. Later, Soviet historians identified and emphasized the similarities between the *shabinar* and Russian feudal serfdom.[15]

The Manchus, who were responsible for the degeneration of the *shabinar* and unconcerned with the stability of the Mongolian economy, became more interested in the protection that the Mongols provided as a buffer zone against the Russians. While the Manchus were quick to take advantage of Mongolian Buddhism, they were hesitant to promote its practice. As a result, very few monasteries were subsidized under Manchu rule.[16]

The Manchus also strove to create solid political ties with the Mongols, and this was done primarily through marriage.[17] As one would imagine, the integration of the Chinese political administration into Mongolia resulted in repercussions in Mongol society, such as the gradual loss of prestige enjoyed by Mongol princes under the Manchus.[18] This political manipulation by the Manchus, together with the gradual imposition of feudalism within the Mongolian Sangha, rendered Mongol polity impotent in the face of Manchu control, even in the highly important system that identified and empowered reincarnations of religious leaders.[19]

For example, very early in his life Zanabazar defined the position of the Bogd Gegeen as a political and religious office.[20] With the leader of the Mongolian Sangha in a position to affect education, religion, and now politics, the Manchus quickly sought to prevent any further possibility of a Mongol Bogd Gegeen after the death of the second Bogd Gegeen. However, this attempt was preempted by a Mongol revolt in 1756 when a Mongol prince, Chingunjav, rallied the people against the Manchus. According to Bawden, this was the most visible sign of Mongol discontent against the Manchus.[21] Because the Mongol populace held the Bogd Gegeen in such high esteem, the Manchus were concerned that a future Bogd Gegeen's remarks against the Chinese would catapult the Mongols into a full-scale revolution. Thus, the Manchus declared that any future incarnations of the Bogd Gegeen must be unveiled first to the Ch'ing emperor. From the beginning, this proved to be contentious:

> After the death of the second incarnation, rumours circulated throughout Khalkha that the third had appeared in one or other of seven different noble Mongol families, but the Emperor intervened to prevent this from happening, and in a curious decree issued in 1761 announced that the Khutukhtu had appeared in Litang in Tibet.[22]

With this kind of political obfuscation, the Manchus achieved their goal. Indeed, from this point on all reincarnations of the Bogd Gegeen were found in parts of Chinese-held Tibet. Furthermore, the Manchus created positions within the Mongolian Sangha especially for their Manchu-appointed officials and were extremely selective about which Mongol figures were allowed to rise and maintain positions within the Sangha.

The Qamba Lama, for example, was the head of a monastery under the Mongolian Sangha, but from the first half of the eighteenth century, with the insertion of Manchu officials, he now shared his power with the Manchu-appointed Shangzudba. Another official position, the Da Lama, was created for the sole purpose of certifying that Chinese laws were followed within the Sangha.[23] Up until this time, religious and political legitimation of the Sangha's authority had made it a basis for intellectual and ideological influence and growth. As the Manchus successfully restricted the function of the *shabinar*, they effectively reduced the possibility that influential people, about whom the Chinese might need to be concerned, would ever rise against them in the future.[24]

Lamas and rebels who were discontented with the Manchu administration were summarily arrested or exiled. This was the most direct and effective means of suppressing the Mongol intelligentsia and controlling Mongolia. Bawden makes an explicit reference to one such occurrence in 1776 after the Manchus had quelled a rebellion. He lists judicial decisions by Chinese officials involved in these kinds of actions, and concludes:

> Such harsh treatment was meted out all over Mongolia. Some rebels were let off, on the pretext that they were only "stupid Mongols", but many were beheaded and had their heads displayed, while others, especially *lamas*, were banished on foot to the distant provinces of south China, a most unhealthy area for Mongols used to the clear cold climate of the steppes.[25]

In urban areas and in the monasteries any show of dissidence was met with harsh treatment, while in the peripheral regions of the nomadic Mongols the weakened Sangha became nothing more than a mouthpiece for the Chinese. Dismantled and disorganized, the Sangha became overly lenient in applying normal Buddhist interdicts both internally and among the laity.[26] The people became so unaccustomed to adhering to the strict doctrinal form of Buddhist doctrine that the Mongols characterized the fourth Bogd Gegeen as being "terrible" because he tried to make them observe Buddhist edicts long outdated.[27]

It should be noted that while under the control of the Manchu administration (1691–1911) the Mongolian Sangha was not socially inactive. Because outright rebellion was unrealistic, some lamas turned instead to important social activities, in an attempt to ameliorate bleak living conditions in a peaceful way. Derek Pritchatt provides this example: "The church worked in close cooperation with the ruling nobility, some of whom themselves introduced modest educational services for commoners—for example, Prince To Wang, in the mid-1800s, who introduced compulsory primary education."[28] Other lamas turned to art as a form of religious expression. In the southern region of Outer Mongolia, the Noyon Qotagt D. Ravjaa engaged in writing poetry and prose.[29]

The Manchus had nurtured a religious, political, and educational system in Mongolia that preempted any form of educational or political evolution; however, this system continued to grow in terms of both revenue and participants. In addition to this, Caroline Humphrey claims that Buddhist missionary work advanced in the nineteenth century at the expense of shamanism, under the direction and work of the lamas.[30] The institutional influence brought about changes within the nobility. Nobles took on the precepts of the lamas while still retaining their secular ranks.[31] Buddhism was the spiritual core of Mongol society, dictating both ethical and moral views for the Mongols, but for the Manchus Buddhism was simply an effective tool used to control the indigenous population, as demonstrated by the selection of ecclesiastical officials.[32] As noted, the Ch'ing dynasty required that it validate any reincarnations of the head of the Mongolian Sangha, the Bogd Gegeen, and this certification generally meant the future compliance of that incarnation.[33] Heissig notes, "All the heroes of the religious biographies written in Mongolian were not only high-ranking church dignitaries, but *personae gratae* with the Manchu court as well."[34]

Although the *shabinar* still performed menial tasks, they did so under a Chinese Buddhist hierarchy. In this sense, the Sangha acted as an educational imprinting system for all its adherents, in particular the *shabinar*. This growing class of Chinese-educated and Chinese-influenced *shabinar* resulted in a greater number of people holding official positions who were directly affected by Chinese policies, another factor that broadened the sphere of Manchu influence.

Furthermore, with an increased number of *shabinar* the income generated for the Sangha increased as well. Moses reports the following statistics on the Mongolian Sangha by the beginning of the 1900s: "Scattered across the great expanse of Outer Mongolia were some 583 temple complexes, plus an additional 260 religious meeting places of various kinds. Around them were more than 6,000 buildings of which 2,962 were for strictly religious purposes."[35] This estimate indicates just how pervasively the Mongolian Sangha was enmeshed within Mongol culture and the resulting importance it played in the political maneuverings of the Manchus.

Like all previous dynasties, the power of the Manchus soon began to decline. At this time, the eighth incarnation of the Bogd Gegeen was the leader of the Mongolian Sangha. He was a Tibetan, born in Lhasa to a family connected to the Dalai Lama; however, the Eighth Bogd Gegeen's resistance to Manchu oppression and political savvy won the Mongol nobles' admiration. Onan and Pritchatt claim that:

[The Eighth Bogd Gegeen] was brutal, suspicious towards his subordinates and extravagant, but his political skill and political ambition were far beyond those of his contemporaries. . . . Although he was not a Mongol by birth, he was able to control all the Mongol nobles and hold them together.[36]

The Eighth Bogd Gegeen realized that he could control much more than just the leadership of the Mongolian Sangha. Like Zanabazar before him, he realized that without the Chinese Jabzandamba ruling over him, his *qotagt* could enjoy uncontested sovereignty.

The Eighth Bogd Gegeen commanded incredible respect from the Mongols. Since the time of Zanabazar, the succeeding Bogd Gegeen incarnations remained the undisputed leaders of Mongolian Buddhism and continued to enjoy special powers and privileges. The Mongols regarded his position as comparable to that of Tibet's Dalai Lama. Robert Rupen cites Russian explorer A. M. Pozdneev in 1892:

Crowds of worshippers stretch toward the Khutukhtu from all sides, and not only Khalkhas, but also southern Mongols as well. . . . He was perhaps the only Mongolian personality known to all the generally illiterate and often apathetic Mongols throughout the land . . .[37]

This undiminished admiration for the Bogd Gegeen and the corresponding decline of the Manchus presented the Bogd Gegeen with an unquestionable opportunity. However, at this time Mongolia was still too weak to challenge the Manchus militarily. The alliance with another country was essential and Russia was the most accessible and viable candidate.

According to Soviet records of the period, public discontent with the Manchus extended well into the twentieth century.[38] Russian contact that began in the seventeenth century was under close scrutiny by the Chinese during the 1800s. With the dwindling of the Ch'ing dynasty, knowledge of Mongol discontent could have been a motivating factor for increased Russian activity in Mongolia. In 1860, the Russians sent their first representative to Urga to review trade negotiations between

Mongolia, China, and Russia.[39] The Bogd Gegeen did not overlook the possibility of Russian support. In 1895, he sent an envoy to Russia to determine whether or not the czar would agree to conspire with the Mongolian Sangha against the Manchus.[40] Apparently, the Bogd Gegeen was overly optimistic. The Russians were unable to lend support and the Bogd Gegeen was forced to wait.

Similarly, any hope of an alliance with neighboring Tibet also met with failure. When the Dalai Lama came to Mongolia in 1904, the Bogd Gegeen deliberately treated him with what can be called "inattentive diplomacy." Rupen suggests that the Bogd Gegeen could have felt threatened by the visit. As in the past, the Mongols clearly revered the Dalai Lama, although it is impossible to say who held more of the public's admiration, the Dalai Lama or the Bogd Gegeen.[41]

By the twentieth century, the Chinese had controlled Mongolia for more than two hundred years. The Mongolian Sangha had not experienced another wave of influence from Tibet, nor had any other commanding Mongol figure arisen since Zanabazar's death in 1723. Mongolia was left with a Sangha that was led by a collection of mediocre figureheads who were served by a multitude of overworked *shabi*. Unlike the nomadic aggressors of old, the Manchus neither added nor contributed to Mongol culture. Instead, they kept a healthy distance, leaving the country without leaders and with a largely ineffective Buddhist polity.[42] If it had not been for the weakening of the Ch'ing dynasty, Mongolia might still be under Chinese rule. However, the Ch'ing dynasty finally did weaken, and by 1911 the Bogd Gegeen regained his status as the most prominent Mongol political figure by freeing himself from the constraints of the Manchu court. This was a highly advantageous position for Mongolia, and for the first time in centuries the Mongols found themselves unified.

4

PERIODS OF AUTONOMY IN
EARLY TWENTIETH CENTURY MONGOLIA
(1911–1921)

When Mongolia arrived on the international scene in the early 1900s, the country fluctuated between being autonomous and being under Chinese control. Within a span of ten short years, the Mongols established a new autonomous theocratic government only to have it overtaken by the Chinese, attacked by the White Guard, and finally occupied by the Red Army. At the beginning of the twentieth century, nearly one seventh of the Mongolian population was ordained as lamas in the Mongolian Sangha.[1] Buddhism remained active within Mongolia during these years, but the focus of the Sangha began to lean toward Mongolian political figures who also served as religious leaders. Robert Rupen claims that at this time,

> Buddhism so permeated Mongolian society, and religious leaders exercised so much political and economic power, that the most critical questions concerned the retention or elimination of the church, or to some degree of compromise with it. Mongolian nationalism was almost inseparable from Buddhism.[2]

In essence, to speak of the Mongol polity during this period of autonomy would be the same as speaking of Mongolian Buddhism.

For this reason, it is important to examine the intellectual figures that emerged from and around the Manchu-influenced Mongolian Sangha throughout the period of autonomy. Most of the intelligentsia came to constitute a new third group of lamas led by the Bogd Gegeen, who along with the Sain Noyon Qaan was perhaps the most influential leader within the Sangha during the Mongol fight for independence.[3]

Under the auspices of the Bogd Gegeen, monasteries continued to prosper and remained unaffected by the political instability that was otherwise threatening Mongolia. The educational system underwent slight modification. According to Kaplonski, both China and Japan influenced the educational reforms that were attempted by some high-ranking lamas and nobles.[4] By now the Sangha's pedagogical system had led to a cultural trend wherein the lamas were regarded as the intellectual representatives of Mongol society. This monopoly allowed Mongolian Buddhism to continue to increase its dominant role in medical practices.[5] Mongolian art and craftsmanship became another venue for the Mongolian Sangha. In addition to the many Buddhist paintings and religious paraphernalia generated, the lamas were known as the best tailors, dyers, and manufacturers of *ger*, which were the common dwellings for most Mongols.[6]

The *shabinar* had not stopped growing. By 1918 the Bogd Gegeen had 8,833 *shabi* families and the Sain Noyon Qaan had almost 2,000, and their numbers became political assets for the two Buddhist leaders.[7] The noted increase of Mongolian lamas most likely was the direct result of the Mongolian Sangha's separation from China and the subsequent increase in the political potential of the Mongolian lama. Overall, this was a period of real resurgence for Buddhists in Mongolia, as Rupen states:

> The huge Buddhist sector consisted of 115,000 lamas and 750 resident monasteries (another 1,850 temples were not lived in). . . . In Urga alone, thirteen thousand lamas lived at *Da Khure* [monastery], and another seven thousand at *Gandang* [Gandan Monastery].[8]

It must be noted that there were also periodic accusations and claims of corruption involving the Bogd Gegeen, all of which were systematically censored. Considering the situation, it would have been unlikely not to find corruption within the Buddhist hierarchy. Today, however, Mongols think highly of the Bogd Gegeen's presence during the autonomous period. While they note his improprieties, they also give him credit for his role in proclaiming Mongolia's independence.[9]

On October 10, 1911, a civil war broke out in China that resulted in the ousting of the Manchus, who had ruled Mongolia for over 297 years. China was now a republic.[10] The political turmoil within China resulted in a new administration that the Bogd Gegeen was disinclined to obey.[11] With the urging of the Sain Noyon Qaan, Rupen reports, the Bogd Gegeen and his congress sent a letter to Russia again requesting support: "This congress resolved to turn to Russia for help, and sent a small delegation (Qangda Dorji Wang, Da Lama Tseren Chimit, and Qaisan) to St. Petersburg with a letter to the Tsar, dated July 7, 1911, and signed by the four Qalkha *Qaan*, lay princes of Mongolia."[12]

In an effort to terminate Chinese political control in Mongolia, the Bogd Gegeen made a bold move in December 1911. With full recognition of the surrounding princes, the Bogd Gegeen was inaugurated as the Bogd Qaan, ruler of Mongolia.[13] This act was accomplished through the support of the Russians, who sent an infantry battalion to the capital under the pretext of protecting Russian diplomats.[14] This act of independence was not simply confined to what is now known as Outer Mongolia, but pertained to all Mongols, including those who were residing in Inner Mongolia. In effect, Mongols from northern Mongolia and those living north of the Great Wall were now emancipated from the Chinese.[15]

Throughout his transition from religious leader to king, the Bogd Gegeen commanded the respect of both the Mongol nomads and the Buddhist laity.[16] His private affairs, however, produced strife among the lamas. According to Larry Moses:

> There was an atmosphere of degeneration about the fin-de-siecle court of the eighth Khutukhtu, the first and last King of Mongolia. After the death of his consort he decided to take another wife and sent emissaries to collect suitable names: his choice fell on the wife of a wrestler. . . . The Khutukhtu himself maintained for some time a liaison with one of his attendants, a man called Legtseg: the two used to change clothes and reverse their roles and had a homosexual relationship. . . . In the end Legtseg was arrested, apparently at the Khutukhtu's instigation.[17]

Previous incarnations of the Bogd Gegeen had enjoyed consorts as well. Although the Mongolian Sangha tacitly condoned this custom, it was unacceptable according to Mongolian Buddhist tenets. The promiscuous actions of the Eighth Bogd Gegeen essentially pushed the boundaries of what was already a lenient Mongolian Sangha.

Aside from his personal life, the newly appointed Qaan of Mongolia had a plethora of political issues with which to concern himself. Initially the Bogd Qaan had hoped to convince the new president of the Chinese republic that Outer Mongolia's independence meant only self-preservation, and that the Chinese should not be concerned with Mongolia's alliance with the Russians. In his pleas, the Bogd Qaan used the transition to independence as a means of preserving Mongolia's economy and religion:

> To President Yüan, Republic of China . . . Due to crises last winter, Outer Mongolia proclaimed its independence and I, Javzundamba Khutagt, was elevated by all as the Great Khaan of the Mongol nation, despite my utmost opposition. . . . The reason that Outer Mongolia proclaimed independence on this occasion was to strengthen our nation, defend our religion and retain our territorial integrity. . . . The position of Outer Mongolia, located in the frontier corner, is like "a solitary pile of eggs standing alone, helplessly, between powerful neighboring countries."[18]

The Bogd Qaan's simile of the pile of eggs was not far from the truth. Mongolia's army was neither well trained nor well armed, and a defense of its perimeters was nearly impossible. Being adjacent to two incredibly strong militaries only accentuated Mongolia's fragile state. Unfortunately, the Bogd Qaan's appeals were not heard in the way he had intended. His letters to President Yüan only made Mongolia's weak military apparent and, furthermore, failed to assuage China's fears of Russia taking control of Mongolia. One of the Bogd Qaan's generals, Damdinsüren, expressed grave concern over Mongolia's tenuous and vulnerable position:

> The enemy soldiers could penetrate the capital, Khüree, from three directions. There are many Chinese and Russians whose exact origins

are not clear and are gathering everywhere in the vicinity seeking profit. Therefore I beg you to consider seriously the question of the defence of this area and I beg you to issue a decree ordering the prompt training of the soldiers of the area.[19]

Damdinsüren had cause for concern. The Chinese refused to recognize Mongolia's autonomy and interpreted Russian diplomacy regarding Mongolia's moves towards independence as suspiciously overactive.[20] Aside from the Chinese, who now saw the retaking of Mongolia as feasible, it could be safely asserted that the Russians had more to gain from an autonomous Mongolia than Mongolia itself. Mongolia's geographic location could serve as an excellent buffer for either Russia or China. Chinese withdrawal from Mongolia provided Russia with the ideal opportunity for Russia to exert its influence, which had been kept to a minimum until the twentieth century.[21]

Despite this volatile international framework, it was imperative for the Bogd Qaan to assemble a legitimate government. Once Mongolia was no longer under the political auspices of the Chinese, it was the Bogd Qaan's task to create a government that reflected both Mongol religious and political sovereignty. According to Baabar, debates arose over who would act as prime minister and oversee both religious and state affairs. If the tradition of the Mongolian Sangha was to be followed, then the head of the Sangha would oversee both, but this was an option that was stridently rejected by the nobility:

> According to the Lamaist religious canon, the head of the church was to oversee both religious and state affairs, but a conflict arose between the secular nobles and lamas as to whom would oversee state affairs—a layman from the Golden Lineage or a religious figure.[22]

The disagreement was finally resolved with the nomination of the Sain Noyon Qaan, who was believed to be a direct descendent of Chinggis Qaan, thereby satisfying both political and religious contenders.[23] This new government was comprised of ministries and a bilateral legislature called the Great Qural and the Lesser Qural. The majority of the ministers and members of these Qurals were princes or landowners. According to Moses, this legislature served more as an advisory committee than as a lawmaking body. He further notes that surprisingly few high-ranking lamas were appointed to the new government.[24] There are several possible reasons for this. One reason may be the duplicity surrounding Chinese-placed ecclesiastical figures in the Mongolian Sangha. Another reason may be due to the fact that the Bogd Qaan was wary of any religious figure that might threaten his position. This attitude could have resulted from the Qaan's insecurity concerning his political improprieties. Soviet sources support this latter theory, claiming that the Bogd Qaan poisoned rival figures, the Sain Noyon Qaan (who had received the command of the Ministry of the Interior as well as the Office of Prime Minister) and Qangda Dorji (who had been awarded the Ministry of Foreign Affairs in order to avoid closer relations with Russia).[25]

As a result of his high social stature and his deft, though sometimes improper, political dealings, the enormous power enjoyed by the Bogd Qaan during the autonomous period virtually went unchecked and resulted in uncontested and unequal distributions of power. Consequently, disparities between the laity and the Sangha increased at a steady rate in a fashion comparable to the Manchu period, largely due to the increased size of the *shabinar*. Under the Bogd Qaan's government it was such an economic advantage to be a *shabi* that some princes elected to become *shabi* just to avoid state taxes, which served to further centralize the economic and political power of the Mongolian Sangha.

> It is significant for the changing state of Mongol society that, during the years of autonomy (1911 to 1919), the economic advantages of being subject to the jurisdiction of the Great Shabi, as the estate of the Jebtsundamba Khututkhtu, at that time the King of Mongolia, was known, rather than the secular administration, were such that whole groups of people transferred from one to the other. . . . An extreme example of such a voluntary transfer is that of the high lama known as the Mergen Bandida Khutukhtu, who in 1914, took fifty families of his own shabi with him to become shabi of the Jebtsundamba Khutukhtu's estate.[26]

With his power clearly established, the Bogd Qaan turned his attention to expanding the boundaries of his dominion, just like his Mongol theocratic predecessors. He recognized that the Mongols of Outer Mongolia had sought to unite with those of Inner Mongolia for some time. Unfortunately, the Chinese remained in control of Inner Mongolia. Therefore, in order for the Bogd Qaan to unite Inner and Outer Mongolia, he would need the support of the Russian government.[27] At this time the Russians were still negotiating with the Chinese for the autonomy of Outer Mongolia. Under their new administration, the Chinese refused to recognize the separation of Mongolia. Soviet records indicate that:

> Voicing the views of the trading, usurer and bureaucratic circles of China, the government of Yüan Shih-kai categorically refused to recognize the separation of Mongolia from China. An equally decisive refusal was given to tsarist Russia's proposal that Mongolia be given internal autonomy.[28]

Thus, the possibility of a unified Inner and Outer Mongolia became out of the question. Without the presence of a religious leader, Inner Mongolia was left factious, with various princes vying for control, even though in the minds of the Inner Mongolians the Bogd Qaan's status was just as prominent as it was for the Outer Mongolians. The mere fact that the Bogd Qaan commanded a unified and autonomous front in opposition to the Chinese elevated him in the eyes of the Inner Mongols and this threatened Chinese authority.[29] In the end, though, it was the Russians, in tenuous diplomatic negotiations with the Chinese over Outer Mongolia's autonomy, who forced the Bogd Qaan and Outer Mongolia to accept the finality of the separation from Inner Mongolia.[30]

The failure of the Bogd Qaan administration to unite Mongolia and his own failure to abide by Buddhist principles, interestingly, appeared to cause no significant political repercussions among the Mongol populace. However, the Sangha reacted strongly to the Bogd Gegeen's dissolute behavior. Bawden notes that during the corruptive incarnations of the Bogd Gegeen there emerged a third party of lamas.[31] Whereas before this time there was a two-party split (the high-ranking lamas and the low-ranking *shabinar*), a third group now came into existence made up of the lama intellectuals and the *shabinar*.[32] This group found the actions of the Bogd Qaan unacceptable and strove for a more enlightened form of Buddhism:

> The last Khutukhtu's [Bogd *Gegeen*] vices and excesses may not have affected his standing among the ordinary faithful, but did lower him in the estimation of the lamas of Urga, and there was a vocal, though ineffective, opposition both among the learned lamas and the lower orders, to his displays of immorality. The clergy was losing faith in its leaders, not only in the Khutukhtu, but also in other high lamas who were despised for their drunkenness and lasciviousness.[33]

The presence of the intellectual lamas was de-emphasized during the socialist period in Mongolia because it detracted from the Soviet political position that the Mongolian Sangha was, in its entirety, feudalistic. In order to avoid ambiguity, it was necessary for Soviet and socialist Mongol historians to say that an economic tyranny was derived from a Mongolian Sangha whose feudal high-ranking lamas oppressed a second group of lower-ranking lamas. This was a binary system devoid of intellectual diversity. In reality, however, this was not the case. By 1915 there was only one secular school compared to a Sangha with over one hundred thousand lamas, all of whom had at least eight to ten years of education.[34] Although the majority of lamas were not intellectuals, any intellectual, especially those with socialist sentiments, had acquired some form of Buddhist pedagogical training. High-ranking lamas were taxed heavily before the intense purges of the 1930s in the hopes of "freeing" the low-ranking lamas and *shabi* from the feudal "clergy." This philosophy began shortly after the socialist revolution of 1921 and was expounded upon in Soviet history:

> The ordinary, lower-ranking lamas formed part of the class of *arats*, constituting a special stratum in it. As Academician B. Ya. Vladimirtsov has correctly pointed out, lamas can be subdivided into two groups. "One

group comprises the re-incarnated Great lamas, all closely connected with the class of the Mongol feudal aristocracy. . . . The second group includes monks from the ordinary people, the *albatu* and *shabi*; they, of course, do belong to the class of simple, ordinary people."[35]

At the same time, in 1927, Siklos states that in the first edition of the *Great Soviet Encyclopaedia*, it says that in the opinion of the Russians, the interactions between the Mongolian Sangha and the laity were, to some degree, egalitarian.[36]

Both of these views, while problematic, are extreme in that the socialist view of the Mongolian Sangha categorically considered high-ranking lamas as feudal lords who oppressed the masses, although in reality some were activists who were involved in the early socialist movement. It is important to note that Buddhist nations, which have not experienced successful, strong socialist movements in comparison, view the Sangha as sacred and, to some extent, as a symbol of nationhood. In this vein, the Sangha's appropriation of land and the wealth of its members would be exempt, for the most part, from political derision, and its growth would be seen as emblematic of the nation's growth.[37]

The other view comes from a nascent Soviet perspective that considered the Mongolian Buddhist hierarchy to be fluid and one in which any person could rise. In reality, it was extremely difficult for a *shabi* to rise to the level of a lama. Some key Buddhist intellectuals and lamas were not selected to serve in the Bogd Qaan's administration. As a result, these individuals focused their efforts on forming a new government that would, nonetheless, remain Buddhist. These figures included: Dogsomiin Bodoo, B. Puntsagdorj, and D. Losol, three of the seven elite leaders of the socialist revolution who were lamas; Qasbaatar, another lama who was a commander in the socialist revolution; and intellectual leaders such as Damba Dorji and Dja-Damba, socialist congressmen who fought for a different form of Buddhism that was more egalitarian, a concept that is present in classical Buddhist doctrine but obviously implemented during this period in Mongolia.[38]

The last and perhaps most influential figure was a Buriat (ethnic group in Mongolia) by the name of Tsiben Jamtsarano, the initial mentor of

Choibalsan. According to Stephen Kotkin, Tsiben Jamtsarano was the most prominent Buriat intellectual of his time. As an intellectual with many social causes, Jamtsarano was also the leading voice for a new form of Buddhism that was compatible with socialism.[39] Aside from teaching Mongolian language and culture in St. Petersburg, he helped found the Mongol Scientific Committee in 1921 (which later became the Mongolian Academy of Sciences).[40]

Later, many of these figures became influential members within the socialist government. It is conceivable that they could have been more instrumental in preventing later governmental attempts to eliminate Mongolian Buddhism; however, during the autonomous period, the political climate was never conducive for them to take this type of action. This was, in part, because the Manchu infrastructure of the Mongolian Sangha left no room for rising intellectual lamas.

Furthermore, the Bogd Qaan continued this political policy within his government by excluding many lamas from his legislature. Ironically, some of these lamas' actions directly led to the Bogd Qaan's dismissal.[41] The lifestyle of the Mongols had not changed substantially for over two thousand years, and the only development Mongolia could boast about was its rising religiosity. Contemporary Mongol historians look somewhat disdainfully on this period of Mongolian Buddhism, seeing the religion as one of the reasons for Mongolia's lack of technological expertise and economic development into the early twentieth century:

> When Lamaism first came to Mongolia it promoted social progress, but it developed to become superstition, outdated symbolism and stumbling block to social progress. Under the oppressive teachings of Lamaism, a form of Buddhist philosophy adopted by the backward nomads, the Mongols were prevented from enjoying the fruits of twentieth century civilization.[42]

During this time period public opinion of the Mongolian Sangha wavered and secularism began to rise; popular secular intellectuals, such as Jamtsarano, continued to succeed in the academic community but were neglected under the Bogd Qaan's administration: "Some Outer Mongolians had come under the influence of an outstanding Buriad

Mongol intellectual, Tsyben Zhamtsarano, who ran a newspaper and a school during the period of autonomy."[43] Many early socialist revolutionaries found one another within this academic community, with some encounters orchestrated under the guidance of Bodoo and Jamtsarano.[44] Bodoo was a teacher at a Mongolian language school during the autonomous period. Through this job he met Qorlogiin Choibalsan, whom he brought to his home and adopted as a son.[45] Choibalsan, the most influential Mongol figure to emerge from the early seven revolutionaries of the Mongolian People's Revolutionary Party, later became Mongolia's prime minister.[46]

The ending of the autonomous period is not entirely understood. Essentially, how the Chinese regained control of Mongolia is under dispute. Although the Bogd Qaan's *shabinar* were impressive in number, his military force was not. Moses writes: "At Urga itself, the rule of the Jebtsun Damba Qutugtu was not backed by a military force sufficient to counter a determined assault by any of the modern warlord armies in North China. When the challenge came in 1919, the government collapsed . . ."[47] Some records indicate that the Bogd Qaan was persuaded to relinquish control, while others state that he and his government had no choice but to abdicate authority to the Chinese.[48]

The Soviet Union was in the process of its own internal struggles during the Chinese advance, an occurrence that was more than just a coincidence. Russia had recently survived a revolution and was fighting against a renegade faction of the old government, the White Guard, led by Ungern-Sternberg. Unable to provide military assistance in sustaining its hold on Outer Mongolia, the Soviet Union issued a special proclamation directed more toward the Chinese and the White Guard than the Mongols:

> On August 3, 1919, the Soviet government addressed a special appeal to the government and people of Autonomous Mongolia stating that it completely renounced the advantages and privileges which had been seized by tsarist Russia under the unequal treaties imposed by the latter. "Mongolia" the appeal said, "is a free country. All authority in the country must belong to the Mongolian people. No single foreigner has the right to interfere in the internal affairs of Mongolia."[49]

A single foreigner, however, did interfere with Mongolia's internal affairs, Russian Baron Ungern-Sternberg. One of Ungern-Sternberg's chief armies, under the command of Semenov, found its way to Outer Mongolia in an attempt to capitalize on the Mongolian Sangha's large reservoir of livestock and other wealth.[50] The Chinese, who commanded a firm hold over the Mongol polity, directed the Bogd Gegeen to disperse troops to combat the White Guard. The Bogd Gegeen complied, appointing two *qotagt* to oversee and engage Russian troops in combat on the western and eastern frontiers.[51]

The devastation caused by the White Guard was severe. A Mongol recalled seeing old men, women, and children burned alive, their property confiscated.[52] These occurrences were not uncommon, a direct result of the White Guard's destructive and frantic rush towards Siberia. The vast wealth that had been accumulated by the Mongolian Sangha (from the *shabinar*) was seized to fund Ungern-Sternberg's planned invasion of the Soviet Union. Murphy acknowledges Sternberg's actions were those of an insane man:

> Ungern Sternberg's plans were clearly those of a disturbed man, and, in fact, his ruthless and demented activities in Urga clearly indicate his state of mind. . . . Because Sternberg planned a northward strike to destroy Bolshevism, Ungern-Sternberg planned a northward strike against Russia and the Bolsheviks he hated. No fully rational man soberly assessing his forces and the means at his disposal would have made such plans.[53]

These coinciding invasions by the Chinese and the White Guard left much of the Mongol countryside stripped and barren. Lamas were killed, monastery structures were destroyed, and cattle were butchered or stolen.[54]

Third-party lamas considered these occurrences to be a confirmation of the Bogd Gegeen's political ineptitude. They then initiated talks with Soviet Russia over a possible revolt against the Bogd Qaan's administration. The Soviets saw this as a perfect opportunity to position their military in Outer Mongolia. This last infiltration of Mongolia catalyzed what may be the most dramatic social change in Mongolian history and propelled events that led to the demise of the Mongolian Sangha. In a letter to George G. S. Murphy on July 4, 1963, Soviet academician I. M. Maiskii wrote:

> You ask me what were the considerations, and who were the chief decision-makers in the decision to commit Soviet troops to enter Mongolia in July 1921 to destroy Ungern Sternberg? My reply to this question is as follows: The chief decision-makers were the Soviet Government of the day headed by V. I. Lenin; the main consideration for taking such a decision consisted in the necessity to destroy Baron Ungern-Sternberg, an arch-enemy of the Soviet Russia.[55]

As is often the case, socialist and western scholars have hotly debated the main purpose for the Red Army's invasion. Regardless of the motive, the results proved disastrous for Mongolian Buddhism.

5

THE BEGINNINGS OF THE
MONGOLIAN PEOPLE'S REVOLUTIONARY PARTY
(1921–1929)[1]

In 1921 the new Mongolian government, the Mongolian People's Republic (MPR), stabilized itself through the presence of the Red Army. Following the revolution, sudden radical events occurred that led to perhaps the most intense political transformation in Mongol history. From 1921 to 1929, these events were determined by the evolution of the young Mongolian People's Republic and its sole political party, the Mongolian People's Revolutionary Party (MPRP). As the MPRP increasingly aligned itself with Soviet sentiments, the relationship between the Mongol polity and Buddhism became more and more strained.[2]

Politically, the foremost reason for the deteriorating relationship was the redistribution of members from the Mongolian Sangha "party" to the socialist party. The socialist government began to lure *shabinar* and potential lamas away from the Sangha and relocate them into socialist political structures. In terms of cultural politics, an example of this shift is exemplified by the renaming of the capital from Urga, an indigenous Mongol term, to Ulaanbaatar (The Red Hero), a name full of Soviet overtones.

This period marked the political ascent of the MPRP and the political descent of the Mongolian Sangha.[3] This chapter will focus on the MPRP's political growth and its impact on the Mongolian Sangha. It is important to note the balance of power in the ranks of the Mongolian People's Revolutionary Party, which violently shifted away from the intellectual lamas and secular moderates to the radicals.

POLITICAL IMBROGLIO

The exact details concerning the formation of the MPRP are cloaked in socialist propaganda, Western refutations, and archival information currently inaccessible for verification.[4] Soviet and socialist historians depict the MPRP as a social phenomena evolving from Mongol thought, as a government created by working-class Mongols who were dissatisfied with the Bogd Qaan and the Mongolian Sangha. Discrepancies in this claim surfaced later in the works of Western historians such as Robert Rupen and George G. S. Murphy, who cite evidence of only an appearance of Mongol control.[5] Rupen and Murphy assert that the Russians encouraged, motivated, and eventually led influential Mongol figures to revolt against the Bogd Qaan and the Buddhist-influenced polity.

There are varying accounts concerning the number of Mongol soldiers who participated in the revolution of 1921, but by their very inconsistencies these accounts seem to buttress the claims of Murphy and Rupen. Socialist records indicate that both Mongols and Russians were heavily involved in the fighting;[6] however, Murphy contends that only a small number of participants were Mongol, with the overwhelming majority being Russian.[7]

Both socialist and Western scholars concur that the key Mongol figures during the 1921 revolution were Dogsomiin Bodoo, Soliin Danzan, Damsranbelegiin Dogsom, D. Losol, Dambiin Chagdarjav, Qorlogiin Choibalsan, and Damdinii Suqbaatar.[8] Among these seven figures, Choibalsan and Suqbaatar currently are regarded as the most notorious by contemporary Mongol accounts, partly due to their own socialist propaganda.[9] In fact, each of these men survived the democratic process of the 1990s, each supported by a cult of followers.[10]

It is important to remember that this incipient period of Mongol socialism is most correctly characterized as turbulent and uncertain even though its effectiveness was quite profound. These years marked the end to the Buddhist polity and the Sangha's ability to alter Mongolia's political evolution. Thus, the future of the Mongolian Sangha rested in the hands of the political leaders who succeeded the Buddhist polity.

Whereas members of the MPRP such as Qorlogiin Choibalsan were supported heavily by the Soviet Union and therefore interested in the disenfranchisement of the Mongolian Sangha, others such as Iapon Danzan were supported by the bourgeoisie and the middle-ranking lamas, who favored an autonomous Mongolia.

An analysis of the socialist construct of the 1920s provides a window into the more recent incarnations of the MPRP and its perspective on the Mongolian Sangha, although one must carefully take into consideration the respective orientations of one's sources, namely Soviet sources.

To understand the MPRP's political agenda in the 1920s, it is important to examine its political origins. For this examination, I will draw mainly upon D. Dashpurev and other socialist historians who portray the MPRP as a coalescence of two groups: the Urga and the Consul.[11] The Urga group, a coalition associated with progressive and patriotic feudals who wished to free themselves from Chinese dominance, was the first to form, with Danzan as its leader and Suqbaatar and Dogsom as founding members.[12] The Consul group was composed shortly afterward, led by Bodoo with Choibalsan, Losol, and Chagdarjav as its founding members.[13] The exact time when these groups merged is hotly debated by both socialist and non-socialist scholars. Socialist scholars believe that these two groups were created in the summer of 1919, whereas the non-socialist scholars favor an earlier date.[14] Regardless of the precise date, members of both groups became preeminent in Mongol politics for the next thirty years.

Dashpurev maintains that when the Urga and the Consul groups joined, the latter was the more influenced by Russian ideology:

> On 25 June 1920, when the two revolutionary groups coalesced into a united group, i.e. "Mongolian People's Party," some of its members, particularly Bodoo's group, already was under the influence of Russian Marxism (Bolshevism).[15]

With the Urga group consisting of intellectuals opposed to Chinese rule and the Consul group influenced by Russian thought, it was merely a matter of time before the two convened to seek Russian assistance.

The new MPRP held its first official congress at Kiakhta in 1921. In addition to the elite seven revolutionary leaders, other intellectuals and underground political figures came together to discuss the objectives of the new political party. During this congress, the Buriat intellectual Jamtsarano, won a key argument in favor of allowing the Bogd Qaan to retain his position in the future government.[16] This decision was a testament to the young MPRP's loyalty to the Mongolian Sangha but, at the same time, it demonstrated a potential divide regarding that very sentiment.

In fact, the loyalty of the MPRP was tested shortly after this conference ended. When the MPRP initially asked the Soviet Union for support, its members were told to bring a letter requesting assistance, certified to be authentic by the Bogd Qaan's seal. At this time the MPRP was not interested in soliciting the help of Soviet troops, feeling that, with the assistance of Soviet weaponry alone, they would be able to claim Mongolia and protect themselves against the Chinese:

> The Mongol envoys, like Handdorj and Nanmansuren in the past, said they needed military instructors, arms and weapons, but not troops. . . . They asked for ten thousand rifles, twenty canons and three hundred machine guns.[17]

The request for a letter from the Bogd Qaan administration may have been a means for the Soviet Union to protect itself in the event of an unsuccessful revolution and an agitated Bogd Qaan administration. Although the Red Army was a sufficient force in immobilizing and eliminating the White Guard and freeing the Mongols from Chinese control, the Soviets could not be sure which Mongol administration would emerge victorious in the fight for independence.

The request for a letter proved to be only a nominal obstacle. One of the MPRP's rising leaders, Choibalsan Puntsagdorj, a lama who was a member of the Bogd Qaan's government and a MPRP sympathizer, helped to secure an official seal from the Bogd Qaan. However, when the party reached Irkutsk and met with Kupun, who was the Soviet head for Far Eastern affairs, the Soviet representative tested the Mongols, saying:

You delegates have brought a document with the Bogdo's seal. It is something that will be in the record for you in the future. But in this matter it is important that you delegates should submit a document, which makes clear your own desires and carries the seal of your own party.[18]

This was the first time that the Russians had publicly suggested the idea of revolting against the Bogd Qaan. In Mongol culture a move against the Bogd Qaan was more than just a political coup; it constituted religious treason.

According to Murphy, at this point Dogsom, Danzan, and Bodoo resolutely opposed the idea of differentiating themselves from the Bogd Qaan administration.[19] Out of the seven founding members of the MPRP, Bodoo and Losol were lamas and Danzan and Dogsom were part of the Bogd Qaan's original administration. Dashpurev states that Dogsom, Danzan, and Bodoo's resistance to revolting against the Bogd Qaan at this time was inconsequential. Prior to this meeting the other more compliant members of the MPRP had already agreed upon a set of guidelines and accords with the Soviets.[20] Apparently, the desire for a change in government was reason enough for Danzan, Bodoo, and Dogsom to remain loyal to the revolutionary party, allowing for a separation from the Bogd Qaan. As seen in this episode—essentially the MPRP's first collective interaction with the Soviets—there were intimations of a division between Buddhist and socialist supporters that would eventually become quite evident.

It is clear that by the Kiakhta meeting in 1921 the Russians were prepared for an invasion of Mongolia. It was during Mongolia's autonomous period that the Russians were given their first chance to enter into Mongol culture and economy without significant political impediments from the Chinese, for any hold that the Chinese had on the Mongols had dissipated under the pressure of the White Guard. In fact, one could speculate that the Russians already had invested time and money assessing their chances for a successful invasion of Mongolia prior to meeting with the MPRP. This theory is based on accounts of an expedition led by Russian Ivan M. Maiskii to Outer Mongolia in 1919:

D. P. Pershin, a reputable eyewitness and at that time a director of the Mongolian National Bank, had no doubt that Maiskii masterminded the events that led to the invasion of 1921. Perhaps we should not neglect other members of Maiskii's expedition, for they were to play important roles in Soviet Mongolia. There was the Mongol, Erdeni Batukhan, who was later to be Minister of Education . . .[21]

Maiskii's account provided the Soviets with accurate information concerning Mongol terrain and its topography. Officially, his expedition was sent for the purpose of trading; however, it has been noted that the areas his expedition visited later became key sites for the Red Army during the revolution.[22]

While the geographic location of Mongolia and the elimination of the renegade White Guard certainly were unofficial motives for the Soviet invasion of Outer Mongolia, the only official reason the Soviets gave was that they acted in response to the MPRP's request for aid.[23] Soviet scholars state that just prior to the invasion of the Red Army, the renegade Baron Ungern-Sternberg used the Bogd Qaan to gain the confidence of the Mongol princes.[24] Whether or not the reports concerning complicity by the Bogd Qaan are true, they further justified the Soviet's involvement and gave the MPRP cause to restrict the Bogd Quaan's power. Then, upon establishing the MPRP, one of the first steps was to distinguish the revolutionary group from the preexisting Buddhist polity, effectively reducing the Qaan's political power:

On July 9, 1921 the People's Revolutionary Government sent the Bogd Government an ultimatum. In this document, after mentioning the harm created by the *gamin* and Ungernists and the goals of the People's Party and Government, it was stated that all ministries and offices of the Bogd Government must bring their seals and badges of office to the Interior Ministry by noon, July 10, 1921 and hand them over to the representatives of the People's Party and Government as well as the Commander-in-Chief of Army who would be gathered there to decide governmental questions.[25]

The purpose of these directives was to demonstrate publicly the end of the Bogd Qaan administration and the beginning of the Mongolian People's Republic.[26] Interestingly, this decree met little resistance. During the creation of the Mongolian People's Republic, MPRP moderates such as Danzan and Jamtsarano won appeal from the bourgeoisie, the middle-ranking lamas, and even some of the high-ranking lamas.[27]

The Mongolian nomads, who were affiliated with neither the Sangha nor the wealthy class, remained largely apathetic to these proceedings. After centuries of disjointed Manchu rule, the Mongol populace became indifferent toward the changing political climates. At the time, the only kind of change that may have aroused a reaction at the popular level would have been one that affected the practice of Buddhism "on the ground":

> The Outer Mongolian was loyal to his religion and to his prince; he had no notion of loyalty to a state. . . . So long as any foreign power was careful to rule through the traditional nobility and through the Urga Khutukhtu and other religious dignitaries, the population was compliant.[28]

Still, the publicly issued ultimatum was part of the gradual process that allowed the MPRP to distance itself politically from the previous ecclesiastical system. In this light, Larry Moses characterizes the MPRP's initial steps as anticlerical but not antireligious.[29] The early MPRP wanted a new government, but not necessarily a new culture. At this point, it would have been extremely dangerous for the MPRP to oppose Buddhism. The Bogd Qaan's earlier improprieties may have weakened his personal credibility, but they had not diminished Mongolia's respect for Buddhism.

THE RISE OF THE MPRP

When the MPRP organized its initial administration, many of the Bogd Qaan sympathizers received important positions in the government. This was not an accident. Many influential Mongol figures who assisted in the MPRP's rise to power were, in fact, lamas. In addition, Bulag credits the lamas and the social roles they played for solidifying Mongolian culture during this nascent nation-building period:

> The reason the lamas played so large a role in the early revolutionary process was that they were recruited from all "classes" and all groups. Lamas were perhaps the only group that could move between administrative boundaries.[30]

Bodoo became the first prime minister, and Danzan the first finance minister. Puntsagdorj, a lama like Bodoo, was the first minister of internal affairs under the MPRP, a position he had held during the autonomous period.[31] However, opponents to Buddhists were already active in the new government. According to the State Historical Archives, there were forty-two Russian specialists working under Puntsagdorj at the Ministry of Internal Affairs.[32] Later, it was to become clear that although the initial MPRP stance toward Buddhism was favorable, this attitude was entirely contingent upon the sentiments of the seven revolutionary leaders. Thanks to the support of Jamtsarano and other Qaan supporters, the Bogd Qaan still retained some authority in the new MPR, even though the religious administration had technically been replaced by the MPR. Yet, the Russians, with help from the Mongolian radical socialists, did not give up trying to strip the Bogd Qaan of his political powers.

After eliminating the Bogd Qaan administration, the next step for the MPRP radicals was to reduce the power of the Bogd Qaan's office. This was a gradual process, and at times less effective than might have been desired. The radicals continually urged the MPRP to limit the power of the Bogd Qaan through public declarations and agreements, as seen, for example, by the Oath-Taking Treaty in November 1921.[33] This declaration removed the power of the Bogd Qaan to veto resolutions and decisions made by the MPR. The offerings to the Bogd Qaan, a standard custom for Mongolian government officials, were also greatly reduced, thus effectively restricting the Bogd Qaan's revenue and expenditures. Yet, even after limiting the Bogd Qaan's power, the Mongolian Sangha and the MPRP remained at a standstill. Due to the presence and status of the Mongolian Sangha, the MPRP did not dare eliminate ecclesiastical figures entirely from Mongol polity, even while they were curtailing the Bogd Qaan's influence on the current political structure.

The true stratification of power between the Bogd Qaan and the MPRP became more apparent shortly afterward. In December 1921, the Bogd Qaan's bodyguard, the Saj Lama, staged a small revolt against the MPR.[34] The Saj Lama was arrested, but the Bogd Qaan, despite his limited power, managed to pardon the Saj Lama, which indicated that the Bogd Qaan still retained power, albeit a marginal amount. However, as the Qaan's nominal power dwindled in the ensuing months, his power to protect the Saj Lama dwindled as well. Ultimately, the shift in power favored the MPRP enough that they could have their way with the Saj Lama. The following summer the Bogd Qaan's authority was not strong enough to prevent the Saj Lama's execution, along with other political figures.[35]

Although the Bogd Qaan was reduced in stature, the Mongolian Sangha was by no means impotent during this period. By denying their medical expertise, the Sangha was able to postpone the formation of an army until Russian doctors became available.[36] As the sole political party in Mongolia, the MPRP's only competitor for social influence was the Mongolian Sangha. The MPRP had good reason to be apprehensive of the Sangha's power. Unfortunately, this power was often marked by maladroitness in the hands of the lamas, as Moses aptly states:

> Because the power of the Church pervaded all Mongolia and because its hold over the people was both ecclesiastic and economic, it, the Church, could well have become a force for modernization. . . . Instead, it perpetuated its centuries-old educational and hierarchical hold over its initiates, who received only the meagerest education in Tibetan scriptures and were completely subservient to the will of the individual high lamas. As a result the Church was not capable of supplying innovative leadership in the face of the threats of the MPRP and made no attempt to introduce change within the traditional lines of Mongol patterns of authority.[37]

Without any efficacious leadership, the Mongolian Sangha remained collectively inactive. The Bogd Qaan and the Manchus had unwittingly alienated the very people who were now in the greatest position to support the Mongolian Sangha—the middle- and low-ranking lamas.

For several centuries, the Sangha had existed through perfunctory duties and the levying of taxes, but its hierarchy remained static. The Chinese supported this restricted stratification by appointing religious figures they could trust, those who could assure them that the Sangha would remain aligned with the Ch'ing dynasty. The low-ranking lamas, who comprised the overwhelming majority in the Sangha, remained confined to their role, which was the functional equivalent of a temple servant.[38] Economically, they were similar to the *shabinar* in that a *shabi* was not supported by a monastery but relied instead on family support or herding.[39] Whereas low-ranking lamas held economic grievances, the middle-ranking lamas held ideological ones.[40]

In 1922, after the first months of revolution had passed, the MPRP resolved to target once and for all the Mongolian Sangha and reduce its influence through laws and regulations. Throughout this period of reduction, the MPRP carefully monitored the Sangha's activities and numbers.[41] Without finding any solidified resistance to their policies, the MPRP escalated their political and economic assault and, in 1923, access to *shabinar* land came to a complete halt. This caused yet another serious financial setback for the Sangha.[42]

However, even with these obstacles the Mongolian Sangha, supported by more than one hundred thousand followers, constituted at least 44 percent of the Mongolian population. By 1924 the Mongol economy was still closely linked to the Mongolian Sangha, which controlled 20 percent of the country's livestock.[43] Even though the Mongolian Sangha lacked the leadership as well as the power of the Bogd Qaan, it nevertheless was an economic and political machine waiting to be harnessed. In the past, the Tibetans and then the Manchus had provided the Sangha with its leadership and then capitalized on the resulting political influence. In the 1920s, however, the MPRP was forgoing this process, and set their course solely on the elimination of Buddhist influence.

As a result of certain purges within its own administration, the MPRP's political stance regarding Buddhism dramatically shifted. Those targeted during these purges were mainly third-party lamas and intellectuals who had facilitated the transition from the Bogd Qaan administration to that of the MPR. Lamas, Bodoo and Puntsagdorj, who held high offices in the new government, were accused of secret activities with the Bogd Qaan. C. R. Bawden, a scholar of Mongol history, had difficulty substantiating Bodoo's alleged actions:

> [Bodoo] had had to resign early in 1922 and was then supposed, partly out of pique, to have engaged in a plot to overthrow the revolution he had helped to bring about . . . Bodoo testified that he had sent a partisan's cap and some hand grenades as a gift, and that he had suggested to Chagdarjav that they should go and ask [Dambijantsan] to join them in a direct revolt against the government. What can have possessed these men, experienced revolutionaries and politicians, to engage in such an ill-found plot, if indeed they did, is hard to fathom.[44]

It is apparent that political motivation existed behind these accusations. Puntsagdorj and Bodoo were convicted and then executed on August 30, 1922, along with a small group of political leaders, including the Saj Lama.[45] Among these leaders were Togtoq, the minister of justice, and Chagdarjav, the vice prime minister, who were both removed from office under similar pretexts.[46] Rupen states, "Thirteen months after the new regime was established in July 1921, fifteen major political figures—including the prime minister and two members of the Khalkha Seven . . . were shot, and twenty-six others were arrested."[47] This was one of many critical purges for the MPRP, and it dealt a severe blow to the cause of Mongolian Buddhism in the new nation.

The elimination of these party officials was the first incident for the MPRP in which the Ministry of Internal Affairs publicly executed officials and altered Mongol political structure.[48] Ironically, one of its first victims was the Ministry of Internal Affairs' first minister, lama Puntsagdorj, who was implicated by another lama for using the Bogd Qaan's seal.[49] This new role for the Ministry of Internal Affairs threatened the Mongolian Sangha and provided the MPRP with unrestrained power. From this point on, the term, Dotood Yaam (Mongolian for Ministry of Internal Affairs) elicited incredibly high levels of respect and fear by the Mongol people. Bawden claims that "hardly a year passed when there were not plots discovered and others rumored, and in 1922 it was necessary to enlist Soviet experience in organizing an Office of Internal Security and a secret police force."[50] The Internal Security and secret police were subdivisions within the Dotood Yaam, which consisted of investigators, enforcers, and informants for the MPRP, who later assisted in the fight against the Buddhists. In the case of Vice Prime Minister Chagdarjav, the use of the Dotood Yaam was not restricted to Buddhists; it was also highly effective in manipulating the leadership of the MPRP itself.

Finally, the last vestige of Buddhist control vanished from Mongolia in 1924 with the death of the Eighth Bogd Qaan. The Mongolian Sangha attempted to find the ninth reincarnation, but the MPRP was quick to prevent this. "The Urga Khutukhtu had died in May, 1924, but a search for a ninth reincarnation was forbidden by [MPR] law."[51] This one law effectively emasculated the possibility of a Buddhist polity and ended the Mongolian monarchy: "On November 26, 1924, the First State Ih Hural proclaimed the Mongolian People's Republic and adopted the first Mongolian constitution."[52] The Soviet Union supported this bold move by the MPRP and, for the first time in centuries, lamas were absent from all political offices.[53]

Sandag postulates that the Bogd Qaan was assassinated, and part of his theory rests on the fact that both the Qaan and one of the revolutionary heroes, Suqbaatar, had died within a brief period of time.[54] Whether their deaths were planned or natural, Mongolian leadership altered dramatically in that year. The MPRP's confidence in radicalism grew rapidly following the deaths of the Bogd Qaan and Suqbaatar, which previously had been met only with passivity from the Mongolian Sangha, making way for a major transformation of the Buddhist social structure. Monasteries were converted into schools, and steps were taken to strip the wealth from the high-ranking and middle-ranking lamas.[55] The Sangha's lack of resistance only further encouraged the more radical MPRP members, who then successfully purged the party of any third-party lamas, leaving the moderate intellectuals as the sole surviving supporters of the Mongolian Sangha in the MPR. Danzan was perhaps the most influential of these moderate members in the MPRP and, in truth, he was the Mongolian Sangha's last hope for survival. He was also the most prominent moderate from the first group of seven MPRP representatives. After Bodoo's death, Danzan rose from the office of minister of finance to that of vice prime minister and, with the death of Suqbaatar in 1923, another former political adversary was removed. At that point Danzan assumed the role of minister of war and commander-in-chief of the Mongol army.[56]

Although initially Danzan was sympathetic to the Soviet cause, he began to distance himself from the Soviet Union with his idea for a capitalist-based economy. Unlike his Russian counterparts, he felt that in order for Mongolia to make the transition to a communist society, it must first realize a capitalist economy.[57] In addition to his differences regarding the economy, he soon became skeptical of Soviet motivations, as Sandag writes: "Danzan recognized the gap between Soviet words and actions when some of their representatives began to openly interfere in Mongolia's internal party and state affairs."[58] Wary as he was of Soviet motivations, Danzan became a threat to the kind of Soviet-Mongol relations that the Soviets wanted. Thus, it was necessary for the Soviets to find another figure, one who could neutralize Danzen's views and influence. The Buriat El'bekdor Rinchino, of the radical socialists, matched Danzan's rising power:

> In political terms the basic disunity within the party leadership expressed itself as a disagreement between those who wanted Mongolia to follow the Soviet path straight away, and those who considered she was not ripe for an experiment in communism. In personal terms it was a duel between the Buriat Rinchino and the Khalkha Danzan. It was common knowledge that the two simply could not stand each other.[59]

Rinchino was powerful in his own right and his position in the Dotood Yaam made him a dangerous opponent.[60] Furthermore, the Soviet's growing concern over Danzan's allegiance gave Rinchino the political leverage for which he had been waiting. With the aid of Choibalsan and his "Youth Death Squad," Rinchino accused Danzan of conspiring against the state.[61] On August 30, 1924, Choibalsan's men dragged

Danzan outside the Great Qural where he was summarily executed, allegedly for plotting with the Chinese against the Soviet Union.[62]

THE FALL OF THE MONGOLIAN SANGHA

With Danzan's removal, there were no further threats of liberal socialist ideas that might deter the MPRP from its attack on the Mongolian Sangha. The Soviet Union and the Dotood Yaam now were able to direct their full attention to their first and last remaining threat. This battle was meticulously planned and required background research on the Sangha so that the socialists understood just what it was that they were fighting. A retired Dotood Yaam worker, Luvsanchültem Sodov, gives this account of their preparation:

> We became secretaries of the representatives of the Government official Losol. One day he called us in and said that we must follow Gombodoo. He said to us, "You should calculate all the livestock in 30 *aimag*s for 1926 and 1927. This is a secret job. You need to work with this old man, Bari." We started our job. We were done in 1928. Then, a representative of the Dotood Yaam person came and said we should not reveal the information. We had two copies of the calculations. I gave one of them to the Dotood Yaam official.[63]

This intelligence was used a year later when government workers abruptly began to secretly tax the lamas. Jamsrangiin Sambuu gives a personal account of how they seized the assets of high-ranking and middle-ranking lamas:[64]

> In all secrecy we divided these nobles into three groups, and before dawn we went off in various directions on ready horses from the relay station, and before midday we had seized and sealed the fixed assets of those nobles, and then we registered their cattle, warning them that if they suppressed any, or got rid of them by surreptitiously passing them on to others, they would be committing a criminal offense.[65]

The Soviet Union directly supported these actions and Mongols such as Sambuu were rewarded for their loyalty and sent to Moscow.[66]

In 1925, the party issued a pamphlet entitled *The Historic Decree on Party Policy towards Religion.*[67] On the surface it appeared simply to be an attempt to publicly recognize the Buddhist hierarchy, but in reality, this was a shrewd way to ascertain the Sangha's composition and its operating structure, as well as a means to understand the Mongolian Sangha's inherent class structure, which consisted of the *shabinar*, low-ranking lamas, middle-ranking, and high-ranking lamas. The information proved extremely useful because it demonstrated to the MPRP that there were disproportionate numbers of low-ranking lamas and *shabinar* compared with the middle- and high-ranking and land-owning lamas.

The MPRP recognized that in order to eliminate the Mongolian Sangha it was first necessary to create a schism between the land-owning lamas and the *shabinar* on the one hand and the low-ranking lamas on the other. The most distinctive difference between these two groups was their economic position—the high-ranking and middle-ranking lamas owned land and usually held more cattle. By carefully targeting only the high-ranking lamas, the MPRP taxed and confiscated the lamas' cattle. Through these taxes and confiscations, a dramatic shift in ownership began to occur between the Mongolian Sangha and the MPR. "Properties belonging to nobles and lamaseries were confiscated; sliding scale and high taxation of lamas and temples were introduced to impede the recruitment of monks and to redistribute church herd."[68] The MPRP was untroubled by the Sangha's discontent. The MPR continued to tax and confiscate lama property, which finally roused the land-owning lamas from their lethargy. In 1926, hundreds of high-ranking lamas revolted against the taxation of their land and herds. A lama named Yondon, from the Bogd Qaan administration, stirred up trouble by starting a rumor that the ninth incarnation of the Bogd Gegeen had been discovered.[69] These disturbances were quickly quashed, of course, but lama discontent escalated.

The high-ranking and some low-ranking lamas then found a new way of fighting the MPRP's influence. Both the MPRP and the Mongolian Sangha dispersed propaganda, but in this tactic the MPRP was at a disadvantage.[70]

For many years the Mongolian Sangha maintained a printing system with a well-connected group of monasteries and *shabinar* in place for the dissemination of Buddhist ideas. In addition to these practical advantages, the people also supported the Mongolian Sangha. Thus, the MPRP was urged to take stronger actions.

Yet in order for the MPRP to take up this stronger stance to the Mongolian Sangha it required a removal of its international "eye." On August 1, 1927, in an effort to remove all international objections to Soviet plans, Stalin told the Mongols that any international person or organization that did not support the Soviet Union (and its designs) would be considered an enemy of the Soviet Union. Furthermore, whoever opposed the Soviet Union also opposed revolutions and, therefore, was an enemy of the Mongolian People's Republic.[71] At that time, many international organizations were operating in Ulaanbaatar. According to Shirin Akiner, they included Scandinavian missionaries, European technicians, and American business firms. Mongols were encouraged to go abroad and develop international ties, and as a result, many of the brightest minds were sent to study in France and Germany. Six months after Stalin's decree in 1928, all such activity abruptly ceased. Foreign businessmen were expelled from Mongolia and the Mongols studying abroad were recalled.[72]

Once the perceived threat from international quarters had been removed, the MPRP escalated its attack on the Mongolian Sangha by attacking its educational system. It was through the educational system that the Mongolian Sangha was able to attract new low- and middle-ranking lamas, and for centuries the laity had depended on the Mongolian Sangha to educate its people. At that time, the number of students studying within the Mongolian Sangha was greater than all students studying in MPRP public institutions.[73] If the MPRP hoped to gain favorable public opinion, monastic education had to be eliminated. In 1928, the MPR mandated a separation between the Sangha and the state.[74] One of the results of this mandate was prohibiting lamas from teaching in the monasteries without the consent of the local, secular administrative officer.[75] This severely limited the Sangha's influence on the people and, by limiting teaching within the monasteries, a devastating blow was dealt to the rural Mongol on many levels. Even so, the appeal of Buddhism prevailed.

Education was only one of the many assets of Mongolian Buddhism. As late as the nineteenth century, the majority of written literature was in the Tibetan language.[76] This monopolization of literacy and educational theory allowed Buddhism to be more than just a religion to the Mongols; it became a venue for education and a repository for Mongol history. Lamas were among Mongolia's doctors, astronomers, and, in many cases, its artists.[77] The Mongolian Sangha, as an institutional authority, embodied Mongolian culture. What is important to discern is that Mongolian society, much like Tibetan and other non-Western societies, was devoid of the impetus that would divide the secular from the sacred. Buddhism pervaded every aspect of Mongolian culture, projecting its far-ranging influence into provincial habits and routines that Westerners normally view as the domain of the secular.[78]

In addition to removing the Mongolian Sangha from its monopoly on education, the MPRP invested energy in the growing Mongolian Youth Revolutionary League, which was comprised of prominent young Mongols who were interested in learning socialist doctrine.[79] In this way, the MPRP hoped to decrease the numbers of new scholars entering the Mongolian Sangha and likewise increase the number of scholars interested in socialism. Although the MPRP's efforts did affect the numbers entering the Mongolian Sangha, Buddhism still managed to attract a majority of young minds with its traditional educational system and religious authority.[80]

Unable to halt the influx of low- and middle-ranking lamas, the MPRP finally found another means to end the continuing power of the high-ranking lamas. In 1929 the MPRP effectively thwarted the future growth of high-ranking lamas by decreeing an immediate halt to searches for reincarnations.[81] Some prominent Mongols tried to resist these increasingly oppressive reforms, but their efforts were lost amidst a veritable storm of crippling and restrictive legislation. Similar to Jamtsarano's earlier efforts, a proposal to create a new form of Buddhism that could be merged with Marxist ideals was put before the Mongolian *qural*:

Right-wing elements in the MPRP, headed by Damba-Dorzhi and Dja-Demba aimed to switch the MPR to the capitalist path of development. . . . They preached in favour of bourgeois nationalism and the reactionary ideas of Pan-Mongolianism and tried to preserve and adapt Lamaism to the new conditions.[82]

Djademba and Dambadorj, two of those who hoped to affect some form of harmonization between the disparate worldviews, were both removed from office shortly after these proposals were made, allegedly for conspiring with the Japanese.[83]

By the end of 1929, any and all resistance to the MPRP's escalating aggression was quelled. The winds of change now blew in favor of the Soviets, socialism, and the Dotood Yaam. Danzan's death marked the end of Mongolian nationalism. Repeated purges of the ministers and the legislature effectively intimidated most future idealists or intellectuals. Few attempted to curb the MPR from its viciously aggressive political agenda.[84] The next period of history, in fact, was a horrific time for Mongol Buddhists and the Sangha. After the movement toward democracy began in 1990, this earlier era came to be known as a nightmare about which no Mongol wished to talk.

6

VOICES FROM THE REIGN OF TERROR
IN BUDDHIST MONGOLIA
(1929–1940)

The MPRP's polity mirrored Stalin's Soviet Union in the 1930s with its emphasis on propaganda and collectivization, and its implementation of new economic programs.[1] Following the prohibition on searches for reincarnations and the levying of special taxes for lamas, the MPRP was able to launch its ultimate assault on the Mongolian Sangha. It was during this period that the MPRP publicly denounced Buddhism, claiming it to be a "backward concept" that had manipulated the Mongols for centuries.[2] The MPRP began a war on the Mongolian Sangha that would benefit the interests of the Soviet Union as well as the Mongolian People's Revolutionary Party. This era marked the beginning of an unremitting reign of terror upon Buddhist Mongolia until its demise in 1940.[3]

By the early 1930s, the Mongolian Sangha was completely disenfranchised from the Mongol polity. Furthermore, its tenuous relationship with an apathetic laity yielded only meager support from the people. The MPRP's economic pressure on the Mongolian Sangha had intensified, causing minor uprisings that in 1932 culminated in a full-scale revolt on the Mongol polity. High-ranking lamas led the revolt and promised a reemergence of a Buddhist polity. It was this possibility that caught Soviet attention and eventually led to their sending forces to Mongolia. With Soviet troops in Ulaanbaatar, the MPRP managed to regain control; however, the Soviets needed reassurance that this control would last. This reassurance was to come in the guise of Qorlogiin Choibalsan's leadership and the Mongol's secret police, the Dotood Yaam.

After a decade of terror, Choibalsan and the Dotood Yaam effectively silenced ecclesiastical challenges and completely effaced Buddhism from Mongolian culture. This was accomplished by an all-out assault upon Buddhist culture. Lamas were beaten, thrown into labor camps, or shot, their bodies left to rot in uncovered pits. Monasteries were torn down, burned, or used as prisons camps or to house Russian soldiers. The MPRP's administration did not change significantly until Choibalsan's death in 1952. By then, the Mongol polity was firmly anchored in a religious apathy, an atheistic socialism that left no room for institutional Buddhism.

The impetus for the anti-lama campaign that began in the late 1920s clearly came from the Soviet Union. As early as 1927, the Kremlin exerted pressure on the young MPRP to eradicate the Mongolian Sangha. At this point, however, the MPRP was still divided in its relationship with the Sangha. Sandag writes:

> The Mongolians tried to disregard the Comintern demand, indicating that the lamas and their centuries-long ideology were a substantial portion of the population. The Soviets would not listen. They increased the pressure.[4]

By 1929, the MPRP was focused on the task of uprooting the Mongolian Sangha. Results from the MPRP analysis of the Buddhist hierarchy disclosed that the majority of Sangha members primarily were drawn from the low-ranking lamas and *shabinar*. The MPRP had already isolated the *shabinar* from the Mongolian Sangha with laws that mandated the separation of Sangha and state. These laws prevented the Sangha from taxing the *shabinar* and using their land, a restriction that reduced the Mongolian Sangha's *jas* (property). Furthermore, even the ability to remain in robes was made nearly impossible as the MPRP lured the low-ranking lamas and loyal *shabinar* away from the Mongolian Sangha and blocked the training of new lamas. However, before these policies could be completely effective for the MPRP, it was necessary to gain the support of the people by promoting their own public image.

To accomplish these goals, the MPRP published propagandist newspapers that targeted particular segments of Mongol society.[5] In order to maximize the effectiveness of socialist propaganda, it was necessary to restrict all external influences, especially education. Just like the previous political administrations, the MPRP knew how education could be used as a means of redirecting the youth. A ban restricting any Mongol under the age of eighteen from studying at a monastery was imposed while another restriction was directed toward health care for a simple reason. For centuries the Mongol lama was respected as a religious figure, an educator, and a Tibetan "doctor"[6]; but under the new laws the realms of education and medicine were confined to the secular.[7]

Sociological changes were also designed to specifically target segments of the populace. The education of Mongol youth had become an early preoccupation for the MPRP. For example, the Mongolian Youth Revolutionary League (MYRL) launched in 1921 had been formed, in part, to create a controlled group of rising socialist intellectuals. In its early stages, Qorlogiin Choibalsan initially presided over it.[8] The MYRL served as an excellent conduit for socialist propaganda. As the propaganda intensified against the Mongolian Sangha, MYRL participants began exhibiting malicious behavior towards the lamas. In 1929, MYRL purged its members of those against or even ambivalent toward the MPRP.[9] The result was a group so extreme in their views that their actions became detrimental to the benign and less radical movements of the MPRP. In order to save face, the MYRL's Central Committee was forced to reprimand its members publicly in 1930 via an official letter. This letter, while reprimanding its members, simultaneously revealed MYRL's actions:

> The arbitrary expulsion of young lamas from their monasteries has taken place in almost every *aimag*, and other actions contrary to policy have occurred, offending the piety of the people and the lamas. Such activities include: the destruction of stupas, the gouging out of the eyes of statues of the Buddha, stopping people from giving free-will offerings to the monasteries, and so on. Offensive actions of this sort have proved a great hindrance to the work of getting the poor lamas on the side of the People's government, and attracting the people away from the authority of the monasteries.[10]

"The Lama Devourer," Political Repression Museum of Ulaanbaatar.
Artist and date of painting unknown.

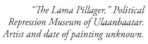*"The Lama Pillager," Political*
Repression Museum of Ulaanbaatar.
Artist and date of painting unknown.

This iconoclastic behavior toward Buddhism derived from the socialist and MPRP propaganda. As the MYRL show, it was not only the Mongolian Sangha that was under attack, but also Mongolian Buddhism's signification. Along with the influx of Marxist symbols and doctrine came its condemnation of religion and its denigration of Mongolian Buddhism, which it sought to replace. Booklets such as *Ways for the Anti-Buddhist League to Carry Out Propaganda against Religion* were widely distributed, offering advice on how to disseminate propaganda.[11] The illustrations serve as examples of how Mongolian lamas were regarded and depicted in this kind of propaganda. They were the devourers and destroyers of land and property, and the mortal enemy of the workers.

The propaganda program was so successful that the social animosity generated in reaction to MYRL's actions hindered the MPRP's efforts to persuade lamas to apostatize. A retired lama, Rentsendavaa Danzanshagdar, recounts how attendance at a MYRL meeting distanced him from the MPRP movement. A MYRL representative instructed the members to build a fire and burn the contents of a monastery. "So, we young people had no choice. We did everything that [the representative] said. And they said that we were fulfilling the responsibilities of the Youth Revolutionary Party."[12]

The MPRP's propaganda program affected Mongols other than those belonging to the MYRL, and led to the formation of organizations such as the Anti-Buddhist League, which fashioned itself after the League of Militant Godless in the Soviet Union.[13]

By 1930, the MPRP was resolutely and completely compliant to Soviet thinking. The eighth MPRP congress passed a resolution that attacked the idea of neo-Buddhism and declared the Mongolian Sangha to be an enemy of the state.[14] Religious political figures were removed during this period and accused of conspiring against the Mongolian People's Republic. For example, the Eguzer Qotagt, a high-ranking lama who worked as the minister for governing the southeastern region of Mongolia, was killed in 1930 along with seven others, all of whom were accused of conspiring against the government.[15]

The MPRP's motivation for collectivization also changed. They no longer wished to impede the growth of the Mongolian Sangha for the sake of socialist principles; rather, they sought to become economic competitors. Aggressive taxing and confiscation of property became malicious and relentless:

> Cadres sent into the countryside to force collectivization, forced rebellion instead by their brutality and ignorance of local customs. . . . The cadre had a clear writ for their act, no matter how violent. The Eighth Party Congress empowered them to take whatever steps required to prohibit the masses from worshipping, to prevent veneration of Buddhist scriptures, to destroy or close monasteries, to forcibly take over administration of local governments, and finally, expel all lamas under 18.[16]

In previous centuries, high-ranking lamas enjoyed an economic advantage. They were able to acquire capital through labor and the imposition of taxes under the *shabinar* system. Because of these advantages, they were classified among Mongolia's rich "feudals." Many of the holdings that the MPRP originally seized included property from these high-ranking lamas, such as revenue accumulated through taxes, herding, or trading. After these changes were implemented, however, even low-ranking lamas who needed additional income from an outside job were targeted to lose their benefits as well as their position. Low-ranking lamas were given the choice of either paying a steep tax or joining the army.

These seizures were known officially as the *jas* campaign. Although the campaign was disguised in ideological language, the real goal was to funnel the economic power of the Mongolian Sangha into the MPRP by confiscating its funds. To this end, the confiscated funds were used as incentives for low-ranking lamas who apostatized.[17] This campaign implemented a strategy derived from the MPRP's research on the Buddhist hierarchy and it did produce results, but it was not as successful as the party had hoped it would be.

Thus, these economic cutbacks were systematized with increasingly lower-ranking targets. The MPRP began by attacking the Buddhist construct through its leaders. First, they eliminated the leader of the Mongolian Sangha, the Eighth Bogd Qaan, and then, tey targeted the high-ranking lamas, followed by the low-ranking lamas. If the MPRP had been able to conceive of any other strategy for destroying the Mongolian Sangha, they could have found none better.

Because of the prior amalgamation of Sangha and state, it was almost impossible to distinguish the feudals from the clergy, yet the socialists did so successfully and vigorously. A common misconception of this period is a distinction drawn between the Mongols classified as "feudals" and the high-ranking lamas. Murphy states that:

> In 1929, 699 feudal estates (comprising herds and fixed property rather than land) were distributed to lay Mongols and to lamas who wished to leave their monasteries. In 1931 and 1932 the property of 837 clerical and lay lords were expropriated. This measure was carried out in two waves, the secular group being expropriated first and the religious next.[18]

Mongolian records may provide clues that explain this distinction between secular and religious groups. As stated previously in chapter 5, the MPRP attempted to justify politically the "emancipation from the shackles of capitalism."[19] The Chinese government had encouraged a prosperous, albeit religiously lax, Mongolian Sangha as the most obvious institution to be opposed by a socialist polity. It was politically advantageous for the MPRP to record in the history books that feudals were being stripped of their property. It would have been much more difficult to justify this action against pious mendicant lamas. It is also likely that wealthy Mongols, who could be considered secular, were financially integral to the Mongolian Sangha because of their donations, who like much of the nobility, had joined the Sangha to avoid paying taxes.[20]

Previously under the Bogd Qaan's administration, the economic elements of the Mongolian Sangha were protected under a sacred blanket. Now, under the new socialist administration with the separation of the Sangha from the state, economic luxuries and necessities under the Sangha system were eliminated by the MPRP. Whether we speak of Murphy's first (secular) or second (religious) stage, the Mongolian Sangha was fundamentally under attack from all sides.

In response to this aggressive socialism in 1932, lamas congregated outside monasteries and retaliated. Part of the difficulty in suppressing these uprisings was in finding soldiers who would oppose the lamas. Charles Bell writes:

> According to an Outer Mongol monk, two Red Mongols washed their clothes in a cauldron, being one used for boiling the tea for the monks. The monks, enraged, beat the two Reds so severely that they died. The matter was reported to Urga, which sent forty carloads of soldiers, but these soldiers joined the monks. The officer in charge of them fled and returned to Urga.[21]

The very Mongols who responded with passivity during the 1921 revolution now demonstrated the same behavior towards the Buddhist rebellion. In 1931, lamas appealed to the Panchen Lama to help in an uprising, but received only verbal support.[22] From 1930 to 1932, revolts occurred across Mongolia; the *aimag* (provinces) of Qövsgöl, Arqangai, Övörqangai, Bulgan, and Üvs all recorded rebellions.[23] These rebellions were not without repercussions. Baabar disdainfully reflects on the words of Russian communism's founder, Vladimir Lenin, as they came to life in the steppes of Outer Mongolia: "Here [at] the secret urging of Lenin given ten years before, 'The more cruel lamas and representatives of cruel capitalism we kill, the more it will benefit us,' were executed verbatim."[24]

Moses states that although the most intense revolts occurred where oppression was the most severe, in Qövsgöl and Üvs *aimag*, lama leaders from Arqangai and Övörqangai *aimag* led the most effective rebellion against the MPRP in 1932.[25] After failing to upset the MPRP by establishing their own political party, the lamas rallied together and staged a revolt. This revolt was so successful that the MPRP was forced for a second time to rely on the Soviet military: "This time it was beyond the capacity of the Mongolian Army to deal with the situation—many of its members fought [as allies] with the rebels—so the Soviet Army was called in to help prevent the complete collapse of Party authority."[26] In July 1932, tanks, the Red Army, and the forces of the NKVD (Narodnyi Komissariat Vnutrennikh Del), a Soviet department overseeing various governmental affairs, were rushed into Outer Mongolia to protect the MPRP from the lama revolutionaries.[27] This Soviet action finally dispelled any previous misconceptions that the Soviets were Buddhist allies and discredited the theory that the Red Army was the legendary army from the ethereal land of Tibet's Shambhala. Moses writes:

> But of greatest appeal was the promise of achieving an earthly utopia with the aid of an apocalyptic army from the unearthly realm of Shambhala. Shambhala, a heavenly kingdom, lay somewhere in the undefined north. The lack of precise geographical definition allowed Comintern propagandists to identify Russia as Shambhala . . .[28]

Today there is a visual illustration of this revolt at the Political Repression Museum in Ulaanbaatar in a painting that depicts a tank attacking the lamas. Reports of this occurrence are still remembered by Mongols, including a young Mongol teacher at the Pedagogical University, who recalls the event:

> I read somewhere when I was young (everyone knows this) that the lamas fought a tank in Tariat Arqangai around 1929–1932. They thought that they could hold the tank with hemp rope. They tried, but the tank was too strong.[29]

It was evident that the MPRP had moved too quickly and too harshly. They realized that, in order to destroy the Mongolian Sangha, they needed to reexamine their strategy and change their methods. The capture and execution of the rebellious leaders were the last extreme acts taken at this time.[30] Recognizing that they had failed to win popular support, the MPRP was determined to improve its public image. Forced secularization of lamas ceased, and those who wanted to return to the Sangha were allowed to do so. The relentless confiscation of property subsided, but there was still a hidden agenda behind the MPRP's conciliatory actions. Brown writes:

> The Special Religious Commission attached to the Presidium of the MPR Little Khural pointed out in a propaganda document that 'The proper path to combat religious belief is revolutionary ideology and we should inculcate revolutionary ideology into the minds of the *ard* [lit., people]

masses; when their lives change (improve), the road to abandoning (religious faith) will be opened automatically in the future.[31]

These reforms were part of the New Turn, a policy implemented by the MPRP that mirrored the actions of the Soviet Union at the time. As a result of the New Turn, Outer Mongolia appeared as a more welcoming country to both Mongolian intellectuals and Buddhists from abroad. Emigrants were assured that their herds and property would be returned to them.[32] However, the MPRP had not truly rehabilitated itself. Its new attitude was adopted only while it waited for a more opportune time to dismantle the Mongolian Sangha. Meanwhile, its apparent acceptance of Buddhism alleviated the social pressure on low-ranking lamas because of the MPRP's reduction of propaganda output and the cessation of anti-Buddhist sentiments. Taxes, however, were still levied on high-ranking lamas. Additionally, within the Mongolian Sangha ranks of novices were still effectively limited by the age restriction.

Further restrictions were based on two motives: first, to affect the high-ranking lamas; and second, to provide an incentive for lamas to move out of the monasteries. Because high-ranking lamas had always benefited economically, they remained in the monastery. However, low-ranking lamas, who sometimes were forced to live outside the monastery, always had difficulty surviving. Thus, subsequent restrictions that were imposed on the Mongolian Sangha targeted only lamas inside the monastery, since those outside the monastery were barely able to survive in the first place. As Brown writes,

> A resolution further clarifying the question of lama electoral rights issued on May 22, 1934 by the Presidium of the MPR Little Khural and the Council of the Ministry ordered that . . . low lamas who participated in work such as livestock economy and caravan transport have electoral right . . . and lamas permanently staying in temples and monasteries as disciples have no electoral rights.[33]

In 1932, according to Moses, in an attempt to reduce the high-ranking lamas' *jas*, the tax on the Sangha's livestock, was doubled and then doubled again.[34] More important, according to Brown, the MPRP's decree of religious tolerance did little to bring about a decline in Soviet influence:

> The Party itself was faced by a thoroughgoing crisis of confidence, which affected all classes in the country, not least its own adherents. It was the belated recognition of this by the Comintern and the Soviet communist party, which dictated Russian intervention to make the Mongol party see reason and beat a retreat.[35]

Indeed, this statement by Brown and other socialist historians implies that the Soviets controlled the implementation of the New Turn. Indeed, the Soviet Union was involved in numerous Mongolian governmental sectors, as seen by the fact that almost all young Mongols studying abroad went to the Soviet Union. Another example of Soviet involvement was the Mongolian People's Army, which was created and commanded by the Soviets in 1921. The army was solely dependent on the Soviet Union for military training and equipment.[36] In addition, the Soviet Union controlled Mongolia's foreign trade and, like the Manchus, used trade as a way to block or limit outside influence.[37] This trade monopoly with Mongolia was so effective, Murphy says, that the country became completely sealed off from the world:

> Until the 1950s, Outer Mongolia was a region hidden even from most Soviet citizens. Soviet control over Outer Mongolia's press, intellectual life, public opinion, and libraries archives—in fact, all the sources for unbiased historical writing—was complete.[38]

Although the 1932 revolt forced the MPRP to mitigate their attacks on Buddhism, it was only a matter of time before the MPRP succeeded. The rise and fall of MPRP Prime Minister Genden serves as an unfortunate example of the futility of resistance.

Genden was unique for having survived the political purges of the 1920s, and, while others were either eliminated or retired, he rose steadily within the ranks of the Mongolian People's Republic. In the 1920s he was elected chairman of the Lesser Qural and remained aligned with the radical socialists until the early 1930s.[39] However, with the New Turn, Genden began to distance himself from the radical MPRP movement. He is quoted as saying: "When there is posed the question, does the Party lead the Government or does the Government lead the Party, then the Party has no business in leading the Government."[40] When he assumed the post of prime minister (1932–1936), Genden became another example of the paramount influence the Soviets exercised over the MPRP:

> In December 1933, Stalin personally met with Genden and requested that he alter the course of Mongolian economic development. This request included the eradication of the lamas and monasteries and the conversion of their property and capital into cooperatives. Genden refused, giving the excuse that it would take a century to accomplish such a task. His reply, however, was not an absolute refusal to comply with Stalin's request.[41]

Laws relating to lamas and monasteries were subsequently changed to allow for greater discrimination and punishment during Genden's administration.[42] Sandag implicates the KGB in the mass arrests and executions during this period, indicating that the MPRP and Genden were not the sole perpetrators in many of the religious attacks. Although the KGB may have been involved in substantial plots, such as the Jambin Lhumbe affair, KGB involvement does undercut Mongolia's and the Dotood Yaam's responsibility and the part they played during this tumultuous period.[43] Importantly, there was a struggle within the MPRP between Genden's followers and the radicals regarding the amount of support given to Soviet foreign policies and suggestions. However, Genden and the moderates were winning the battle. Yet, as Baabar claims, his open defiance against socialist atheism and Joseph Stalin was to mold his destiny:

> In 1933 Genden openly declared his desire "not to fight with religion." Genden stopped hiding his religious beliefs, he set free lamas who had been arrested on false accusations, and he forbade the arrest of lamas who were maintaining a relationship with the Panchen Bogd.[44]

His open disregard for Stalin's policy on religion and his further refusal to comply with Stalin's requests eventually led to Genden's death.[45]

In an account by Genden's daughter, Tserendulam, Genden died of suspicious causes while he was in the Soviet Union in 1936:

> On our first day back, some people blocked our way into our house. My father was inside. At first, I thought that they were kidding. My mother also wanted to go inside, but they refused to let her in as well. Soon my father came out looking very upset. He told us that we had to go back to Mongolia and not to make a fuss. Then he was ordered not to say anymore and they took him away. . . .
>
> One day I went out to the park to meet some Mongolians. I saw that there was a funeral flag on the door outside of the Mongolian embassy.[46]

One of the trademarks of this reign of terror, which is apparent from the account of Genden's death, was subterfuge. When Stalin needed someone to take Genden's place, it was required that this person be intelligent, ruthless, and, most important, subservient to the Soviet Union. He found that person in Qorlogiin Choibalsan.[47] Choibalsan, who was in charge of the Dotood Yaam at the time of Genden's removal, is credited with Genden's demise as well as many other potential political rivals.[48] Indeed, it was a long road for Choibalsan in his quest for the leadership of the MPRP.

Choibalsan was born on February 8, 1893, to Qorloo and the lama Butemji.[49] They sent him to a monastery at an early age to become a lama. Choibalsan stayed for two years until, reportedly, he ran away to Urga.[50] It was in Urga that he met Bodoo, the future leader of the Consul group. The exact nature of the relationship between Choibalsan and Bodoo is disputed among scholars. Some say he was Bodoo's younger brother, while others maintain that Bodoo adopted him.[51] In either case, there was a strong relationship between the heavily Russian-influenced Bodoo and Choibalsan before the emergence of the MPRP. It was with Bodoo's help that Choibalsan enrolled in the Foreign Ministry School, one of the first institutions to offer a Russian education, where he was to spend a brief time under the tutelage of Jamtsarano.

From the Foreign Ministry School Choibalsan was sent with six other

Mongols to a college in Irkutsk to continue his studies and sharpen his Russian.[52] By 1918 he was back in Mongolia and active as one of the founding members of the MPRP and the MYRL. When the Mongolian People's Republic was officially established in 1921, most of the founding members assumed active roles in the new government. Yet, according to Murphy, Choibalsan's role was initially nominal: "Transcripts of the earlier Mongolian party congresses show Choibalsan to have been an almost silent participant."[53] In 1924, after assisting in Danzan's death, Choibalsan became commander-in-chief of the Mongolian army and was elected to the Lesser Qural by the Great Qural.

For a time Choibalsan's presence was quietly felt, but in 1929 he was appointed to a special commission that was responsible for confiscating properties from the lamas and feudals.[54] However, Choibalsan and his radical group were attacked when Genden rose to power in the MPRP. In 1934, Choibalsan was sent with others to Moscow by a resolution of the Central Committee of the Great Qural. According to Dashpurev, it was during this time that Choibalsan met Stalin and became acquainted with his administration:

> In 1934, when Givaapil and Choibalsan were under the custody of Soviet Secret Police in Moscow and a judicial investigation was going on, they met each other. It is an established fact that after some time, Choibalsan became a supporter of Stalin's terror in Mongolia and it is probable that he learnt the finer points of communist terrorism at the KGB headquarters in Moscow.[55]

There was an additional factor that might have played a role in Choibalsan's manner and intense lack of tolerance. As is still the case in Mongolia today, alcoholism was of epidemic proportions in Mongolia, and MPRP members were no exception. An employee of the state, Erdembileg Gompil, who worked under Choibalsan during Genden's administration, also noticed Choibalsan's proclivity to abuse alcohol:

> In 1932, the beginning of May, in Arqangai aimag, there was a counter-revolutionary uprising. Because of this, we formed a volunteer committee.

Approximately 350 people were involved. Choibalsan was the committee leader. . . . During the time I worked with Choibalsan, it was typical for him to drink a lot. He had a Tibetan cook, and he [Choibalsan] was always drunk. When I visited him at his wooden house in the steppes, he would be drunk and so was his wife, Bortolgoi.[56]

Friends and coworkers alike considered Choibalsan to be an alcoholic, so much so that his reader (commissioned by Choibalsan as a reviewer) Tsedev Dash comments on Choibalsan's tendency to drink and notes several occasions at which he drank excessively:

In 1934 Choibalsan became vice prime minister and in 1936 he held the title of Marshall. At that time his wife, Bortolgoi, supposedly said, "Both of us drink too much. You are now in a high position, but you do not need to drink. Stop drinking."[57]

Alcohol may have been a way for Choibalsan to cope with Stalin's orders. It could have been just a bad habit that he picked up. Nevertheless, it impacted on his judgment and his temperament. His relationships with members of the MPRP were often tense because of his immense power and erratic temper. One Mongol, a train stationmaster, offers his opinion of Choibalsan and his involvement during the "reign of terror":

Now, many people said that Choibalsan was a very bad person. If Choibalsan was a good, though very brutal, person, then I had indeed led a dissolute life and our country would have been fine. Back then many people said that all these internal problems were due to Choibalsan. Choibalsan was very smart, but he used his intelligence in the wrong way. . . . He was an alcoholic. Partisan Demberel said that Choibalsan did not listen to anyone and that he was a rather strange person.[58]

Choibalsan quickly took steps to fill the office vacated by Genden. Between 1936 and 1939, Choibalsan served as head of the Dotood Yaam, minister of war, commander-in-chief of the army, prime minister, and minister of foreign affairs. These were the years when the Dotood Yaam's

Green Hats became infamous.[59] The many governmental positions Choibalsan held allowed him to provoke fear and force compliance in every Mongol. During this time, a Mongolian border guard stated in an interview that Choibalsan was "everything," the head of the Dotood Yaam and the MPRP. No one could refute or disagree with Choibalsan or else they were arrested or killed:

> Before me there had been a metal factory director, Demberel. He was say-ing to the other people, "When I met Choibalsan, I said to him that it was foolishness to arrest so many innocent people." He was so angry and asked, "Do you think that I am blind?" Demberel was arrested after this.[60]

According to this same border guard, Choibalsan appointed many Russians to the Mongolian government. This was no accident. Unlike Genden, Choibalsan maintained close ties with Stalin, which was a dip-lomatic necessity for any Mongol who wished to remain in power during this time. Occasionally, Stalin would reward Choibalsan's loyalty with gifts. Sometimes the gifts were not rewards, but rather subtle suggestions. For example: "In 1935, Choibalsan was appointed first deputy prime minister. He received a gift of 20 Soviet GAZ automobiles from the Soviet Union at the time, indicative of his rising status."[61] The next year Stalin gave Choibalsan four rifles and thirty thousand bullets. The number presaged the number of executions that Choibalsan ordered shortly afterward.[62]

By 1937 the Soviet Union had invested a considerable amount of effort and capital in Choibalsan and in the destruction of the Mon-golian Sangha. At the same time, political activities around the world were slowly affecting the Soviet Union for the worse:

> The Soviet Union recognized the grave threat of the Japanese to the south and east into Inner Mongolia. Not only would it lose its broad buffer protecting the Trans-Siberian line, it would be cut off from contact with North China and Chinese communists.[63]

It was because of Mongolia's geography that Soviet interests intensi-fied during Choibalsan's administration. Mongols became the primary recruits for the Soviet defense forces, and Mongol soldiers became spies who guarded the Mongolian borders on behalf of the Soviets.[64]

The Soviets soon realized that the Mongolian support forces needed to be protected. According to Tserendorj, at the time an assistant to a Mongol general, a Russian delegate spoke at a banquet and requested assistance from every MPRP member present in supporting Choibalsan's policies:

> At the banquet this Russian delegate said, "In your country there are many people against the revolution. You should kill them all as soon as possible." He [Frinovskii] also said, "In this business, Choibalsan is really lonely. So please, please help him, especially Prime Minister Amar. You should take it upon yourself to help Choibalsan in this effort." He ended by saying, "I am saying this in the name of Russia."[65]

Time was no longer a luxury and the situation was becoming dire for the Soviets. Thus, in order to use recent events to their advantage, the Soviets declared that lamas and ethnic minorities (for example, the Buriats along the northeastern border) were conspiring with Japanese spies.[66]

When news of this conspiracy became known, it allowed the MPRP the leverage it needed to eliminate the political opposition. Certainly, ethnicity was an issue for the Mongols, since ethnic consciousness is intrinsic to any socialist cultural construction. The Qalq ethnic minority, which constituted the largest and the poorest class, ultimately was favored by the socialist administration.[67]

As an illustration of these events, it might be noted that Zanabazar's prestige under the socialist period suffered from both the Qalq and Buddhist issues.[68] However, religious issues overshadowed ethnic ones. Even though the Qalq were given preferential treatment, the importance of ethnicity remained a secondary issue to the one of religion. Next to the means of production, it was religion that shaped the core of socialist doctrine. Because religion was so antithetical to the purported nature of socialism, it became part of the very paradigm that socialism sought to escape.

The Mongolian Sangha was portrayed as the cause of economic exploitation in socialist propaganda, just as the Qalq were framed as the exploited. More important, contrary to the case of Mongol ethnicities, religious identity served no useful purpose in the new socialist identity. Highlighting this distinction, Bulag cites the following statement by Choibalsan: "About the Buryats [Buriats]: The Japanese have been seeking agents among them just like among the lamas; as far as they are concerned, I am not referring to the entire Buryats, I should not say so."[69]

The Mongolian Sangha, now identified as the enemy, had aligned itself with the Japanese, whose military forces had recently advanced into Inner Mongolia. In an effort to drive home the Soviet idea of the duplicity of the Sangha, the MPRP began to disseminate propaganda material that implicated the lamas and the Sangha. The propaganda was so persuasive that lay Mongols began to accept the accusations as true.[70]

The MPRP followed whatever policies or propaganda Choibalsan accepted and could pass on to the populace. An MPRP member, Tseren Tserendorj, states:

> At the end of the meeting some people stood up and spoke. Most of them said that they wanted to congratulate Mr. Choibalsan and his assistant Damba for a job well done. They truly were trying to eradicate all the people who were against the party and that this was the right thing to do.[71]

During this time Mongolia was experiencing a cult of personality. With complete Soviet backing, Choibalsan found that he held as much control as had the Bogd Qaan before him.[72]

Choibalsan, unlike his predecessors, had no reservations about using terror to the fullest extent possible. He strategically brought border guards and other important subordinates to witness an execution of fourteen men as a visual example of his power and lack of tolerance.[73] If it proved necessary, Choibalsan's tactics could be deceitful and merciless. In 1937, to clear up any doubt as to who were his supporters in the aftermath of the deaths of Genden and Demid, another well-known political figure, Choibalsan stated, "If anybody exposes someone he would be free from execution." His promise was just another charade. After this proclamation, Choibalsan killed over ten thousand people, many of whom had been promised immunity.[74] Even Mongol socialist historians who defend the MPRP and its efforts to destroy the Mongolian Sangha acknowledge the ruthlessness with which Choibalsan ruled:

> However, during the course of the above-mentioned struggles, Kh. Choi-balsan committed serious errors which violated revolutionary law in the operations of the Ministry of the Interior which he instituted through his own direct leadership and orders.[75]

Choibalsan felt no remorse, nor did he object to the destruction of the Mongolian Sangha. This was one of the determining factors that ultimately won Stalin's favor.[76] Laws continued to escalate against lamas during Choibalsan's rule. The military tax that was placed on lamas who were of the age to join the army increased over 1,000 percent between 1933 and 1938,[77] and the law separating Sangha and state was amended in 1936 to prevent the first and second sons of a family from becoming lamas.[78] Under Choibalsan, tactical use of terror intensified, making possible for the first time the eradication of the Mongolian Sangha. Thousands of lamas were forced to join the military, apostatize, or, if they chose defiance, arrested and shot.[79] All of this was made possible through Choibalsan's most effective tool, the Dotood Yaam.

The Dotood Yaam provoked fear in the everyday Mongol during the reign of terror.[80] The fear was justified. The Dotood Yaam was an incredibly powerful and unmonitored segment of the Mongol polity consisting of informants, researchers, inspectors, and special police forces. The Dotood Yaam had already been granted extra freedoms during Genden's administration:

> The Special Part of the 1934 Criminal Law consisted of nine chapters and 132 articles. The number and scope of counter-revolutionary crimes was substantially enlarged, a distinction was drawn in the structure of the Code between especially dangerous crimes against the administrative order and simply "other" such crimes . . .[81]

Detail of "One Day in the Life," by Irjnee, Political Repression Museum, Ulaanbaatar. This section of the large wall painting depicts the state-sponsored genocide, 1936–1940, when Mongol lamas were arrested, interrogated, and executed for their religious identity.

This new change in criminal law allowed the Dotood Yaam a certain license, particularly in arrests and severe punishments that required little or no justification. Genden himself had sought to turn the Dotood Yaam against the MPRP radicals, and this was not the first time the Dotood Yaam had been used in this way.[82] Danzan's death, among others, was ordered by the Dotood Yaam. After 1936, under Choibalsan's supervision, the Dotood Yaam became a finely tuned organization that was charged primarily with the eradication of the Mongolian Sangha.

Furthermore, Russian influence was constantly applied to the Dotood Yaam. The Soviets had, in fact, been involved with the Dotood Yaam's operations for over twenty years. They were present at the beginning of the Dotood Yaam in 1921 and, in the last years of the reign of terror, Soviet troops often accompanied the Dotood Yaam during mass arrests:

> All the central and provincial branches of the Mongolian Secret Police [Dotood Yaam] started to work for the planned liquidation of the Buddhist monks. For instance, in the summer of 1937, all provincial branches received a cipher (message) directing the arrest of several hundred lamas; and to pursue their political objectives Russian instructors along with their interpreters arrived at the branches from the centre.[83]

As expected, segments of the Dotood Yaam were reserved solely for espionage purposes. Luvsanchültem Sodov was employed in 1937 by the Dotood Yaam to investigate the amount of livestock and salaries of officials in Dornogov and Ömnögov *aimag*.[84] It was also Luvsanchültem's job to keep an eye on the Buddhists. The Dotood Yaam closely scrutinized the Sangha's funds, the extent of public support, and its members. Another member, Tsogt Luvsansamdan, was in charge of categorizing lamas and questioning them:

> We started registering lamas in 1936. There were two kinds of registration. The first group included the high-ranking lamas and also the lamas who usually spread rumors. The second group included the Gavj, the Zurqaich Choijin and the Gürtems. Bayasgalan and Qaimchig were in charge of questioning these people. Each person had to inspect ten lamas,

without fail, every day. Bayasgalan himself questioned ninety lamas a day. Luvsansharav insisted that we should arrest the lamas. . . . A Russian by the name of Gichikov always said criminals should be beaten to get them to talk. If they were beaten, they would tell the truth.[85]

The absolute obedience of the lamas bears testament to the power and effective use of terror by the Dotood Yaam.

Even if the lamas wished to resist the Dotood Yaam, they did not know whom to trust. Unlike the Mongolian army, the Dotood Yaam was filled with spies who carefully watched each other. Baabar writes that some of the Dotood Yaam's cruelest investigators were ex-lamas who had turned themselves in: "Haimchig, who used to read prayers in the monastery, came to be known as the 'butcher of lamas.' One of the leaders of the purge, Luvsansharav, had also been a lama."[86] Penalties for resisting orders usually resulted in execution.[87] In an interview conducted in Ulaanbaatar by Christopher Kaplonski, a border guard was asked about the justification for arrests made by the Dotood Yaam:

"Did arrests require permission from above," [Christopher Kaplonski] asked. He said, "Yes, they did, but it was relatively easy to get. You just told your superiors in the *Dotood Yaam* that you suspected so-and-so of being a Japanese spy, or a counter-revolutionary, or something. People in the Ministry were mainly concerned about getting promoted and they wanted to have 'a good name.' They never thought about the people they arrested, but rather about their own personal life and advancement. They were like animals."[88]

Tsogt Luvsansamdan, also in the role of a spy, when he was young was recruited to instigate fights between the lamas:

I went to the places where many lamas gathered and I would create a problem. Because of this, they would start to beat each other. After this, the police would come and take them. We used this kind of strategy or method to arrest lamas. I would write things up with ten other people. Usually I would choose the place, which would be close to the police.[89]

Always careful of how many people knew what was occurring under his administration, Choibalsan would eventually eliminate those who did the investigating and research. During 1937 and 1938 there were many Mongolian inspectors who worked for the Dotood Yaam. However, in October of 1939, when the destruction of the Mongolian Sangha was still in process, they were all removed from Mongolia and sent to Moscow. In 1949, they were all killed.[90]

Clearly, the methods of the Dotood Yaam were quick and thorough, and the increased intensity under Choibalsan was evident to all Mongols. Survivors and family members of those taken by the Dotood Yaam have compared the visits of the Dotood Yaam before and during Choibalsan's administration:

> The Internal Ministry [Ministry of Internal Affairs] first arrived in Sainshand in 1931. They wore green uniforms. They seized only the head lamas then, about ten of them. When they returned in 1938, there were four Internal Ministry officers, thirty Russian and thirty Mongolian soldiers who came to round up the two hundred lamas.[91]

Surprisingly, the arrests made before the New Turn were usually reversed during this period of Choibalsan's reign, resulting in the release of thousands of lamas. However, many of these same lamas were then re-arrested and, with thousands of newly arrested lamas, simply disappeared:

> My uncle Navaanshiirav was a *tsorg* lama for Jalqanz Qüree. They arrested him in 1932 and sentenced him to ten years in prison, but he came back after [serving] five years. So that means he came back at the end of the summer of 1937. In the spring of 1937 they started to arrest many lamas. Then, in 1939, my uncle was arrested again. To this day I still do not know what happened to him.[92]

The Dotood Yaam was not only powerful and unmonitored, but all possible opposition to it had been eliminated. The Mongolian army was silenced in 1937 because Choibalsan did not want to experience any of the same problems with the army that occurred during the 1932 revolt.[93]

So when the Dotood Yaam's arrests occurred they were, in accordance with terror tactics, sudden and without notice:

> It all changed in 1936. Suddenly, many people came to my home in the countryside on horseback and gathered up all the high-ranking lamas into a wagon. The party members did not say why or where they were going, but they demanded that the lamas leave with them. It was the Dotood Yaam. They had guns and wore green hats. I remember those green hats. At this time, animals and property were confiscated.
>
> The Dotood Yaam bound the high-ranking lamas' hands and feet together and threw them into the wagon.[94]

The green hats were worn exclusively by the Dotood Yaam and the name quickly developed into a nickname, as seen when a Mongol professor recalls his childhood and the chilling memory of the Green Hats:

> The Green Hats came at night to make arrests. They were known as Nogoo Malgai. I was very afraid of the Dotood Yaam. This fear was present all across the country, especially in adults. Anyone could be arrested; fear was everywhere. If there was ever a knock at the door during the night, we were scared. They came with flashlights, and this instrument became one of their trademarks. Children were forbidden to play with these things.[95]

Mongols lived each day with the fear of being arrested by the Dotood Yaam. The number of lamas who were imprisoned or killed was so great that every Mongol family felt the effects. The magnitude of the arrests can be seen in Sandag's statistics, cited by Robert Rupen to be over 120,000 lamas in 1921, 112,000 lamas in 1924, 75,500 in 1930. Rupen writes, "by the late 1930s the lamas had been totally eliminated or dispersed with all monasteries closed and most of them devastated." These numbers alone underscore how many lamas were alive in the 1930s during the reign of terror.[96] The number of lamas killed is still not definitive, but Sandag estimates that about fifty thousand executions occurred.[97]

After being arrested, the Dotood Yaam usually forced their prisoners to confess that in some way they had conspired against, and were enemies of, the state. Conditions were harsh during the questioning period, which could last for many months under terrible living conditions. Admission of guilt was not a declaration of truth; it was simply a matter of attrition. Erdembileg Gompil recounts his experience during the interrogations:

> Usually they asked the intelligentsia four questions: What sort of pan-Mongolist ideas did you spread? What are the counterrevolutionaries up to? Who are you affiliated with? What kind of destruction are you responsible for? . . .
>
> During that time, the Dotood Yaam's methods of interrogation were well known to everyone. There was no one who could help or protect me. Therefore, sometimes I mixed some truth and some false information together. For almost a whole year I did not see the sun. For nearly six months I was not allowed to walk or lie down. I was so hungry that my whole body became swollen.
>
> Only death could end my suffering. Therefore, I agreed to do anything they wanted.[98]

Erdembileg's experience was not unique, nor was it extreme. In fact, Erdembileg can be considered fortunate since he was held for questioning. Many people never lived to be interrogated.

By this time the Mongolian Sangha, crippled by both dwindling finances and loss of prestige, was so overwhelmed by the Dotood Yaam that it failed to become a unified entity. Instead, it merely disintegrated into a plethora of individual monasteries and lamas. There were no unified revolts during this time period, nor was there any Buddhist propaganda. Under the circumstances, this situation is certainly understandable. Many lamas were simply rounded up, brought to a pit, and shot one by one. An example of mass execution was recalled in explicit detail:

> The *Dotood Yaam* wore green hats at this time and there were a lot of green hats around. They brought the people up, and lined them up facing the open grave. Their hands were tied behind their back and they were gagged, but not blindfolded. For each person shot, there was a

person with a gun. "*Neg hün, neg buutai hün*" [Mongolian for "There is one person, for each person with a gun"]. The command to shoot was given. Each person was shot one time. They were shot in the back of the head at point-blank range. . . . After the first group was shot, the second group—who had seen what happened—was lined up and shot.[99]

The memoirs of a medical assistant of forensic science adds this account of the mass executions:

> There have been strange happenings during 1937–1940. Every day in the mid-night hours they (Dotood Yaam investigating officers) used to call me and when I reached there, I saw every time about 30 to 40 prisoners lying in a lorry. They were pushed into the lorry in a throwing manner by some tall men who were working and covered their faces and body with white masks and cloaks. After that the prisoners were taken to the mountain and were shot down by those tall men . . .[100]

It can be said that the only times that mass executions occurred was when the Dotood Yaam visited the monasteries, a statement which highlights the extreme measures taken in the effacement of the Mongolian Sangha. For example, in 1938 there were three hundred lamas residing at the Qamariin Qiid monastery in Arqangai *aimag* (province). The Dotood Yaam arrested two hundred, and another eighty-nine were shot ten kilometers north of the monastery.[101] A contemporary Mongolian reporter, Rinchin, accidentally discovered the location of one of these mass executions. In 1992, when Rinchin was filming a documentary on Mongolia's previous era of political repression, he found seven pits that were dug for bodies in Qövsgöl *aimag*. The corpses were apparently never buried properly but had been preserved for decades by the cold winters. After witnessing this sight with its sickening stench, Rinchin ended his documentary. An occurrence such as this leaves no question as to whether or not Choibalsan used all of Stalin's gift of thirty thousand bullets.

At the Memorial Museum for the Victims of the Political Repressions in Ulaanbaatar, a plaque reads: "1937–1939, there were 767 monasteries. There were around 70,000 lamas, 17,000 of whom were arrested and

13,680 of whom were shot." These figures are the only statistics that have been officially tabulated. Mongolian accounts of the deaths of lamas are still incomplete because the Ministry of Internal Affairs has made some of their archival information inaccessible.[102] The statistics from the plaque also reflect the percentage of lamas who apostatized. According to the numbers above, at least 40,000 lamas left the Mongolian Sangha. Most disrobed out of fear and became herdsmen. Yasanjav, a sixty-year-old teacher in Arqangai *aimag*, tells how his father abandoned the Mongolian Sangha:

> In 1936 my father was a lama in Bolgan *aimag* [province]. He told me about Ganga, my grandfather, who was a high-ranking lama. One hundred and eighty lamas were killed, including my grandfather. Eighty lamas were sent to prison for ten years. After this happened, my father was frightened. So, even though he was a lama, he quit being a lama, and went to work as a herdsman in the countryside.[103]

For those monks who did not disrobe and were not shot, the labor camps in Ulaanbaatar awaited where they would work on the construction of Russian-designed buildings. Lamas, who had been arrested and were now being directed by the Dotood Yaam, exclusively filled these camps.[104] These lamas were generally younger and not high-ranking ones, but old enough to have strong Buddhist roots.[105] Murphy credits Mongolia's increased industrial output in 1937 and 1938 to the increased labor output brought about by lamas who were forced to apostatize.[106] The transformation of religious followers into soldiers and laborers was a tremendous blow to the Mongolian Sangha. However, to the MPRP it was a symbol of victory.[107] One example of this was the Qalqin Gol war in 1939, when Russians and Mongols fought against the Japanese. Over seven hundred Mongolians reportedly died in this battle, significantly less than their opponents.[108] Yet, of these seven hundred, many were ex-lamas who were forced to join the army and, it is said, placed in the frontlines of battle.[109]

Remarkably, in 1939 there still were some lamas in the monasteries who could afford to pay the exorbitant taxes. Public sentiment had altered so completely during Choibalsan's campaign, however, that people started to kill lamas on sight. This forced these lamas to change their clothes and their professions, and enlist as soldiers. By the end of 1939, the high taxes forced all lamas to join the military.[110] Namuubu-daa, an eighty-one-year-old lama, remembers the effects of the taxes and his own final submission to its pressure:

> I was eighteen years old when the socialist period began. I was working at a monastery at that time. Before that time, upon turning eighteen, lamas had to pay a tax to the government to remain a lama. If not, they had to leave and join the army.
>
> Then the law changed so that everyone had to go into the army. Around 1936, there were three hundred lamas and all of them had to become laymen. Before this law was enacted, the tax was between thirty and forty tögrög to remain a lama, which in 1999 was the equivalent of thirty thousand to forty thousand tögrögs.1 It was a very strict law and a very expensive one. Young lamas joined the army and old ones stayed at the monastery. I was in the army from 1939 to 1944.[111]

Choibalsan's objective was not only to eliminate the lamas, but also to remove any special public relationship to and reverence for Buddhism. The Dotood Yaam was extremely successful in its sweep, destroying, and burning relics everywhere it went. During the process of these sweeps, the Dotood Yaam also seized the last of the Mongolian Sangha's wealth and deposited it directly into the coffers of the MPRP.[112] Those who tried to prevent this were arrested or shot:

> Dashzevegn and Qaizen, who were representatives of the Dotood Yaam, came to his home, arrested him, and took his things. Just before his arrest my uncle told me that I should hide the mountain bell with the golden finial and the silver *damar* [hand drum]. So I went to Burenqaan Ulaan Uzuur Mountain, made something to hold them in, and stored them together in it.
>
> When my uncle went to prison, I told my mother what I did for him and she asked me to go back to the mountain and bring back the

items. She felt that they should be at home. So I brought them [back]. Then my mother told other people about this. Very soon after this I was called to the central headquarters of Burenqaan *süm* [district]. Jantsan questioned me. . . .[113]

Even apostatized lamas were sometimes killed simply because of their prior occupation. The Setsen Qaan, Navaanneren, was a lama at a monastery in Qentii *aimag*. He left the Mongolian Sangha and worked for the MPRP as a deputy chairman at the Institute of Sciences in Ulaanbaatar. However, in 1937 he was arrested as an enemy of the state.[114]

By 1938, some 760 of the 771 places of Buddhist worship were closed down.[115] Some monasteries, which had been relocated at first, were later closed:

> The Party started by ordering the relocation of 16 Gobi monasteries in early 1937, and the relocation of a further 59 in the winter of the same year. . . . The year 1938 saw the enforced closure of a further 760 major monasteries out of a remaining total of 771, the rest closing in the following year.[116]

Most of these monasteries were completely razed, such as the monastery of D. Dugersuren, from Zavqan *aimag*, who reports that his own monastery, Shumuultain Qüree, was completely burned to the ground.[117] Thus, on an architectural level, Buddhism had been practically wiped out. Baabar writes that out of the eight hundred or so religious structures, almost none remain, signifying a greater loss than just temples: "Within these monastery compounds were included 1,229 separate buildings and 2,887 prayer halls. Some figures indicated that the 767 temples and monasteries included 5,953 buildings and structures."[118]

By 1940, all monasteries had been closed but one. Gandan, the capital monastery, became the exception when it reopened in 1944. From 1938 to 1940 it was used as a Russian barracks and for the next four years was unoccupied. In 1944, when the United States announced the visit of vice president of the US, Henry Wallace, the Mongols felt it necessary to give the impression that Buddhism was still active.[119] Stalin suggested opening one monastery to prevent the US from knowing the truth—that Buddhism had been erased from Mongolia. This suggestion attests to the MPRP's overwhelming success in removing all public vestiges of Mongolian Buddhism. Rupen locates the motivations for these actions in the 1940 constitution, which depicted institutional Buddhism to be diametrically opposed to the new polity:

> The Constitution of 1940 marked the end of feudalism in Mongolia and the elimination of the influence and power of the Buddhist Church. The Communist regime considered Buddhism the main force of feudalism, and the principal enemy to be destroyed in the process of the development of socialism. The regime in Ulan Bator presented the campaign to eliminate Buddhism in the MPR as a "historic accomplishment of the Mongolian people on their non-capitalist path of development" . . .[120]

The end of this period marked the end of practicing lamas in Mongolia. Anyone who attempted to continue to worship and practice Buddhism was simply exiled from society. Some Mongols managed to hide books or bury artifacts, but acts such as these were rare and, in any case, these Buddhist artifacts were inaccessible to most Mongols because of the need for absolute secrecy.

Of the few monasteries left standing, some were used to house Japanese prisoners of war during World War II but others were left to rot.[121] Gandan was kept open with a puppet community of lamas, a mockery to the Mongolian Sangha: "The lamas are not allowed to give instruction, with the exception of a tiny number of lamas, chosen by a method not clearly stated."[122] No Mongol was allowed to speak about Buddhism or refer to the slaughter of lamas during this period. By the middle of the twentieth century following the reign of terror, generations of Mongols were completely removed from their religious history and culture. The sham practice at Gandan was the only public testament to Buddhism. Indeed, any hope for a Buddhist polity or a public proliferation of Buddhism was completely lost.

7

SOCIALISM TO DEMOCRACY
(1940–2000)

Under the leadership of Choibalsan (1937–1952) and his successor, Tsedenbal (1952–1984), Mongolia remained under the governance of the socialists and suffered continual indignities as these two leaders suppressed any intellectual or religious growth of the Mongols, and thereby also inhibited any revival of Buddhism. In this way, Mongolian Buddhism was disconnected from the Sangha and the economic elites and became relegated to the domestic sphere of the Mongol nomad.[1] Supplementing this socioreligious alteration was the engendering of a new social structure of both *class* and *ethnicity*, which arose out of a socialist environment that prohibited any form of religious expression.[2] Under their administrations, the number of Dotood Yaam employees grew, particularly the informants. This growth allowed the Dotood Yaam to become more effective in monitoring the Mongols and, through this close surveillance, the Dotood Yaam able to fulfill one of its prime objectives: to suppress Buddhism, an objective that was most successful in the urban areas. The Soviet Union also continued to influence Mongols by controlling both their foreign trade and foreign policy. However, because of Gorbachev's new democratic implementations within the Soviet Union in the 1980s, the composition of Mongolia's government also began to change.

After the Mongolian People's Republic ceased to exist, and as Soviet changes were beginning to take hold, Mongolia held its first democratic election in 1990. This marked the end of the suppression of Buddhism, but by then there was little Mongolian Buddhism left to suppress. In an effort to redress this situation, under the leadership of the Indian ambassador to Mongolia, Bakula Rinpoche, Tibetan lamas searched for reincarnations and trained new lamas as early as 1992. These efforts signaled the fourth wave of Buddhism in Mongolia.[3]

THE ERA OF CHOIBALSAN

In 1940, following the collapse of the Mongolian Sangha, Mongolia under Choibalsan became enmeshed in the global struggle of World War II. The Japanese presence in Inner Mongolia was of great concern to the Soviet Union, and World War II only heightened the Japanese threat. Interestingly, linguistics provided the Soviet Union with a way to prevent a Mongol-Japanese revolution within Mongolia. When the Mongols officially adopted the Cyrillic script in March 1941 and Russian became the country's second language, Qochiin Bichiq (the classical language of the Buddhist era) was eliminated.[4] Once again, another remnant of the Buddhist polity was replaced with a socialist one, namely, the Cyrillic script; however, a more pressing reason for this change relates to the Japanese. Stalin regarded the Japanese creation of the script, Manchukuo, in 1931–32 as a threat, "since Japanese-sponsored propaganda called on the Mongol people to break with the USSR."[5] By implementing the use of Cyrillic throughout Outer Mongolia, the Soviet Union was able to tighten its control on international influence as well as activities of the Mongolian intelligentsia.

During several meetings between Choibalsan and Stalin, they constructed a plan of defense against the growing Japanese army.[6] The plan was successful and the Japanese were repelled. After the war, the MPRP, under Choibalsan, relaxed its control and the number of political arrests declined, but the Dotood Yaam still maintained strict control over the Mongols. According to Dashpurev, in 1942 Choibalsan and a then rising political figure, Tsedenbal, signed a secret resolution permitting the Dotood Yaam to torture prisoners.[7] This was proof that a dictatorship was still in place in Mongolia.

Aside from his attempt to unify Inner and Outer Mongolia, Choibalsan was relatively inactive until his death in 1952.[8] He developed a malignant stomach tumor, a hereditary disease that finally claimed his life at the age of fifty-seven.[9] His death came as a shock to the nation and a wave of public sentiment poured in expressing sorrow:

> Choibalsan was widely mourned at his passing and suggestions flooded into the government on ways to honour him. Eleven days after his death, an official in the government reported that eight *aimags* (provinces), 41 groups and 428 individuals had written to suggest his body be preserved like Lenin's was.[10]

It is certain that Choibalsan left a very profound legacy, but an ambivalent one in the eyes of his peers. Some regarded him as a hero for preserving Outer Mongolia's freedom and assisting in the defeat of the Japanese during World War II. Others saw his death as the end of the reign of terror. This period of intense fear and repression drove most religious practice underground.

Prior to repression of the Buddhists in Mongolia, shamanistic practices had already been driven underground. Having sustained doctrinal attacks by the Mongolian Sangha during the Manchu and autonomous periods, Shamanism was outlawed under the MPR's constitution in 1924, and suffered continual religious purges throughout the socialist period.[11] These actions proved to be ultimately devastating to shamanism.[12] In the previous chapter we saw how all representational signs of religion were removed from public spaces in an effort to "protect" Mongolian culture from any outside influences, whether Buddhist or shamanist, by closely monitoring its borders.[13] Even *ovoo* (a grouping of stones and religious artifacts used as both a landmark or a shrine) worship of ritual cairns was prohibited until 1990.[14] In urban areas,[15] terror precluded public veneration and intensive state surveillance quieted any reference to or practice of Buddhism. The state's constant monitoring of Buddhist discourse removed Buddhism from the general Mongol consciousness, relegating it to the status of "public secret." As Michael Taussig explains, the public secret is a particular social knowledge of knowing what not to disclose—what is inferred in society, but not publicized.[16] Here in the Mongol context, the known but unperformed knowledge of Mongolian Buddhism became scarce and untenable.

Formal religious training and teaching were minimal, but they still existed, mostly within the non-industrialized countryside and among the pastoral Mongols. Tsendgiin Düsh, a lama in Arqangai, recounts how he began learning about Buddhism in secret at midnight in 1960. By day he would herd his cattle but by night he would study with a teacher. Although he received instruction in Buddhist doctrine in the 1960s, he was required to further his studies under Bakula Rinpoche in 1992.[17] MPRP reports show evidence of lay Buddhist practice in the 1950s along the western frontier. According to a report filed with the party's Central Committee and Central Inspection Committee, Bayan-qongor *aimag* (province) suffered from a lack of MPRP "fervor." In two districts, a lama who had been granted refuge by members of the local party taught Buddhist doctrine and made astrological divinations.[18]

Humphrey offers the Dayan Derke cave as an example of how shamanistic practices managed to survive. Adherents of both Buddhism and shamanism frequented the Dayan Derke cave for religious rites. The monastery was destroyed in the 1930s, but "a complex syncretic cult continues, perhaps largely for reasons of secrecy, inside the cave where, at this time (1980s), there are Buddhist paintings, a statue of Dayan Derke as a warrior, and a long text painted on a cloth."[19]

Apostatized lamas were still able to offer spiritual advice to herders. Soninbayar, once a lama in Arqangai, continued to counsel herders until the fall of socialism, even though he led a secular life.[20] One could posit that, although institutional religious practice grew more quickly and was more widespread, popular practices endured much longer.[21] Just as the herders comprised the largest group of Buddhist adherents during the communist period, they were also the largest group of shamanist adherents during the Buddhist period. Humphrey comments that, throughout the Manchu period, many Mongols on the periphery remained shamanist even during the time when Buddhism was constantly being promoted. Although the Mongol herder became the new vessel for Mongolian Buddhism in the countryside, the institutional needs left by the Mongolian Sangha could not be filled. As Ole Bruun notes, "Mongolian herders have not been inclined to gather around any movement, be it of a spiritual or secular orientation."[22]

Although some Buddhist practices continued to be observed, most rituals did not survive. The performance of any religious ceremony or practice normally would result in severe repercussions. When Yasanjav's father died, someone was needed to bury him properly. The only person available to deliver the rites was a music teacher. Not long after, the teacher vanished, presumably another victim of the Dotood Yaam.[23] As evidence is found in the Mongolian historical archives, a more comprehensive picture of the extent of pastoral and lay practice of Buddhism during this period can be made known.

When one reflects on the role of Buddhism in Mongolia's history, it is tragically ironic how circumstances repeat themselves. Buddhism, which was meant to replace shamanism in Mongolia, now has been replaced by socialism. David Sneath notes how the political-ritual sphere

> has seen a change from "Shamanic" to Lamaist Buddhist, and then to State-Marxist faiths. In each case, sacred images were placed in the high-status section at the back of the *ger*. The Shamanic *ongon*—small felt idols—were replaced by *burkhan*—Buddhist icons, which were then replaced by State-Marxist political symbols and images.[24]

Some of the memories involving lama disappearances and arrests are so painfully emotional to family members that they are only able to recount them with a stoic countenance and a dispassionate voice. One interviewee was asked to speak about family members who were arrested by the Dotood Yaam. He replied that he had only one relative, an uncle, and that his loss was not as horrible as most. The subject then began to talk about his uncle, a lama, who was taken away by the Dotood Yaam. But in the process of retelling what had happened to his uncle, he added that his brother (also a lama), his brother-in-law, and his father were taken as well. Because he mentioned these deaths in such a matter-of-fact way, it only made the revelations all the more disturbing:

> My mother could not understand. She always expected her son and husband to return. For two years, she would wait in the street. We lived close to the Dotood Yaam, so she expected them to come out. They should

come back, she said. They did not do anything wrong. She suffered a great deal. She was always crying. I think she died from the suffering.[25]

Clearly the interviewee rarely talked about his great losses, yet his tone and countenance never changed during the interview. This kind of stoic manner can be attributed to the long-repressive political state during the socialist period, a legacy of Choibalsan's intense campaign of terror.

THE ERA OF TSEDENBAL

Although the level of terror experienced in the 1930s did not return, Mongolia's oppression still continued after Choibalsan's death. The new political leader, Tsedenbal, emerged within a similar governance style and instituted his own reign of terror:

> Tsedenbal's terror was basically realized by adopting such repressive measures that could exploit Mongolian intellectuals ideologically and morally. This was, however, started in 1949 by adopting two important resolutions of the MPRP Central Committee: the first one, dealing with the teaching of Mongolian history and literature at school level; and the second one about the Textbook for *Arats*.[26]

Soviet influence also continued under Tsedenbal's administration. Before Tsedenbal succeeded Choibalsan, he married a Russian, Anastasia Philatova, a marriage arranged by a Russian named B. Vajnov. There were rumors that Anastasia and Vajnov were part of the Soviet secret police and that this marriage served some ulterior motive.[27] Although that theory is unsubstantiated, Tsedenbal's marriage to a Russian exemplified his preference for Soviet culture and likewise perhaps his disdain for his own:

> But the influence of this marriage had its beginning with hatred for his own countrymen particularly for the Mongolian intellectuals who resisted against Tsedenbal by putting various obstacles in the way of his continuing the practice of terror."[28]

As the terror persisted throughout the 1950s, lay Mongols were driven to extreme measures to preserve their Buddhist heritage, doing so without the help of its traditional proprietor, the Mongolian Sangha. It can be argued that a socioeconomic shift in Buddhist support took place during the second half of the twentieth century. Prior to the socialist period, the high-ranking lamas and wealthy Buddhist adherents controlled the direction of Mongolian Buddhism. However, due to the economic directives under the MPRP, wealthy Buddhists suffered the most, whereas the pastoral laity enjoyed more religious freedom. A common method of preserving Mongolian Buddhist heritage was to hide sacred relics. It was a long-standing tradition to protect the Noyon Qotagt's religious treasures by hiding them inside seventeen different caves in the Gobi desert. The curator of a museum devoted to the Noyon Qotagt Ravjaa brought sixty-five books, pictures, and Buddhist artifacts into the Gobi desert and hid them in caves. He said:

> My grandfather had been a lama for twenty years. He managed to hide or bury most of Ravjaa's valuable items. Ravjaa's body [which was mummified] had to be cremated. In 1969 the Internal Ministry discovered one of the caves and confiscated everything. There were seventeen caves and the one they found had his plays and poems in it. I brought everything back from the remaining caves with help in 1991.[29]

Members of the Dara Eq Qiid in Ulaanbaatar managed to bury some artifacts in the ground just before their nunnery was converted into a prison.[30] Namuubudaa, a lama for eight years before enlisting in the army, managed to hide some books before his monastery was burnt down.[31] Other lamas, like Yasanjav's father, apostatized, but was able to save some Buddhist artifacts and continued his practice of Buddhism; however, like the majority, he never passed on his teachings, even to his own children.[32] While the concealment of Buddhist practice and relic preservation did advance the successful public effacement of Buddhism in most areas of Mongolia, fortunately, it also preserved a remnant of its past. Still, the religious *habitus* had changed. The Buddhism that existed during this period was devoid of any interpretive meaning and contained very little pedagogical activity.[33] Mongolian Buddhism, which for many years had been an institutional religion, had now become a religion of individual practice.[34]

In 1953 Khrushchev began "rehabilitations" in the Soviet Union and the practice of Mongolia's political shadowing by the USSR, briefly implemented "rehabilitations" in Mongolia as well. The rehabilitation process began with a committee that reviewed prior arrests and executions and then decided whether or not the family name, which would have been blacklisted due to a family arrest, should be rehabilitated. This was one of those short-lived moments in which Mongolia was able to reflect on its past political activities. The Mongolian committee conducted a series of interviews and uncovered numerous violations by the MPRP. Yet, because there was the possibility that Tsedenbal's administration might be discredited, the MPRP ordered the committee to abandon its work. Some of the papers were never filed. They disappeared or were destroyed, preventing any future attempt to rehabilitate the names of those families.[35]

During and after the rehabilitation experiment, the Dotood Yaam was still actively engaged in quelling efforts to reinstate Buddhism to the Mongols. After Choibalsan's administration, the Dotood Yaam was renamed Niigmiin Ayoulaas Qamgaalaq Yaam (Ministry of Public Service), but to this day, the Mongols still refer to it as the Dotood Yaam.[36] The ministry's efforts to subdue the Mongols were assisted by the KGB near the Mongol-Soviet borders:

> The arrest in 1972 of the religious leader Bidya Dandaron in Buryat Mongolia for practicing and propagating his Buddhist faith and attempting to maintain Buddhist studies as a discipline was an example of the Russian desire to stifle Mongolian identity there. . . . Four pupils studying Buddhism with him were committed to psychiatric hospitals. The *stupas* he erected to honor his father and teacher (Tsedenov, a famous Buryat lama) were destroyed by the authorities.[37]

Until the 1980s, the control of the Dotood Yaam followed the pattern established during Choibalsan's command, a pattern which continued to rely on the basic tenets of Choibalsan's regime: propaganda and terror.[38]

Mongols were told that Buddhism was a poison, a drug that was both addictive and destructive, and as they say, the opiate of the masses. A Qamba Lama remembers his childhood and the animosity generated towards Buddhism. "The Dotood Yaam said to people that Buddha was the false dream, that he was not real. That religion is a drug."[39] Such propaganda had a great impact on Mongolian children, who used the word *lama* as an insult:

> Maybe when I was ten or twelve, children used to play together. If you wanted to insult somebody, then you would just call them a big lama or something like that. In that way, children would take it as an insult. Why? Because, on TV all these lamas were mainly very, very bad personalities. They poisoned the water and instead of curing people they poisoned them. Then they sometimes beat their disciples and did other things. We saw all of this at school and in the movies. So when you said, "hey, lama" children would get upset.[40]

Jagchid and Hyer provide evidence of how literature influenced this socialized trend, noting the subtle criticism of the Mongolian Sangha: "Another genre of Mongolian literature is short tales or anecdotes of an ironic nature intended to make fun of lamas, nobles, or other elites."[41]

Even during this latter period, a vast number of workers belonged to the Dotood Yaam. After 1955, the number of Dotood Yaam workers decreased to 30,000, but these were only official government workers.[42] In the 1980s, it reportedly employed up to 60,000 informants.[43] Between the public distaste for Buddhism and the Dotood Yaam employees, there was still no safe haven for a Buddhist practitioner:

> Being the ruling party, the MPRP did not allow anybody to write or raise his voice against its exploitative system. Only during the process of democratization of Mongolian society, have we found an opportunity to present a true picture of terrorism and its repercussions throughout the country.[44]

Russian involvement remained strong during Tsedenbal's administration, which lasted until 1984. Soviet propaganda within Mongolia promoted the policy of exclusive trade with Soviet bloc countries.[45] In 1980, Mongolia's economy was heavily dependent on the Soviet Union and its external debt to the Soviets amounted to 3.4 billion rubles. By 1991, Mongolian debt had increased to 10.9 billion rubles.[46] The extent of Soviet influence was predicated upon Mongolia's economic reliance and reinforced by the constant presence of the Soviet military. The Soviet Union stationed troops in Mongolia as early as 1921, incrementally increasing its numbers during Choibalsan's administration. Until 1990, Soviet troops remained under the pretense of defending Mongolian borders.[47]

Interestingly, Mongols were ambivalent about Soviet involvement in their country, due mostly to their socioeconomic standing under the socialist regime. As previously noted, the pastoral Mongols were able to enjoy the most religious freedom during this period. Many pastoral Mongols continued their work under new collective systems instigated by the MPRP, having suffered under previous sociopolitical regimes.[48] Starting in the late 1950s, Morris Rossabi notes how herders enjoyed benefits under the new Soviet-influenced system:

> The government resumed the policy of collectivization through the imposition of higher taxes on private herds, and by the late 1950s the vast majority of herders had been compelled to join *negdels* (or collectives). . . . The government initiated compulsory education and provided free boarding schools for the herders' children. It also furnished the herders with medical care, maternity leave, and pensions. In addition, the new policy, ironically, did not deviate too sharply from traditional practices.[49]

Whereas the herder was distanced from Mongolian political elements, intellectuals were not. During this time, Mongol intellectuals studied Russian and many scholars studied in the Soviet Union. However, most Mongol intellectuals resisted the MPRP's cultural revisionist claims, in particular, historians and sociologists. Tom Ginsberg writes that the MPRP's attitude toward intellectuals was ambivalent:

> On the one hand . . . the Soviet-era intellectuals played a key role as translators of Socialist values and "modern" know-how. On the other hand, for

the communist party to claim to be the vehicle of Mongolian nationalism, it needed to suppress independent proponents of that nationalism.[50]

The middle-class Mongol remained uneasy over Russian presence and influence but, despite the common knowledge that Russian agents and KGB were involved in the government during the rule of Choibalsan and Tsedenbal, the average middle-class Mongol was still hesitant to blame the Soviet Union for the eradication of the Mongolian Sangha and the subsequent political purges, because the middle class enjoyed the benefits of urbanization and an improved infrastructure under the Soviets.

The Soviet Union's influence on Mongolia remained strong during the years of its own reforms. In fact, it was Mikhail Gorbachev's *perestroika* that triggered Mongolia's change to democracy.[51] Uradyn E. Bulag states, "Mongolian political and economic reforms started in 1984 when Gorbachev took over power in the Soviet Union."[52] Tsedenbal was replaced and a reformist, Batmönq, took office. Reforms had a slow but significant impact on religious repression, which began to decrease in the late 1980s. One Mongol recalls an encounter with the police who were responding to reports that he was producing Buddhist art and selling *thangka* (religious scroll paintings). After explaining to the police the meaning of the *thangka* and his efforts to restore them, they let him go.[53] As early as December 1989, a democratic convention convened in Mongolia. Shortly afterward, the Mongolian Social Democratic Party was established at Mongolian National University on March 2, 1990. Within several months, freedom of religious expression was restored.[54]

DEMOCRACY

Democracy in Mongolia has undoubtedly brought with it economic hardships in addition to ideological freedom.[55] The removal of the Dotood Yaam has encouraged intellectual growth and, since the move to democracy, intellectuals have begun to emerge on the political scene in increasing numbers. The newspaper *The Mongol Messenger* reported that "in June 1992, 98 percent of the candidates for parliament in Ulaanbaatar were intellectuals, including lawyers, writers, teachers, and economists."[56] It also was in 1992 when the new democratic government established the constitutional *tsets* (court), which has since become an advocate for and a defender of human rights.[57]

For some Mongols, however, the conversion to democracy came too suddenly. One Mongolian history professor was uncomfortable as he recalled the removal of the prior regime. The source of his discomfort was not democracy per se, but the complete replacement of the previous government. The removal of Buddhism from Mongolian culture engendered a respect for the preservation of Mongol history. As T. Nanjil says:

> In 1946, Stalin helped protect Mongolia against a Chinese takeover. However, from 1932 to 1939 Stalin was responsible for more than 41,000 Mongolian deaths. There would be no Mongolia right now were it not for Stalin. But because of the bad things he did, his commemorative statue in Ulaanbaatar was removed. A tank and soldiers took it away in 1991 or 1992. It was five meters high and made of bronze. It was part of our culture; it was who we are. They did not need to take it away.[58]

Professor Namjil of the Pedagogical University of Mongolia exemplifies a unique form of nationalism that emerged from the previous tumultuous events in Mongolian politics and religion. Mongols like Namjil acknowledge the dark history of Mongolia, but also consider this period essential in understanding themselves today.

Amid these issues of national integration is Buddhism, a traditionally rich cultural source with considerable political influence. Bulag considers Mongolia during the post-socialist period to be immersed in a "myriad of social problems, one of which is the issue of national integration."[59] Another challenge has been demarcating the religious realm. Kaplonski, documenting the early period of democratization, offers an example of Buddhism's involvement in the construction of a new nationalism. He cites religious rallies staged in an effort to link Buddhism with, "the concept of 'Mongol-ness.'"[60] These efforts finally culminated in 1992, when a new constitution was ratified and the drafting committee considered proclaiming Buddhism as the state religion. During this process, Mark Juergensmeyer underscores the support and restrictions placed on the religious sphere. The drafting committee seriously considered a clause that would have proclaimed Buddhism the state religion

> . . . but ultimately rejected the idea in favor of the more vague wording respecting "the traditions of [Mongolia's] history and culture." Despite this show of support for traditional religion, the constitution explicitly prohibits monasteries from assuming political power. Presumably this clause is intended to guard against the resumption of the sort of theocratic power once enjoyed by the Bogda Khan.[61]

This political move did not prevent other groups from calling for a revival of the Bogd Qaan's political office. Political Buddhist organizations, such as the Association of Buddhist Believers and the Mongolian Buddhist Party, came into being and called for the right of religious organizations to participate in politics. Bayantsagaan, founder of the Mongolian Buddhist Party, longed for a restoration of the Bogd Qaan's imperial power, his justification being that Buddhism's doctrines are democratic due to the fact that "Buddhism is the highest form of democracy."[62]

Buddhism was allowed to flourish under the new democracy but, as we have seen, the Buddhism that was left in Mongolia was largely individualized and, therefore, difficult to nurture. Tibetan Buddhism fueled Mongolian Buddhism in the second and third waves, and is playing an active role in the fourth wave. Most of the religious texts in Mongolia are in the Tibetan language, and prestigious lamas are recognized by their training in Dharmasala and by their association with the Dalai Lama.

Although there are doctrinal as well as linguistic influences from Tibetan culture and religion, there remains a definitive Mongolian flavor to the Buddhism that is reemerging. Most of these elements are found in rituals and the Mongol *habitus.* As in the time prior to socialism, one can find the presence of shamanic icons, such as the White Old Man, a character in the traditional cultural dance, the *tsam,* in the Mongolian Buddhist pantheon. On a more informal, but nonetheless cultural level, Mongols give different interpretations to dietary restrictions in place since the time of Bogd Gegeens. The typical Mongolian lama diet, which consists mainly of imported flour, meat, milk, and noodles, is sometimes accompanied by alcohol, which is prohibited in the *vinaya*, the Buddhist book of rules for lamas. This non-doctrinal *praxis* is reappearing in the contemporary revival and purportedly is regarded as pragmatic: "Mongolian Buddhism has a reputation for pragmatism, most obviously concerning issues of celibacy, consumption of meat and alcohol, and formalized training of lamas."[63]

Yet, as Mongolia returns to its form of Buddhism and embraces capitalism, there exist significant obstacles for these new lamas. Many Mongols and curators sold Buddhist relics before the lamas could retrieve them. For example, in July 1999, a curator at the Dzayayn Gegeen Qiid in Tsetserlig, the capital city in Arqangai *aimag*, sold a five hundred-year-old book written in Tibetan and some ancient Buddhist instruments to a tourist for only one hundred US dollars. In the late 1990s, at the famed monastery in Erdene Zuu, any tourist could enter the art shop and purchase centuries-old *thangka* for less than forty US dollars.[64] When faced with these economic hurdles, some monasteries have found it difficult to reacquire their possessions. Badan-Qand, who heads a Buddhist nunnery in Ulaanbaatar, cannot afford to buy back the items once owned by her nunnery:

> When the nunnery was being destroyed people hid things, and some of these things are still in their possession. They will not sell these objects [to us] unless we pay a lot of money. When the nunnery was destroyed, some clever Mongolians hid items so they would not be burned. Back then the parents hid the items knowing that they were important and would be needed later. Now their children have grown up in a capitalist environment. They want money.[65]

Currently, the government is in the process of promoting Buddhism, but offers little monetary support toward its revival.[66] Many other needs exist in this fledgling democracy, and funds are scarce. However, in some instances religious paraphernalia has been preserved. Previously, I mentioned a recovery of artifacts from the Ravjaa Museum in Dornogov *aimag*. Sixty-three years after the fifth curator of the Ravjaa Museum hid books, paintings, and artifacts in the Gobi desert, his grandson Zondon Altangerel, now the sixth curator of the Ravjaa Museum, retrieved them:

> When I was five years old [in 1965], my grandfather told me where the artifacts were hidden. The location was never written down. Neither my mother, nor my grandmother, nor my father ever knew the location, only my grandfather and myself. My grandfather became a herdsman when he returned from his arrest. My family made a vow in 1856 to serve [as curators of] the museum and so we take our duty seriously.[67]

Today the revival of Mongolian Buddhism is also the revival of Mongolian culture. Ravjaa was a famed lama whose philosophies embraced both dGe-lugs-pa and Karma-pa bKa'-rgud doctrines. Among his many relics are his paintings and prose, for he was a famous artist as well. Unfortunately, the success of the Ravjaa Museum is uncommon in today's Mongolia. Most relics simply are irrecoverable.

Aside from the recovery of relics, there is a more pressing global issue that presents another impediment to Buddhism's recovery, and that is a new Christian missionary movement in Mongolia. Affluent missionaries, including Mormons, visit Mongolia armed with Christian propaganda that poses a tempting alternative for Mongolian youth. Many of these missionaries herald themselves as modernistic icons, and reflections of an economically successful West. When asked about Mongolian conversion to Christianity, one young Mongolian Buddhist expressed his belief that missionaries profit from the public's lack of knowledge about Buddhism:

> [Missionaries] really convinced young people who could not realize what is wrong and what is right. In addition, young people were too young to realize what is wrong; their parents did not know what Buddhism is about. . . . Missionaries were usually from America and were presumably saying that the strong [economic] development in America was connected with Christianity.[68]

Many Christian movements have benefited from the globalizing effects and have brought Mongols back to Christian homes in the West while broadcasting Christian programs on television in Ulaanbaatar. A lama at Gandan monastery reflects on the lamas' position regarding the influx of Christianity and recognizes the reasons for the conversion of many younger Mongols:

> Buddhism in its first years here had no momentum—it did not have guidance, it didn't have a policy, it did not have anything. The Christians used this to their advantage. You know, these Christian movements that came into Mongolia rushed to every city and town. . . . Every Mongol then saw movies about Jesus Christ and this Bible. It was very powerfully financed by Westerners. . . . Christianity came here and to these young people who had no other influences, it was very easy for them to grasp the Christian ideals and convert. . . . Christians have many highly educated priests that attack Buddhist philosophy and they use powerful words that new lamas are not prepared to deal with yet.[69]

Despite Christian conversion, Buddhism is still growing at a respectable rate. On January 12, 2000, the Ministry of Justice reported that thirty new religious centers had opened in 1999. Of these thirty, twenty were Buddhist, seven were Christian, two were Baha'i, and one was Muslim.[70] Shamanism has also gained some popularity and *ovoo* worship has again become a widely venerated tradition. Mongols will pull up and stop alongside *ovoo* (shamanistic worship of rock cairns) on dirt roads. After circumambulating clockwise three times around the cairn and dropping a stone on the pile with each turn, they get back into their vehicles and drive off. This ritual, although considered meritorious, is historically vapid to the contemporary Mongol, a testament to the legacy left from the socialist era.[71] Lamas are enjoying their previous status among the laity. They have regained their traditional role as counselor for determining the auspicious days to start milking, move the camp, travel, trade, and marry. Modernity has also added to their prestige:[72]

> Modern lamas are seen to make use of the privileges that spontaneously arose from the Buddhist revival. For instance, when everybody else is consistently annoyed by the Mongolian road police, whose officers use

every opportunity to fine people, Dorjtseveen Lama never even obtained a driver's license, but drives uninhibited to and from the capital in his private jeep.[73]

Interestingly, Mongolia's current religious growth is similar to the growth it sustained in 1251 under Möngke's policy of religious tolerance. The number of lamas and active monasteries in Mongolia is constantly increasing and Mongol interest in Buddhism is rising. There also have been outside efforts to rejuvenate Mongolian Buddhism, including the actions of the current Dalai Lama, who has been traveling to Mongolia since 1990, each time generating religious fervor and excitement.[74] The Ninth Bogd Qaan temporarily moved back to Mongolia and at times expressed interest in staying permanently. The Tibetans had located the ninth incarnation in 1939, and the Dalai Lama formerly introduced the reincarnated Bogd Gegeen to Mongolia in 1991. The Bogd Gegeen has experienced some friction with the new Mongolian government. According to Lynne O'Donnell, the *Weekend Australian*'s news correspondent on China:

> Buddhism's attempts to portray a more modern, less self-involved side of their religion were set back in October when the ninth Bogd Lama, who is based in India, visited Mongolia and stayed for a month despite government attempts to keep him out of the country. Notwithstanding the religious tolerance, the Government apparently feared the Bogd's connection with a time when the lamas actually ruled Mongolia could pose a threat to its policy of separating church from state.[75]

Although a return to a Bogd Qaan administration seems highly unlikely, Buddhist momentum appears to be growing. One of the other difficulties that the Mongolian Sangha faces is finding experienced lamas to train new students. A monastery in Qentii *aimag* has only one lama and he is only twenty years old. In 1999 the young lama's teacher passed away at the age of eighty-one before he could complete his studies. Badan-Qand, the director of Mongolia's oldest nunnery, Dara Eq Qiid, estimates that there are three nunneries and seventy-four monasteries active in Mongolia with only twenty *gelenmaa* (nuns) and five hundred lamas.[76] This problem is compounded by Mongolia's struggle to retain their new lamas, some of whom acquire the requisite training only to leave it behind for capitalist riches. Such was the case of a particularly bright young pupil from Gandan monastery, who was one of the few who managed to learn from Gandan's Mongolian lamas before they passed away; however, fifteen years later he apostatized and left for the us.[77]

Most successes of the Buddhist revival were the result of individuals who catalyzed its growth in limited regions, such as Zondon Altangerel and Badan-Qand, who have taken it upon themselves to reintroduce Mongolian culture into Buddhism. Many of these returning lamas play irreplaceable roles in their community as astrological prognosticators and moral authorities. In 1990, a lama named Lambaatar presided over a meeting in Arqangai *aimag* (province) that encouraged apostatized high-ranking lamas in the surrounding areas to embrace Buddhism once again.[78] Due to the long-lived oppression under the Dotood Yaam, many Mongols do not believe that the reign of terror is really over. Some lamas have returned to the Mongolian Sangha while others are being retrained, so that they too can reenter the Sangha. In Qotont Arqangai, Buddhism regained its foothold largely due to the efforts of one man, Dorjtseveen Lama:

> He is the only man who is considered a "real" lama. He has become the entire institution of the old monastery brought to the service of the herding community. An all-purpose religious specialist, he mediates between the spiritual and the mundane. He is the exclusive reader and interpreter of the books, performer of life-cycle rituals, soothsayer, astrologer, and magician. All in one person.[79]

Although Dorjtseveen Lama has made enormous contributions to his community, his teachings have not spawned any institutional growth. As Bruun aptly puts it, he is everything in one person.

Bakula Rinpoche keenly notes this problem in his efforts to expand Buddhist growth in Mongolia. One of the most prominent figures in the Buddhist revival, India's ambassador to Mongolia, Bakula Rinpoche, traveled to different Mongolian *aimag* in an effort to locate reincarnations and train new lamas, but these efforts, as he would have readily agreed, could not easily turn back the displacement that Mongolian Buddhism has experienced.[80] Nonetheless, his efforts spawned successful followers. One of these recent success stories is Tsendgiin Düsh, the current Qamba Lama in Dornogov *aimag*, who was one of Bakula Rinpoche's students in 1992.

Bakula Rinpoche does not expect Buddhism to regain the momentum and prestige it enjoyed prior to the socialist period; for him, his motives are more secular. He realizes the importance institutional religion owes to the past and wants to assist Mongols in reuniting themselves with their heritage, and for some, this means becoming a lama:

> Today there are many Buddhists in Mongolia, but most of them have no opportunity to study Buddhism. Thus, they are only superficial Buddhists. Young people are so proportionally large in numbers, and so disconnected from their culture, that it will be a big loss for the Mongols if their young people never learn of their heritage. They do not realize how important this is, but the world does. Communism left a vacuum and this vacuum must be filled. Young people must be educated about the past. Mongolia had so many monasteries in the past.
>
> All seven hundred or so monasteries do not need to be rebuilt, nor do we need thousands of Buddhist lamas. However, the monasteries that do exist should be properly equipped and maintained by properly trained lamas.[81]

Among his other achievements, in August of 1999 Bakula Rinpoche supported the building of the Beguv Danjai Monastery, a symbolic construction project that joined both Indian and Mongolian efforts to reawaken Mongolian Buddhism. At Bakula's monastery, dGe-lugs-pa Tibetan lamas are brought from India to teach young Mongols and, additionally, some Mongols have been sent to India to learn Buddhism.

As Mongolian Buddhism and the Sangha reemerge in Mongolia, its different facets may resurface as well. Buddhist medicine has returned to the public sphere, gaining popularity due to its relatively inexpensive native medicines. This has opened doors for institutional growth, but, to date, it has been mainly individuals who have capitalized upon this change.[82] Prior to the socialist period, Cheney observes that the Mongolian Sangha was the popular venue to pursue aesthetics:

> The monasteries offered the possibility of a stable, sedentary existence, an atmosphere in which intellectual and aesthetic achievements were not only highly regarded, but were among the primary objectives of life. It is to be expected that young men who had artistic ability or aptitude for manual skills would be inclined to remain in the monasteries.[83]

Now, like medicine, Buddhist art is being pursued once again at monasteries, some of which are being funded by their own students' artistic output. Some of the Buddhist artistic revival is being stimulated by individuals such as Purebat, who managed to receive some training in Mongolia and then journeyed to India for more schooling during the socialist period.[84]

Developments place question marks in front of Buddhism's road to recovery. A good example is that recent events in Mongolian politics have led to the reemergence of the MPRP. In the elections of July 2, 2000, the MPRP returned to power for the first time since 1996. It was an overwhelming victory, with the MPRP securing seventy-two out of the seventy-six seats in parliament. Before the election, the reformed MPRP offered free education, more jobs, and higher salaries for government officials.[85] Dandii Tserenpil, a Mongolian professor at Indiana University in Bloomington, predicted the MPRP success in 1999, saying:

> In April 1999, three Democratic parliament members were arrested for mishandling funds. When the Democrats were elected in 1996, there was great hope and then this happened. It was a big disappointment. Many of us believe that next year's elections will prevail for the communists.[86]

The return of the MPRP has yet to threaten the Buddhist revival. The MPRP has cautiously acknowledged the errors it committed during the Choibalsan and Tsedenbal administrations, but it has maintained that during those times party members were victims as well. MPRP leader, N. Enqbayar, spoke to the Mongols on September 12, 2000, and expressed his condolences for the victims of the socialist era:

> In particular, during the 1930s, many thousands of citizens were falsely repressed through . . . decisions of the State Baga [Little] Hural and People's Council of Ministers. . . . It is an unavoidable (lit: firm) truth that MAHN was itself the most repressed political force, but MAHN did not separate itself from the repressions. . . . MAHN now asks forgiveness because, when it was struggling to achieve its main goals of the country's independence and provide the people with a happy life, it had insufficient political experience and external and internal factors. MAHN lacked the power to stop or actively limit the repressions, and, because of its opinions and political views the party also was unable to prevent repressing people by resolutions of party's leadership organizations during the 1950s, 1960s and after.[87]

In order to distinguish this new MPRP from the previous regime, twenty-first-century Mongols will need to see actions that match the words of this apology.

Clearly, Mongolian Buddhism is dependent upon the sincerity of the MPRP's apology. If the Mongols are to be successful in rediscovering their heritage, they must be permitted to continue to delve into their recent past. To Bakula Rinpoche, the socialist era was a serious blow not only to the Mongols and Buddhism, but also to the whole world:

> If the teachings are lost, they will be lost to the world. Regardless of whether you are a Buddhist or not, it is crucial that we preserve these teachings. Another thing people do not realize is that Buddhism is more than just spirituality here. Of course, you have the teachings, but art, paintings, sculpture, medicine, and astrology are also a part of Buddhism. If Buddhist teachings are lost, these things might be lost as well.[88]

Bakula Rinpoche goes on to argue that Mongolian Buddhism is more than just a receptacle for history; it is also one for education, medicine, art, and the sciences. Mongolian Buddhism has served as a cultural container throughout its four historical waves and, thus, is unquestionably a part of Mongolian history. Being a source of Mongolian culture, in a wider sense, it is also part of the geographical history of Central Asia in general. Because of Bakula Rinpoche and the Tibetans, it is ultimately (and ironically) the new MPRP government that will determine the duration and the *purpose* of Mongolia's fourth wave of Buddhism. This is not unlike the previous waves, all of which required political support for their perpetuation. Although individual efforts have reshaped Mongolian Buddhism in Mongol society, its longevity ultimately will rest upon the future of the Mongolia Sangha and the political administration that governs it.

APPENDIX

MONGOLIA'S VOICES—PERSONAL NARRATIVES

NARRATIVE 1

NAME: Yasanjav   DATE: July 18, 1999
AGE: 60   LOCATION: Arqangai, Tsetserleg
SEX: Male
OCCUPATION: Teacher
BACKGROUND: Both father and uncle were lamas

First of all I would like to talk about my father. My father was a lama, but not a very high-ranking lama.

In 1936 my father was a lama in Bolgan *aimag* [province]. He told me about Ganga, my grandfather, who was a high-ranking lama. One hundred and eighty lamas were killed, including my grandfather. Eighty lamas were sent to prison for ten years. After this happened, my father was frightened. So, even though he was a lama, he quit being a lama, and went to work as a herdsman in the countryside.

Almost all the lamas were rounded up in just a few days. It was June 1936. Everyone was afraid and no one knew that my uncle was killed. I later learned this from some friends in Ulaanbaatar.

The lamas had tried to save themselves. In 1932 they created a political party in Qövsgöl and tried to run against the revolutionary party [MPRP].

Only the high-ranking or powerful lamas were taken. My father was not a big lama. Seven hundred monasteries were destroyed back then. Only Gandan was untouched.

My uncle was fifty-two years old when he was killed. I was not yet born. When the lamas were taken away, their animals, *ger* [yurts], everything was confiscated.

My father kept practicing Buddhism secretly until his death in 1977. If the Dotood Yaam had found out that he was practicing, they would have arrested him.

We gave all the artifacts that my father had kept in secret to the museum.

My father was afraid, as were all the lamas back then, so he never talked or passed along any stories of his life as a lama. His philosophy was that he could secretly practice Buddhism, but his children were not permitted. He did not want to put us in danger.

I am interested in Buddhism, and I have been studying whenever I can.

Many ceremonies were suppressed because they were Buddhist ones. We secretly held a Buddhist funeral for my father. A music teacher did the offerings to the mountain for my father. That teacher disappeared eight months later.

Russians and Mongols are to blame. Russia is such a big country and we are small in comparison. We would have needed a very clever prime minister, and Choibalsan was not clever. My father was not a special man. He was just like any other Mongolian lama.

This interview was conducted and taped by Michael Jerryson and Christopher Kaplonski, and translated from the tape recording by Narangerel, the daughter of the subject, Yasanjav.

NARRATIVE 2

NAME: Namuubudaa   DATE: July 20, 1999
AGE: 81   LOCATION: Arqangai, Tsetserleg
SEX: Male
OCCUPATION: Lama
BACKGROUND: Lama after the socialist period

I was eighteen years old when the socialist period began. I was working at a monastery at that time. Before that time, upon turning eighteen, lamas had to pay a tax to the government to remain a lama. If not, they had to leave and join the army.

Then the law changed so that everyone had to go into the army. Around 1936, there were three hundred lamas and all of them had to become laymen. Before this law was enacted, the tax was between thirty and forty tögrög to remain a lama, which in 1999 was the equivalent of thirty thousand to forty thousand tögrögs.[1] It was a very strict law and a very expensive one. Young lamas joined the army and old ones stayed at the monastery. I was in the army from 1939 to 1944. It was difficult during the war to practice Buddhism, while fighting against the Japanese. I practiced in secret throughout the war.

My monastery was destroyed. They [the Japanese] burned the temple and everything in it. I secretly hid some books. I've kept the books in my home to this day. In my monastery there were high-ranking lamas who were killed or arrested, about twenty of them. The *ger* of all the high-ranking lamas were searched. At that time I was only eighteen years old, so people did not go into my house and search.

There were so many people in the revolutionary party. Just the members participated in these events, but there were so many members. Before 1936, many people came to the monastery to join or pray. There was no fear then.

It all changed in 1936. Suddenly, many people came to my home in the countryside on horseback and gathered up all the high-ranking lamas into a wagon. The party members did not say why or where they were going, but they demanded that the lamas leave with them. It was the Dotood Yaam. They had guns and wore green hats. I remember those green hats. At this time, animals and property were confiscated.

The Dotood Yaam bound the high-ranking lamas' hands and feet together and threw them into the wagon. My teacher was a Buddhist doctor, and he was one of those taken away, leaving me and five brothers and sisters. After serving in the army for five years, I returned to them [brothers and sisters] and became a herdsman. In 1990 there was a big meeting of lamas in Arqangai, and I began to practice again. At this time, Lamabaatar was alive and he gathered fifteen or twenty lamas together for this meeting.

I became a lama when I was nine or ten years old. So for about eight years I was a lama. I was not even a man when I was forced to quit. After service in the army, people were very scared. They talked a lot with each other about what had happened to me and to others, but these conversations occurred only within our family. I know that there are so many religions in the world. Young people in America should study and follow Buddhism. They should respect Buddhism and know that [the city of] Qaraqorum used to be the epicenter of Mongolian Buddhism.

This interview was conducted and taped by Michael Jerryson, with assistance from Christopher Kaplonski, and translated from the tape recording by Narangerel.

NARRATIVE 3

NAME: Süqbat

AGE: 30

SEX: Male

OCCUPATION: Teacher

BACKGROUND: Lama after the socialist period

DATE: July 23, 1999

LOCATION: Ulaanbaatar, Pedagogical University

I read somewhere when I was young, (this is something everyone knows) that the lamas "fought" a tank in Tarilt, in Arqangai [province]. This event occurred sometime between 1929 and 1932. They thought that they could hold the tank with a hemp rope. They tried, but the tank was too strong. At that time, there was an Interior Defense Ministry [Ministry of Internal Affairs] that was known as the Dotoodiik Qamgaalaq Yaam, or the Do[tood] Yaam. The ministry was started in 1922 and lasted until the 1950s, when it was changed to NAQ [Niigmiin Ayoulaas Qamgaalaq] Yaam, which stands for the Ministry of Social Security. My grandfather practiced Buddhism. He was a lama. He has passed away, and so has my father; however, my grandmother is still alive.

This interview was conducted and translated by Michael Jerryson.

NARRATIVE 4

NAME: Namjil
AGE: 54
SEX: Male
OCCUPATION: Professor
BACKGROUND: Witness during the socialist period

DATE: July 29, 1999
LOCATION: Ulaanbaatar, Pedagogical University

I believe that Lenin, Danzan, and the Bogd Qaan all died in or around 1924. However, this was [not] a coincidence. Stalin disliked all three of these men, but Stalin was neither a good nor a bad man in the eyes of Mongolians. In 1946, Stalin helped protect Mongolia against a Chinese takeover. However, from 1932 to 1939 Stalin was responsible for more than forty-one thousand Mongolian deaths. There would be no Mongolia right now were it not for Stalin. But because of the bad things he did, his commemorative statue in Ulaanbaatar was removed. A tank and soldiers took it away in 1991 or 1992. It was five meters high and made of bronze. It was part of our culture; it was who we are. They did not need to take it away.

This interview was conducted and translated by Michael Jerryson.

NARRATIVE 5

NAME: Zondon Altangerel   DATE: August 7, 1999
AGE: 39   LOCATION: Sainshand, Dornogov[3]
SEX: Male
OCCUPATION: Curator[2]
BACKGROUND: Witness during the socialist period

In 1984 I inherited the responsibility for the museum. In 1991, I was able to reopen the museum. There have been six curators, including myself, which cover seven generations of people who have worked at the museum:

CURATOR	NAME	GENERATION	DATES
1	Balchinchoijoo	First	1804–1865
2	Gan Ochir	Second	1837–1889
3	Narya	Third	1861–1900
4	Ongoy	Fourth	1894–1931
5	Ongoy's brother, Gombo/ Tüvdev	Fourth/ Fifth	1931–1935/ 1935–1984
6	Altangerel	Seventh	1984–present

Every curator has been a Red Hat Tibetan Buddhist.[4] The first, the fourth, and my grandfather, Tüvdev, were Red Hat lamas. The museum was closed from 1938 to 1991. In the summer of 1938 my grandfather hid what[5] he could in the caves. Back in 1938, there were around three hundred lamas in Qamariin Qiid. Two hundred were arrested and another eighty-nine were shot ten kilometers north of Sainshand.

The Internal Ministry [Ministry of Internal Affairs] first arrived in Sainshand in 1931. They wore green uniforms. They seized only the head lamas then, about ten of them. When they returned in 1938, there were four Internal Ministry officers, thirty Russian and thirty Mongolian soldiers who came to round up the two hundred lamas.

My grandfather was twenty-five years old when they came. He was arrested, but then released after half a year. Most of the poor and young lamas were released.

My grandfather had been a lama for twenty years. He managed to hide or bury most of Ravjaa's valuable items. Ravjaa's body [which was mummified] had to be cremated. In 1969 the Internal Ministry discovered one of the caves and confiscated everything. There were seventeen caves and the one they found had his plays and poems in it. I brought everything back from the remaining caves with help in 1991.

The first retrieval I did alone. The keepsake of my family's retrieval efforts is a snuff bottle, which I received from my grandfather in 1984. One day I will pass it on, too.

When I was five years old [in 1965], my grandfather told me where the artifacts were hidden. The location was never written down. Neither my mother, nor my grandmother, nor my father ever knew the location, only my grandfather and myself. My grandfather became a herdsman when he returned from his arrest. My family made a vow in 1856 to serve [as curators of] the museum and so we take our duty seriously.

About sixty-five books and many artifacts were buried or hidden by my grandfather. Some items were broken because my grandfather did not get to them in time. The Internal Ministry had already smashed them. When my grandfather came back, he had to leave behind his lama ways and clothes. The museum was turned into a store. There were approximately twenty other lamas who also gave up their lives as lamas.

This interview was conducted and taped by Michael Jerryson, assisted by Christopher Kaplonski, and translated from the tape recording by Michael Jerryson with assistance from Narangerel.

NARRATIVE 6

NAME: Tsendgiin Düsh   DATE: August 7, 1999
AGE: 49   LOCATION: Sainshand, Dornogov[3]
SEX: Male
OCCUPATION: Qamba Lama[6]
BACKGROUND: Lama after the socialist period

I was born in 1950. In 1990 I became a lama again. My ancestors were lamas. I have had eight teachers. My grandfather and two brothers were lamas. They each had a Gavji degree.[8] But in 1937 my brothers were arrested. They were lamas in the Angalant monastery. My grandfather was not arrested. He became a herdsman after 1937. But my brothers did not come back. They were sentenced to death. At that time one of my brothers was forty years old and the other was thirty-seven years old. Their names were Qamdarma Lusansambuu and Qamdarma Agvaans-ambuu. At that time three people came to our house and arrested them. It was in the spring, April 10, 1937. All this information I learned later from my mother. At that time I had not yet been born.

In 1995 my brothers' names were cleared. When they had been arrested, the Dotood Yaam had seized their property. We have no idea what they did with it. Perhaps they gave it to the government or kept it for themselves.

During this time laws were very strict. People were very afraid. That is why relatives of the lamas could not talk to anyone about their missing relatives.

So in 1960 I began to study Buddhism. My teacher and I studied at midnight in secret. In the daytime I took care of the cattle. Bakula Rinpoche came to our *aimag* in 1992. That is when I became his student.[9]

The Dotood Yaam told the people that Buddhism was a false dream, that the Buddha was not a real person, that religion is a drug. All the Dotood Yaam knew how to do was arrest lamas and take them away. The Mongolians believed this propaganda and there was nothing I could do about it. Now it is different. We can practice our religion openly.

I worship the Buddha, which is why I had studied in secret. But nowadays many people believe that there is a world of spirits, spirits with color and weight.

In 1990, Qamariin Qiid [monastery] was unoccupied but it was destroyed by the Dotood Yaam, the Russians, and the soldiers.

Also, we were not to go to Qamariin Qiid. If we did go, the Dotood Yaam would arrest us.

In 1947 the Gandan monastery was restored. In Mongolia, there were 720 monasteries, and most of them were destroyed. Among those [monasteries] left are the Erdene Zuu and the Dünd-Gobi.

After 1990, people said I should become a lama again. And in 1990 I became the highest-ranking lama.

I always pray for all humankind and for their life and health.

This interview was conducted and taped by Michael Jerryson, and assisted by Christopher Kaplonski. It was translated by Michael Jerryson, with assistance from Narangerel.

NARRATIVE 7

NAME: Bakula Rinpoche   DATE: August 7, 1999
AGE: 82   LOCATION: Indian embassy,
SEX: Male   Ulaanbaatar
OCCUPATION: Ambassador/Lama
BACKGROUND: Witness and lama during the socialist period

If you want to get proper information it is important to meet the right people. I have met many people in the many years I've been here. It would be very difficult to recommend the right people. The best way is to go to the monasteries and find out from the lamas who to talk to. It is extremely important to reconnect Mongolians with their past. Mongolians will need the assistance of scholars to do this.

In countries like Tibet, Tibetan Buddhism is practiced, and there are historical records. Unfortunately, in Mongolia it is difficult to find historical information. Buddhism in Mongolia flourished and reached great heights, but now there's almost nothing, no records or any backdrop [history] to turn to.

If the teachings are lost, they will be lost to the world. Regardless of whether you are a Buddhist or not, it is crucial that we preserve these teachings. Another thing people do not realize is that Buddhism is more than just spirituality here. Of course, you have the teachings, but art, paintings, sculpture, medicine, and astrology are also a part of Buddhism. If Buddhist teachings are lost, these things might be lost as well. Everyone should play a role in saving and preserving this culture. I also feel it is the world's turn to help the Mongolians. In the past, Mongolians helped others. You can see from other countries the texts Mongolian scholars left. Now, after so much suffering, it is the world's turn to give back.

Today there are many Buddhists in Mongolia, but most of them have no opportunity to study Buddhism. Thus, they are only superficial Buddhists. Young people are so proportionally large in numbers, and so disconnected from their culture, that it will be a big loss for the Mongols if their young people never learn of their heritage. They do not realize how important this is, but the world does. Communism left a vacuum and this vacuum must be filled. Young people must be educated about the past. Mongolia had so many monasteries in the past.

All seven hundred or so monasteries do not need to be rebuilt, nor do we need thousands of Buddhist lamas. However, the monasteries that do exist should be properly equipped and maintained by properly trained lamas.

Gandan was the only monastery that was not shut down, although for a few years it was closed. The others have just recently reopened.

It has been my privilege to work with the Mongolians on and off for the past thirty years. I have been an ambassador for the past ten years. Recently, I opened a monastery and there are now fifty or sixty young lamas there.[10] My hope is that they will help others.

This is what I can tell you briefly. You must meet the people. Go find out which were the big monasteries back then. Gandan has some old lamas who might be able to help. There are so many laypeople and former lamas, who are old now. Some have returned to being lamas, but there are hundreds who have not. There are eyewitnesses and relatives [of the dead or missing] who will be able to tell you of the atrocities that happened [here].

Please find them.

This interview was conducted and taped by Michael Jerryson, and translated from Hindi to English by Attaché Sonam Wangchuk, who served as the Indian ambassador to Mongolia.

NARRATIVE 8

NAME: Requested anonymity   DATE: August 9, 1999
AGE: 72   LOCATION: Ulaanbaatar
SEX: Male
OCCUPATION: Professor
BACKGROUND: Both the witness and another family member were
lamas during the socialist period

I was born in 1927. I have thirteen brothers and sisters. Most of them died in childhood. I have four sisters and nine brothers. I am the youngest child.

My mother's brother lived at the Gandan monastery. He was a Gants lama, the highest rank for a lama. When he was arrested, he was about seventy years old. It was 1937. I was living with my family, so I did not see him get arrested. At that time, one of my older brothers lived with him. He was twenty years old. My brother was also arrested. He spent ten years in a labor camp before he was released.

When I was five years old, I lived with my uncle and studied Tibetan. I studied only for two years before I left. I was not very interested in Tibetan, and I had to live apart from my family in order to study it. I missed my family; I was only five years old. Today, I can read the Tibetan script, but I do not understand it.

In the early spring of 1937 my father was arrested. My uncle and brother were arrested shortly afterward. I was almost ten years old. My mother died three years later. It was very hard [for me]. I became an orphan and went to live with one of my older sisters.

My brother worked at a labor camp in Ulaanbaatar, constructing some Russian buildings. After my father was taken, he never returned. I found out later that for no apparent reason he was shot after two months [at the camp]. In 1995 I received documents that gave me this information. I received one million tögrög as compensation, and my father was declared rehabilitated.

My older sister's husband was also arrested. I was left with my four sisters. I lived with either my oldest sister, or the second oldest. She was married to a famous linguist. He was an extraordinary scholar. I lived with them. He had a great deal of influence on me. When I was seventeen, he sent me to school.

If children are very young when their parents are arrested, it does not matter that much. Older siblings have it harder. My older sister was expelled [from school]. If I had been older, there might have been some problems. Stalin declared that a son is not responsible for his father ['s deeds]. After this [declaration], those who were expelled [from school] were able to reapply. Entrance exams became easier. If you applied for a job that did not have serious responsibilities, they did not care [about the exams]. But you had to mention any arrests in your family.

I was sent to Moscow to a very good academy and became a scholar.

The Green Hats came at night to make arrests. They were known as the Nogoo Malgai [lit., the Green Hats]. I was very afraid of the Dotood Yaam. This fear was present all across the country, especially in adults. Anyone could be arrested; fear was everywhere. If there was ever a knock at the door during the night, we were scared. They came with flashlights, and this instrument became one of their trademarks. Children were forbidden to play with them.

I was afraid of those flashlights. Everyone was afraid of them.

The Dotood Yaam confiscated all our property, but left us the *ger* and yard. We were fortunate. Some people lost their *ger* as well.

My father was considered to be a rich man and [because he was rich] he was thought of as a feudal. He was first arrested in 1932 or 1933. They took all his cattle. He spent two or three years in prison and was then released. He was a rich herdsman and a trader. Then he was arrested for the second time. My father was born poor and worked for his money. He would bring silk and tea by camel from China to Mongolia to trade.

I was not aware at the time that the Soviet Union was behind my families' arrests. When politicians were arrested, the propaganda was very strong. I thought they might be enemies, spies from Japan.

Before I went to the Russian academy, I knew the part the Russians had played in my family members' arrests. [On the one hand] I was very glad to have the educational opportunity. At that time, only the brightest could attend these institutes. On the other hand, it affected me [negatively]. I'll never forget my father. I used to tell everyone that he had been arrested. Some people tried to keep their pasts a secret. I did not. When I told my Russian friends, they were sad and understood how I felt. The Russian people were not responsible. Their government was just like ours.

When I became a scholar, I was investigated. Everyone was investigated. My letters and books were checked. Sometimes the Dotood Yaam confiscated them. After Khrushchev, it [life] became easier.

I consider myself a Buddhist in name only. I do not believe in it. I respect it; I understand it. But I am too old. It is too late for me to become a real Buddhist. I prayed when I was young. However, it was hard to do this within the atmosphere in which I was raised. My family, my father and mother, were all strong believers.

My mother could not understand. She always expected her son and husband to return. For two years, she would wait in the street. We lived close to the Dotood Yaam [headquarters], so she expected them to come out [at any moment]. They would come back, she said. They did not do anything wrong. She suffered a great deal. She was always crying. I think she died from the suffering. It was psychologically damaging for her.

I would like to know more about my father. It is my fault [that I do not know as much]; I want to learn more. I know very little about my father, and my children criticize me for this. Maybe I can go to the archives and learn something that I can leave for my children.

This interview was conducted in English by Michael Jerryson and Christopher Kaplonski. A tape recording of the interview was denied because the interviewee was too self-conscious. Photography also was denied, and it was asked that the real names be stricken from the record.

NARRATIVE 9

NAME: Badan-Qand
AGE: 32
SEX: Female
OCCUPATION: Director
BACKGROUND: Participant in the Buddhist revival

DATE: August 16, 1999
LOCATION: Dara Eq Qiid,
Ulaanbaatar

I would like to introduce myself. I am Badan-Qand and I was a journalist for a year before I started working at the nunnery, which was ten years ago. My goal is to help poor children, to do good deeds for my people, and to reconstruct this nunnery.

We currently have twenty-one students here. They are poor, and some are orphans. Fifteen just graduated from a Korean school, a two-year college, and are now certified to translate Korean. Some students also graduated with computer skills. Currently, there are four students studying in India.

I have practiced Buddhism for ten years now. There is no one alive who came out of the nunnery [before the reconstruction].

I learned some of the history of the nunnery with the help of a master, who is now deceased. It is really interesting to talk about Buddhist history. Socialism is a recent dark cloud over the history of Mongolian Buddhism. The nunnery's history must be studied in stages.

This nunnery was destroyed and reconstruction began just ten years ago. This main building is the only sound structure we have left. There are many differences between our nunnery and others in Mongolia. Our nunnery accepts children who are homeless, poor, or disadvantaged. Many people outside the nunnery have helped these children. Just recently some children left with Koreans to get an education.

There are two other nunneries in Mongolia. One is located at the beginning of the fourth district, behind the hospital. The Tügs Bayas Golomt is in the third district, near the cinema. This nunnery is the oldest. It was established during the Manchu period. In fact, this used to be an old Chinese district. The other two nunneries were established in the 1990s. During the Manchu rule, Mongolian *gelenmaa* [nuns] prayed here. Even after the Chinese exploitation, Chinese *gelenmaa* prayed here.

After the great revolution [in 1921], this was used as a primary school. During World War II, Japanese prisoners of war were kept here and it was used as a prison. I think it was destroyed in 1947. It was very difficult to find out the history of this nunnery, so I can't say exactly when the Japanese were here. They were last detained here in 1947. One professor, Üldzii, who is now deceased, told me about it. There were Chinese *gelenmaa* and Japanese soldiers held here. The Mongolian government never recognized this nunnery because the Chinese used it. There is nothing in the archives. Only now are we able to begin chronicling its history.

When the nunnery was being destroyed people hid things, and some of these things are still in their possession. They will not sell these objects [to us] unless we pay a lot of money. When the nunnery was destroyed, some clever Mongolians hid items so they would not be burned. Back then the parents hid the items knowing that they were important and would be needed later. Now their children have grown up in a capitalist environment. They want money.

Some things had apparently been buried here. We found some items. We were careful doing this; we noted where and when we found them. Now, I am not a *gelenmaa*. I am just a person who wants to help Mongolia, the children, and Buddhism. I am a Buddhist.

The government did not support the rebuilding; we financed it mostly through local donations. Mongols donated. It is very important to uncover the real history of this nunnery, and of Buddhism. I am very interested in Buddhism from the old days. We have some *gelenmaa*—that is, girls training in India [in Dharmasala].

I could be a manager of some company right now, making money. But instead, I chose this field of work to help others. Nowadays, many Americans study Buddhism. The interest and desire is there. Many people can help reconstruct Buddhism. The Americans can help. So, it is crucial that we connect with Americans who are willing to help and support us, to help the children who need it.

We believe that the girls who come here do not need to become *gelenmaa*. However, it is necessary for them to learn their history and become educated. For now, we educate the children. For example, some are receiving language training right now to be Korean translators. Generally, the children we accept are orphans. These children are taken off the streets.

I would really like to be connected with other colleagues from around the world. For instance, an M-8 peace corps volunteer named Joni helped connect me with the Korean people. Rinpoche Bakula has been here, and the Dalai Lama visited us as well.

I am not married, but I have many children. I am thirty-four years old. I am young. There is still so much more that I can do. I hope you will connect me with people who can help. I would like to be connected with the United Nation's children's division. I am interested in sending my children abroad. The ones that study abroad have quite a different experience.

Currently, I think there are twenty-four monasteries in Ulaanbaatar, with about fifty more in eighteen *aimag* with some five hundred lamas.

There are probably many monasteries in small *süm* [districts][11] I think that there are only twenty certified female *gelenmaa* in all of Mongolia and only four of them have studied professionally.

This interview was conducted and taped by Michael Jerryson, assisted by Christopher Kaplonski, and translated by Oyunt.

NARRATIVE 10

NAME: Erdembileg Gompil   DATE: January 2, 1992
AGE: 85   LOCATION: Ulaanbaatar
SEX: Male
OCCUPATION: Teacher and translator
BACKGROUND: MPRP member and witness during the socialist period

---

I was born in 1907 near Qala Gol. At that time I was working as an errand boy. When the revolutionary party's [MPRP's] first central school was established, I went there with three people from my area. We studied there from May 10 until September 1 of 1925. After that, we were chosen to study at the Orientalistic Institute in Leningrad in a class for Mongols. I graduated in 1929 and started to work as the chief of trained cadres at the Ministry of Education. Between 1932 and 1939 I was a teacher at the Teacher's College.

In December 1939 the Dotood Yaam arrested me. They forced me to confess that I had committed a political crime, that I was a spy, a pan-Mongolist,[12] and a terrorist. They forced me to confess. Many people accused me and persecuted me, but they are all dead now so there is no need to go into details.

During that time, the Dotood Yaam's methods of interrogation were well known to everyone. There was no one who could help or protect me. Therefore, sometimes I mixed some truth and some false information together. For almost a whole year I did not see the sun. For nearly six months I was not allowed to walk or lie down. I was so hungry that my whole body became swollen.

Only death could end my suffering. Therefore, I agreed to do anything they wanted. I did not hide the fact that I had participated in the Barga's [an ethnic group in Mongolia] movement in 1928. Nor did I hide my involvement in the Friendship Party of Russia.

In 1929, the League of Revolutionary Youth purged their membership, but they did not expel me because I never hid the fact that I had participated in the movement. I was righteous.

Now let me talk about how I participated in this movement.

In 1928, when I came back from Russia for a summer vacation, some factions of the Barga rose up against the Chinese, reaching as far as the Mongolian border. They were going to organize some secret meetings in the mountains.

A Comintern representative, Stepanov, went to the [Barga's Revolutionary Party] meeting. I went with him as a translator. The Barga's Revolutionary Party was an offshoot of the Revolutionary Party [MPRP].

In August 1928, Stepanov also accompanied me to the Qalq Golin Ereg Deer Tsogtsmber Gedek People's meeting. The members of the Mongolian People's Revolutionary Party's committee led this meeting.

At the meeting we decided to prepare for the revolution and to engage people in many kinds of activities. Just after this meeting, Stepanov went to the Barga to incite political agitation and to establish a party cell for half a month.[13] At that time some people came from Ulaanbaatar in a counterrevolutionary uprising. One man named Mersee led them. At that time, I was at the border. I worked among one hundred agricultural families from the Barga who had fled Chinese and Japanese oppression and had chosen to live in Mongolia. They were frightened. Their leader was a man named Gongorjav. These families crossed the border and became Mongolians.

When my job ended, I went back to Ulaanbaatar. After that, I went to Leningrad to continue my studies.

When they interrogated me in 1939, the following people were present: Dugarjav (who became a minister among the central district's directors of propaganda), Shijee, Rinchin Byaambaiv, Navaan-Yunden, Erqeiv Sambuu, Dugersuren, and one university teacher, I can't remember the name. Shijee was a righteous man. He was kind of strict, and he did not know Russian very well. He did not represent any particular school of thought, but he read a lot about Marxism.

Eight of us were divided into two groups and were imprisoned. While Shijee was in prison, he translated military rules and laws. In the Dotood Yaam, there were some laws in Russian. I translated these. I translated two or three "Japanese secret agent" records. Also, I translated the history of the Russian Bolshevik party. But Rinchin and Dugarjav translated most of this. Out of the eight of us, Dugarjav and Rinchin disappeared completely. The rest of us were later released. We were in prison from the spring [*qavrac*] of 1939 until August of 1940. We prepared our own meals. We could do our translation work at any time.

I think it may have been autumn of 1949 when two Qalimaks came in at 3:00 AM. They said to us, "Lie down and don't get up," and they cursed. Then they took Shijee. After that, he never came back. We thought that maybe he had gone to Russia. His health was generally very good. He was big and strong. He did not lose his faith in prison. He would always laugh, play, and do [funny] things. We assured each other that, of course, we would be exonerated of every false accusation. We also thought that, maybe, some of us would be punished.

After I was seized in December 1938 I was interrogated three or four times. They game me a pencil and paper to confess to the accusations. A man named Avilov interviewed me first. Tülüülügch Dorj hit me many times. He made me sit on a very high chair. I was between seventy and eighty centimeters high, and my feet could not reach the floor. If I moved, he hit me. He was a bad tempered man. He used to go by the name of Gossöö Dorj. In the spring of 1940, before the Tenth Revolutionary Party meeting, one division of the military became inactive. At that time two important members of the Dotood Yam, Nasantogtoq and Bazarqan, were arrested. In the place of Bazarqan, Dorj was appointed.

After Shijee's disappearance, Dorj moved us to the east because repairs were required there and they needed labor. I stayed in a public prison, called Central prison. Dugersuren was sick. I did not know where Dugarjav was. We were separated like this. We did not talk about this incident. They thought that Dugarjav was connected with the White Guard because he was working in a Buriat *qoroo* [community].

Shijee never confessed to any wrongdoing. He was a leader in the Youth Revolutionary Party. Usually Torguud interrogators questioned him.[14] They did not address [any specific] political or party policy. I knew the secretary of the Central Committee. His name was Baasanjav. He was one of my students at the Teacher's College. After graduation, he wanted to become a teacher, but instead he was promoted to a position in the Central Committee. When I was in a *ger* prison in the autumn of 1940, he was in another *ger*. He suffered some really bad fevers. That is why he always screamed out. We did not meet. As far as I knew, he was not allowed to talk to anyone.

I do not know much about Genden and Luvansharav, but in May 1932 I started to work under Choibalsan. At that time he was the minister of agriculture. In 1932, the beginning of May, in Arqangai *aimag*, there was a counterrevolutionary uprising. Because of this, we formed a volunteer committee. Approximately 350 people were involved. Choibalsan was the committee leader. I served as a translator.

The Arqangai's counterrevolutionary uprising really affected the lamas of the Gandan monastery. During the time I worked with Choibalsan, it was typical for him to drink a lot. He had a Tibetan cook, and he [Choibalsan] was always drunk. When I visited him at his wooden house in the steppes, he would be drunk and so was his wife, Bortolgoi.

Choibalsan was a very strict person. One time a woman was late to a special meeting. He arrested her and put her in prison but not for a long time, just a few minutes; it was very much his style to arrest and punish people. He did not write well in classical Mongolian. He understood Russian, but did not speak it very well. Therefore, I usually translated for him. He was friendly with those who were close to him. Some of his friends said that he was not very friendly, particularly to those with whom he worked.

When I was in prison, Dorj and Bazarqan would hit me a lot. They kicked me and hit me with a ruler. Usually they asked the intelligentsia four questions: What sort of pan-Mongolist ideas did you spread? What are the counterrevolutionaries up to? Who are you affiliated with? What kind of destruction are you responsible for?

The Ministry of Enlightenment, the seat of government, the Ministry of Justice, and the Dotood Yaam were all part of the Political Party [MPRP]. The party's doctrines were completely developed, taught, and disseminated by the Ministry of Trade. . . .[15]

Until December 1938, the party was charged with making arrests and they were carried out. Meetings were held and taxes were assessed.

I knew Losol from the time he was a minister. At the teacher's college there was an evening class on leadership. At the time, I was teaching history at a college and Losol was a colonel.

In prison I was held in room number fifteen. One day Suren came and moved me to number seven. There was no one there; Losol arrived shortly afterward. The next morning they gave me just a bowl of tea, but Losol got bread, butter, sugar, cigarettes, and matches. I stayed there for seven days. Every evening the court called Losol for a special judgment. Once, after he came back he talked to me.

He had been a committee leader in Övörqangai. At that time he had sent a person to spy on Bachinbogd. Bachinbogd was in Inner Mongolia. By the time this spy returned, Losol had become vice prime minister in Ulaanbaatar.[16] The spy wanted to see Losol, but Losol did not want to see him. That is why that person hated him and said, "I met Bachinbogd according to Losol's request."

Losol had told me, "Who is suffering in a prison? Who is living joyfully outside? I already gave almost three hundred names to the courts."

I said, "You are a wolf."

Losol said to me, "I gave all the leaders' names, including Choibalsan."

Once, when he came back from interrogation, he told me, "They tried to find out more names. But, fortunately, today when I was being interrogated, one person came forward. The Dotood Yaam inspector asked his name. That person said his name was Damba and added that Losol had helped him join the Revolutionary Party [MPRP].

It was written down that I only said the "Truth." Right now I am saying this here, to you. Maybe this is a concession for me."

_____

This interview was translated by Michael Jerryson and Narangerel from field notes of an interview conducted by Ölziibaatar.

NARRATIVE 11

NAME: Rentsendavaa Danzanshagdariin   DATE: 1992(?)
AGE: 70   LOCATION: Qövsgöl *aimag*,
SEX: Male   Burenqaan *süm*
OCCUPATION: Ex-lama
BACKGROUND: Lama, and another family member was a lama during
the socialist period

Right now I live in Qövsgöl *aimag* [province], Burenqaan *süm* [district].
I am seventy years old. My uncle Navaanshiirav was a *tsorg* lama for
Jalqanz Qüree. They arrested him in 1932 and sentenced him to ten years
in prison, but he came back after [serving] five years. So that means he
came back at the end of the summer of 1937. In the spring of 1937 they
started to arrest many lamas. Then, in 1939, my uncle was arrested again.
To this day I still do not know what happened to him. They arrested
him just before Tsagaan Sar.[17] My uncle's title was Tsorg [doctor].[18]

Dashzevegn and Qaizen, who were representatives of the Dotood
Yaam, came to his home, arrested him, and took his things. Just before
his arrest my uncle told me that I should hide the mountain bell with
the golden finial and the silver *damar* [hand drum].[19] So I went to
Burenqaan Ulaan Uzuur Mountain, made something to hold them in,
and stored them together in it.

When my uncle went to prison, I told my mother what I did for
him and she asked me to go back to the mountain and bring back the
items. She felt that they should be at home. So I brought them [back].
Then my mother told other people about this. Very soon after this I was
called to the central headquarters of Burenqaan *süm* [district]. Jantsan
questioned me. He was a representative of the department.

He asked about the bell and *damar*, and suggested that I tell him
about anything else I might have in my possession. I told him that
I did not know of anything else. They interrogated me for about a
month. At that time my home was in the country, but I was living in
the center of town. That is why I stayed at Ganjimitav's home. He was

a veterinarian. The person who usually questioned me instructed me to go to the small hill near the city early in the morning and to sit there. I was not to go into town.

It was spring, so I was wearing a thick *del* [a Mongolian robe].[20] It was difficult to survive. I bought food, hot from the *süm*. I really wanted to go to the doctor's home and eat something, but I really was afraid. Then, before night fell, they called me. I was questioned again. I was so tired and hungry that soon I thought I would pass out from heatstroke. My interrogator became very angry and started to scare me. From then on, every day began like this, and this pattern continued for about a month.

After a month I was allowed to return home. But when I got there they already had confiscated the bell and the *damar* and some other things. I do not know what they did with the bell and the *damar*. In 1990, I wrote about it in a newspaper called *Democracy*, which prompted the person who had taken my uncle's bell and *damar* to write back that he had not taken them. He lied.

From the time I was a child, I was a lama in Jalqanz Qiid. But soon I became a layman. I became a member of the Youth Revolutioary Party, although at first some of us hesitated. We did not like it. Soon after, representative Jantsan arrived. After he questioned me, he destroyed the *qüree* [the monastery], saying all party members should set fire to monasteries and destroy everything—books and equipment. So we young people had no choice. We did everything that we were told. They said that we were fulfilling our responsibilities to the Youth Revolutionary Party.

In 1932 in our hometown there was a counterrevolutionary uprising. Jigiid was the leader of this activity.

This interview was translated by Michael Jerryson and Narangerel from field notes of an interview conducted by Ölziibaatar.

NARRATIVE 12

NAME: Tserendulama, Peljee   DATE: December 15, 1988
SEX: Both female   LOCATION: Ulaanbaatar
BACKGROUND: Witnesses during the socialist period,
Tserendulama is Genden's daughter, and Peljee is his sister-in-law

---

TSERENDULAMA: I was ten or eleven years old when my father was arrested. I was his only daughter. That is why he loved me a lot, although he was a strict person. When we lived in Russia my father taught me to read and write and asked his chauffeur to teach me Russian. We went to Russia together with sister Peljee, my mother's sister. It was her responsibility to look after me. Our life was so nice. We had chauffeurs, doctors, translators, and servants. We also had several horses. My father taught me to ride a horse, to swim, and to ride a bicycle. He said that I should be patient and strong. Every day my father spoke with Peljee and she wrote down what he said.

Eldev-Ochir's family lived near our home. His children would come to our house and I would visit them at their house. One day our two families traveled to the Black Sea [area] by train and by ship.

On our first day back, some people blocked our way into our house. My father was inside. At first, I thought that they were kidding. My mother also wanted to go inside, but they refused to let her in as well. Soon my father came out looking very upset. He told us that we had to go back to Mongolia and not to make a fuss. Then he was ordered not to say anymore and they took him away. My mother fainted in the bathroom from the shock [of it all].

We did not eat anything; we just boarded the train to Moscow. We wanted to go to the Mongolian embassy, but they gave us a hundred rubles and told us not go anywhere. I was so afraid.

PELJEE: They arrested him in the middle of the night in July [year unknown]. One Russian suggested that we should take a vacation in G. Sochi [Greater Sochi is the world's second longest city], but we had already finished our vacation and now we wanted to return quickly to our country. They told us that Genden would go by plane, but that we should go by train that evening. Two people accompanied us on the train.

One short Russian man told us not to speak to any Mongols. He also said that he would return in three days. Although we were detained in the hospital, we felt like we were in some [kind of] prison. We stayed there in Moscow until October 20 [year unknown].

TSERENDULAMA: We were so afraid and just stayed in our room all day long. One day I went out to the park to meet some Mongolians. I saw that there was a funeral flag on the door outside of the Mongolian embassy.

PELJEE: That night the doorman came to our room and said that our general had eaten something and died. We told him that we wanted to go back to Mongolia, but he did not respond. One day we discovered that this Russian man could speak Mongolian. Everyday we asked to go back to Mongolia. He said that he had been in Mongolia for about nine years.

Then, on October 20 [year unknown], they allowed us to go back, but they said we had to pay for our own tickets. So some of us sold our clothes. One Buriat man helped us to sell our clothes. Then when we got to the train station, we were not allowed to take our three boxes [on the train]. These boxes contained some carpets and other expensive things. Genden told us that we did not need any money or property, but that we should just take our photos.

We had many photos, but the Russians took them.

TSERENDULAMA: Although I was very young at that time, I remember everything. Our father's bodyguards were so nice; they were like brothers. But, after my father's arrest, they became strict and ruthless. They broke many things at my house.

PELJEE: At the train station we were told not to bring those three boxes.

We had only two options—to leave them or miss our train. But one Buriat man helped us.

This interview was translated by Michael Jerryson and Narangerel from field notes of an interview conducted by Ölziibaatar.

NARRATIVE 13

NAME: Tseren Tserendorj   DATE: February 25, 1988
AGE: 75   LOCATION: Ulaanbaatar
SEX: Male
OCCUPATION: Train conductor
BACKGROUND: MPRP member and witness during the socialist period

When I was arrested I was working as the train master of a Mongol train station. It was our responsibility to transport people from UB to thirteen *aimag*. We also delivered Russian mail from the Ulaan-Ude. If something happened to the mail, we had to notify the Ministry of Foreign Affairs. There were two hundred cars and buses at our station.

At that time I was twenty-seven years old. On January 18, 1939, I was arrested [while asleep] in my bed and taken from my house by people named Lqumbe and Sereeter. They called someone on our phone to say, "501 has been cut." Then they cut our phone line with a knife. After that they took all of our valuables, party documents, some books, my driver's license, and some certificates.

They took me to the backyard of the Dotood Yaam, to the seventh *ger*. In one small *ger* there were about twenty people. In that *ger* were Navaan, Yundan's brother, Chinbat, and the *aimag* officer of the court, Sosor. Also there was a person from the Dotood Yaam, two students from the countryside and Arpak. After twenty days they called me. Many people said it was very dangerous. Also the arrested people said that the director of the Children's Palace died because he was interrogated outside, wearing only his underwear.

Vandan questioned me. He always asked which group I was in. I maintained that I was just a member of the revolutionary party. Even though Vandan was young, he was not so strict. He probably became stricter as he got older. I heard that he is dead now.

At that time there were many strict and powerful people in the Dotood Yaam. Among them were some nice and smart people. But because of the time and circumstances they could not say anything [against the Dotood Yaam].

Then my health deteriorated, which is why I had no choice. I agreed with everything my interrogators were saying. In order to avoid all sorts of trouble, I told the Dotood Yaam the name of a person who already died, the Mongolian transportation director, Jandan. I had no choice. They asked me about him. Even though I had never been to his house, I told them that I had gone there once to play chess and that Jandan told me that soon we would build a kingdom supported by Japan. He also said that we already had the people's support. It was completely false information. But I had to say something like this in order to save myself. Then I added that Jandan had tried to recruit me as a member; he had been so insistent that I finally agreed.

Thinking back, I can't believe they accepted that story. After this report, I had a chance to go to the hospital for prisoners. In the spring of 1939 the Dotood Yaam sent many prisoners to the hospital. In one room there could be fifty or sixty people. Ex-speaker of the Lesser Qural, Laagan, city trade director Zagd and auto office director Jamba Jamzha were in our *ger*. There were so many army officers. In May, many young prisoners shouted that I should be sent to the hospital and so I went to the hospital.

In our hospital room there were twenty people. Before me there had been a metal factory director, Demberel. He was saying to the other people, "When I met Choibalsan, I said to him that it was foolishness to arrest so many innocent people." He was so angry and asked, "Do you think that I am blind?" Demberel was arrested after this.

People said that Demberel's health was very bad. He was mumbling and crawling on all fours and kept shouting that before he died he would meet up with Choibalsan. A soldier finally killed him with the butt of his gun.

I also know about the death of the national artist, Namqaitseren. He was also an inmate, but he helped inoculate the prisoners. At this time there was one Russian doctor who was called "Red Hair." There were many army people, about thirty or forty of them.

A month later I left the hospital and returned to prison. I was sitting with the political officer, Navaan-Luvsan, chief of Omno-Gobi Dambatseren. We talked a lot about my time at the hospital. Once, after Demid's death, there was a Russian called Frinovskii who came and inspected the Dornod army with Choibalsan. Before he left there was a banquet. As political director and assistant to the general, I was there. At the banquet this Russian delegate said, "In your country there are many people against the revolution. You should kill them all as soon as possible." He [Frinovskii] also said, "In this business, Choibalsan is really lonely. So please, please help him, especially Prime Minister Amar. You should take it upon yourself to help Choibalsan in this effort." He ended by saying, "I am saying this in the name of Russia."

I was present at Demid's funeral ceremony, at which the trade union director, Elee, made some remarks. All the party members and army officers gathered in one room; Prime Minister Amar was speaking when I entered this room. He said that Demid had been a very smart, strong, young general. He said that we had lost our young friend and that all Mongolians were sad and the government and the Iq Qural [supreme legislative body in the Mongolian unicameral system] were very sorry.

Darjav was crying a lot. In fact, many people were crying. Choibalsan stood up and reminded us that, while Demid was very special to the Mongolians, we should not mourn his death. Instead, he said, we should work hard and be careful. In reality, Choibalsan was not so sad. I was still young then, so I did not fully understand what was happening around me.

The following week many people were arrested. The Dotood Yaam started rounding people up in very a strict fashion. That week there were fourteen arrests. I heard that on Sunday and Saturday they had started arresting people. On Monday we had a meeting at five o'clock where a party member, Luvsansharav, said that because his health was not very good, he would remain seated.

He told us that in 1933 someone by the name of Lqumb had been against the party. He was sentenced to death, and before he died he implicated Genden and Mend. At that time Mend was the minister of commerce. He said that Mend and Genden were also arrested. Our party was doing a great job.

But one person in the back of the room stood up and asked if he had known about this earlier. Luvsansharav replied that both he and Amar knew about the incident two years earlier. They had been waiting for the details to be verified and for the right time to bring it up. At that time, Amar and Choibalsan were not present.

At the end of the meeting some people stood up and spoke. Most of them said that they wanted to congratulate Mr. Choibalsan and his assistant Damba for a job well done. They truly were trying to eradicate all the people who were against the party and that this was the right thing to do.

After that meeting the three people who had spoken up against this were arrested. Luvsansharav, who had been leading the meeting, said that Choibalsan had been elected to the Ministry of Defense with his assistant Damba.

And then I was arrested too. While I was in the prison, someone by the name of Bat-Ochir pronounced my sentence. Before this, someone had held the position of director of the Old Cultural Center. After I was arrested, Bat-Ochir the partisan, Dash-zeveg's son, Candagdorji, and Gengee were arrested.

The first and second stations of the Mongolian transportation system had their own league within the Revolutionary Party. I was the league's director. So Bat-Ochir told me, "Do not to be afraid. You will not be killed, but you will not be free for some time. We will decide about it at the judicial proceedings of the Iq and the opening Qural. You do not need to say very much." He had a good conscience. But later on he became an alcoholic.

I was sentenced to six years in prison. Actually, I was arrested on January 18 [1939], but somehow [the initial date] became February 18 [1939]. So I was in prison one month extra. After my time in prison I worked very hard for Mongolia and the Revolutionary Party. The government rewarded me many times for my service. Then I became an auto station director and I retired. When I was in prison, for breakfast and lunch we would have one slice of bread, and for dinner we had soup with liver and lung with rice.

In spring 1939, our food became a little bit better and we ate raw onion. Each day there was one meal and it contained horsemeat. Every time we ate, morning and evening, we ate bread. When the war started we went to the central prison. This time there were sixty to seventy people to a *ger*. There were no blankets and mattresses. We just had our *del*. We had to forget about showering and hot water. So many people had lice. One time I saw a young man. He was so skinny. His clothes, everything he owned, had become infested with lice. He died. It was so miserable to see him, such a young guy.

Actually, after [I was released from] prison I met some of the people who used to be hard and strict with the prisoners. These people had become very poor and some of them asked me for help. I helped them, even though they had been brutal to us. I think [I did this] because, during those times [after prison], everyone was so much nicer and kinder than they are today. Otherwise, now it would have been very difficult to see a person who had been brutal to me.

I was interrogated every day. Many people said that it was because of Stalin's very strong influence in Mongolia that people were arrested. Badraq told me that he was arrested while I was in the hospital and that afterwards he was sent to Russia for two months. Some of his guards were [members of] the Russian KGB, which he found out when he was in the prison. Badraq also said that Stalin suspected his wife, and so the Soviets arrested his wife as well. First Russia's Stalinism influenced us. One popular theory held that if socialism were to spread, class conflict would become worse. He also told me, "If a criminal admits his crime there is no need to find evidence for his conviction."[21] This is Vishinski's theory.

Now, many people said that Choibalsan was a very bad person. If Choibalsan was a good, though very brutal, person, then I had indeed led a dissolute life and our country would have been fine. Back then many people said that all these internal problems were due to Choibalsan. Choibalsan was very smart, but he used his intellect in the wrong way. He was associated with Bodoo's crimes and he was publicly criticized many times. There was a time when he did not have a job. He was an alcoholic. Partisan Demberel said that Choibalsan did not listen to anyone and that he was a rather strange person.

I also heard that his two commissars committed suicide because they knew that Choibalsan was very bad person, but they could not tell the truth. That is why they thought it would be better to die.

When Choibalsan was young he made several trips out to talk with tradesmen who spoke Russian. After that experience, he studied Russian, and then it was easy for him to become a translator. Then he suddenly disappeared from his hometown. People said he went to Bogd Qüree. He lived with a lama named Sharavdorji. At that time, he was in an *aimag* in which many people from many places gathered. He was called a thief. There were many Russian traders there so he was very important to them.

That is Choibalsan's brief biography. His biography states that his father, lama Gelen Butemji, offered his grain crop and animals to the revolution.[22] At that time seven young people went to Russia. One of them was from a rich family. His name was Sharavdorji. Choibalsan served those kinds of people. Jambal went with him to Altanbulag. Jambal mentioned this to his closest girlfriend. They used to go there with animal skins and come back with goods from abroad. One day Jambal said to Choibalsan that he should guard the skins, which they had brought, and that he should stay put [stand guard] the whole night. But Choibalsan left and in the evening he came back with a tobacco box and said that he received it [tobacco box] from a Russian [in exchange] for the skins. He said that if problems arose from this, he would not give it back, but would pay him for it.

Jambal was so angry. He said, "Why did you give our goods to a stranger?" They argued and then slept, but at midnight something sparkled in the tobacco box. This box really held some sort of treasure.

At that time Jambal was [living] with a certain woman. But later on Choibalsan and this woman had [sexual] relations. So Jambal said, "I am a lama. That is why it is better for me to leave [the women]." He eventually gave this woman to Choibalsan. This woman was a devout Buddhist. That is why Choibalsan tried to influence her, offering one thousand *dzul* [offering candles].[23] Jambal was not arrested. Choibalsan did not hide anything from him. One day he said that he wanted to divorce his wife and marry this woman, Devee. He said, "Please take my wife back to her home and bring Devee to me. Jambal did what he asked. After that his first wife remarried another man. Then this man was arrested. Choibalsan had many women and Luvsansharav also led this kind of life.

Badraq was the minister of health. Then he too was arrested, along with Punchin Bimbaev, Minister of Enlightenment Dugarjav, translator Dugersuren, Navaan-Yuden, Badraq, and Ja Damba, who was doing translation work. Ja Damba died in 1941 of stomach ailments. In the spring of 1939, when I was in the hospital, Badraq was there. In 1940 and 1941, respectively, Laagan and Badraq were killed.

Badraq came from Russia by train. He had no nourishment other than water, which he drank until he came to Ulaan-Ude. Badraq told me many things, but I have forgotten almost everything. He said many bad things about Stalin and Choibalsan: that Choibalsan was with Bodoo's wife and that Laagan was an old man. He said that Choibalsan should not be prime minister because he was such a bad person. Demid and Choibalsan were awarded the title of "Marshall" in 1939. Originally, only Demid should have earned that recognition. Choibalsan questioned this saying, "Why? I also should have this reward, because I was one of the first revolutionaries." Choibalsan was a jealous and arrogant person.

Once Choibalsan met his friend Losol's wife and the woman asked for his help in the name of a friend with whom he had worked. But Choibalsan claimed to know nothing about it, adding that he would do his best to help.

When I was in prison there was one woman among the political criminals. Her name was Densmaa. She suffered a lot. Sengedorji, the Central League director was also arrested. There were many soldiers and lamas. There also was one Hungarian. He was a mechanic. He appeared to like the Mongols. He always shouted and cursed. I do not know what happened to him. He just disappeared.

Many people were killed in that era. It was very hard work for soldiers. Sometimes young prisoners helped them, but I myself never saw exactly how they helped out. One person, Dorji, committed suicide when he was in the prison. Before his death Baron Dashzever shouted, "I am in [prison] on a false charge. Please remember this, my Mongolian brothers and sisters."

I do not know what happened to Laagan. When we were at the hospital, nobody came to visit him. After he left the hospital, he just disappeared.

This interview was translated by Michael Jerryson and Narangerel from field notes of an interview conducted by Ölziibaatar.

NARRATIVE 14

NAME: Tsedev Dash   DATE: December 27, 1988
SEX: Male   LOCATION: Ulaanbaatar
OCCUPATION: Minister
BACKGROUND: MPRP member during the socialist period

In 1944 I graduated from the Pedagogical University in Irkutsk. After graduation I came here and taught. In October 1944 the government sent for me. When I came, Marshall Choibalsan had one Russian assistant. They wanted me to work as an assigned reader, a reviewer, who would be responsible for schools and medical organizations. By that point Choibalsan did not do the arresting, as he did from 1937 to 1940. From 1944 until Choibalsan's death, many people came and met with him. He spent a lot of time with them, talking about their problems with their local governments. After hearing about their conflicts, Choibalsan would call the chief of central communications and everything would be decided right away. He would say that so-and-so should not be hassled and then there would not be any problems. People say that Choibalsan was drinking heavily from 1928 until 1935.

In 1934 Choibalsan became vice prime minister and in 1936 he held the title of Marshall. At that time his wife, Bortolgoi, supposedly said, "Both of us drink too much. You are now in a high position, but you do not need to drink. Stop drinking. You can divorce me and marry Gündegmaa. But please take care of me." Maybe this rumor was true. As far as I know, from 1944 to 1945 he did not drink except sometimes a little champagne. From 1947 to 1950 when I was a minister I ran into him at a lot at banquets. That time I could see that he was drunk just from champagne. If he needed to talk with the Russian ambassador, usually Ivanov came to the [central] government building. But sometimes he went to the embassy alone.

On May 7 or 9, 1945, Ivanov visited him at his house. It was victory day for the Russian soldiers.

I taught Mongolian to Ivanov. He had asked for someone to find him a Mongolian teacher. As far as I know, Choibalsan went to the Russian embassy just a few times.

At that time there was some resentment about Dandar. In 1945 or 1946 Dandar got into fights with the Russian army chief when he was drunk. Ivanov told Choibalsan all about it. Choibalsan did not punish Dandar severely. But he stayed in prison for one month, during which time he received many honors, including the title of Baatar [hero].

Choibalsan could be strict when he met with the ministers, but as far as I know, he was not strict on a personal level. He was thoughtful about providing people with things. In 1947, during the minister's meeting, Choibalsan mentioned the subject of milk. He said, "Now, in autumn all the dairy workers come close to the city. Is this not true?"

Vice Minister of Education Tudev said, "He knows that at the end of autumn the countryside people sell frozen milk."

After the war the ones who dealt with this were Tsedenbal and Surenjav. Choibalsan met frequently with Rinchin Bayambaa. Choibalsan asked him to bring along books and other documents about Mongolian history. Rinchin explained everything very well. Choibalsan read those books by himself. From 1945 until 1948 their relationship was very close.

In 1945, before the war with Japan, Choibalsan went to Russia with assistant army minister Shagdar and me. We met with Stalin twice. They [Stalin and Choibalsan] planned and coordinated the war with Japan. On our last day in Russia, he [Choibalsan] returned from the banquet sober. When we flew to Russia, Shirendev, the director of the university, together with Rinchin and Dugersuren, accompanied us. When the airplane landed in Irkutsk, people met Choibalsan and welcomed him very politely. At that time there was no tradition of exchanging gifts. That is because, since 1926 or 1927, newspapers and other media had reported this [tradition] and said that it was corruption. People could understand this. That is why when Choibalsan went somewhere he never brought any gifts. Also, he never accepted any gifts from others. So other ministers followed his example and acted in the same manner as Choibalsan. When I accompanied Choibalsan to Russia in 1945 and in 1946 to expand the trade contracts with Russia and then again in 1947 with his family, he never gave or received any gifts.

But after his vacation, the Russian government gave him a truck, a ZiL-110, as a gift. A driver named Sengedorj brought it from Russia. In 1949 Choibalsan went to Russia for the last time, returning at the end of November. In Mongolia we were celebrating Independence Day. We also celebrated the first rail service in our country. That is why after we came back from Russia we had a banquet at the Ministry of Foreign Affairs. Many Russians came to celebrate with us. Maybe there are movies about it.

Choibalsan died in 1952. Shirendev and Sambuu were with him as well as other Mongolian delegates both times that he met with Stalin in Russia. The Dotood Yaam minister, Avakumov, met us at the airport in Molotov. During one of the meetings with Choibalsan, Stalin said, "The Chinese wanted to take [over] Mongolia, but I said that Mongolia is an independent country. That is why Russia cannot decide this. Mongols can make decisions for themselves."

In 1945 Choibalsan told Stalin, "We want to take back Inner Mongolia." Stalin said, "It means that [if you do] you will undermine the interests of the Chinese revolution."

Most of the Russian specialists who were in Mongolia [at the time] returned to Russia after the war. But Ivanov sent some of them back to Russia immediately. Back then, the Russians were really afraid of him.

Choibalsan couldn't write [Russian] but he could speak Russian without an interpreter; he could convey his ideas adequately. However, he was not very good at the classical Mongolian script. Still, he sometimes wrote in his diary, and when he did he would often use the classical script.

In general, he was the most important person in the 1940s. He was busy talking to various people about many different things. Then in the 1950s he began to fall ill. His health was deteriorating. Once in a meeting he put a hot compress on his back. After that, he would usually put it on. But, for a while, he stayed at home.

Then there was a time when the health minister would examine him alone, and sometimes one of the Russian doctors, Brosinko, who was very respectful, would examine him.

On December 3, three doctors came from Russia. Two of them were from Moscow and one was from Irkutsk. This Irkutsk doctor was the same doctor who had operated on Choibalsan's wife, Bortolgoi. Just after the New Year, he took Choibalsan by train to Russia for treatment. Before he left, I went to Choibalsan's house and met with him. He said to me, "Please do your best. You are the [only] person who can help Bumtsend. Please help Tsedenbal. He will have to take care of everything. All of the burden will be on his shoulders. I do not know how long I will stay there. It is not yet clear whether I will come back or not."

Another person, Shagdarsuren, said, "After the operation Choibalsan became better. That is why Stalin was very happy and hugged and kissed me." Still, he died soon afterward.

The doctor said it was a malignant tumor in his stomach. However, after the autopsy they concluded that almost all of his internal organs were badly diseased. In 1949 his brother and sister both died of a stomach disease. Choibalsan had once said, "I too will die of this disease."

Choibalsan's apartment was located in the building, which later became Tsedenbal's, [along with] Tsedenbal's brother, and Sharav, who was Choibalsan's neighbor along with Tsedenbal's wife and brother.

When he went to Russia in 1947, Gündegmaa and one old man named Togoo went too. The exchanging of gifts started during Khrushchev's administration. I came to the ministry in May 1946 and changed my position in February 1949.

In October 1946 I became ill. That is why I went to Russia with my wife in December. I waited for a hospital bed for two months. Then in January 1947 I entered a hospital located ten kilometers from Moscow. That is when I heard that Choibalsan had asked Ivanov to meet with Bakunov and me. So I went with Ivanov to the ministry. Choibalsan asked me if before I met him, I would ask for some trucks for the army. I asked. And as requested, in mid-1947, about ten trucks arrived in Mongolia.

In February 1947 Tsedenbal went to Moscow. His bodyguard was Sodnomdarjaa. Ivanov, the embassy's counselor, Chernoryabov, and the Central Committee's new counselor, Vajnov, met Tsedenbal there.

B. Vajnov introduced Philatova to Tsedenbal and arranged for them to be married. When I was in the hospital, I sometimes got permission to go to my hotel. I had known Tsedenbal since 1929. At this time Tsedenbal was unmarried. Later on, some girls would visit him.

Tsedenbal and Philatova were married in June 1947, when Marshall Choibalsan was in Russia. After that, in early July 1947, they came together to Ulaanbaatar. Also, at that time there was a rumor that Tsedenbal would be married to Tsogzolmaa.

Namsrai and I usually visited him at his home. He did not drink and did not go out so much. Namsrai decided to marry Tsogzolmaa. In autumn of 1945 Tsedenbal, Namsrai, and I visited Tsogzolmaa at her house.

In the beginning Philatova was kind. After I became a speaker of the Iq Qural, she once called me and said, "Tsedenbal's health is not very good. Why do you let him suffer without seeking any medical help?"

I replied, "Do not worry. The doctors will know what to do when it is necessary." People said that she was one of the Kremlin's lieutenant general's daughters.

In 1934 Tsedenbal returned to Irkutsk and in 1938 he graduated from the Financial University of Irkutsk. After that he returned to Mongolia and became a vice director of the Financial University here.

In 1940 I went to Irkutsk to study at the Pedagogical Institute and in 1941 I returned to Mongolia for the New Year holidays. I stayed ten days and when I was to return, I asked to use Tsedenbal's car. He sent me with a letter to take to one of the Russian girls. I found out her address and gave the letter to her. When I got there, her mother was the only one at home. Tsedenbal originally wanted to marry that girl. But she had been appointed to some position in a place far away. That is why it did not work out.

Until 1933, Tsedenbal and some of our friends were in Irkutsk. But in 1932 I became ill and came back. In Russia there was a school that was called The Mongolian Course. But in 1933 the education ministry closed it. Some students moved to Ulaan-Ude. Tsedenbal attended school there. And then he graduated in 1934 and went back to Irkutsk. He graduated from there with honors. During his one-month vacation he went to Kavkaz and Leningrad with two or three Russian friends.

In February 1939 he became a vice minister of finance. After that, in June, he became the minister himself. Between 1939 and 1940 he joined the Revolutionary Party.

In December 1939 Choibalsan went to Russia with Tsedenbal. They came back in January 1940. That was when Stalin turned sixty years old. Tsedenbal sent him a birthday card. When he went to Russia he wanted to have some Russian financial backing. Bat-Ochir knows about this very well because he is a doctor at the Society Institute.

When Tsedenbal came from the countryside in 1929, his name was Tserenpil. But, after 1940 his name changed to Tsedenbal. Maybe the Russians changed his name. In 1940 he returned to his birthplace. His younger siblings, brothers and sisters, were Tsend, Ayush, and Javjandulama. After Choibalsan's death, Tsedenbal started to drink.

This interview was translated by Michael Jerryson and Narangerel from field notes of an interview conducted by Ölziibaatar.

NARRATIVE 15

NAME: Tsogt Luvsansamdan   DATE: September 9, 1988
SEX: Male   LOCATION: Ulaanbaatar
OCCUPATION: Policeman
BACKGROUND: MPRP and Dotood Yaam member during the socialist period

---

There were various claims about lamas, but whether these were truths or lies, it is difficult to say. Guchikov said that Japanese spies were usually from the Gandan monastery. A Russian person told me that soon there would be a rebellion, so it was better to attack Gandan. I do not know about it. But in Gandan there are many lamas.

We started registering lamas in 1936. There were two kinds of registration. The first group included the high-ranking lamas and also the lamas who usually spread rumors. The second group included the Gavj, the Zurqaich Choijin, and the Gürtems.[24]

Bayasgalan and Qaimchig were in charge of questioning these people. Each person had to inspect ten lamas, without fail, every day. Bayasgalan himself questioned ninety lamas each day. Luvsansharav insisted that we should arrest the lamas. Namsrai also insisted. Choibalsan became a minister instead of Namsrai. Amar spoke up and he too became a minister. Luvsansharav accused Namsrai, because Namsrai's attitude toward factory work was lackadaisical. He accused him of being responsible for the combine that burned down. He also said that Namsrai always hesitated to arrest lamas. Luvsansharav noted that Namsrai always said that there were no *ger* for lamas.

A Russian by the name of Gichikov always said criminals should be beaten to get them to talk. If they were beaten, they would tell the truth.

After the war I was the director of the army division stationed in Dornod *aimag*.

The Seventeenth Army Division had Russian soldiers [in it]. I do not know where their jail was located. Natsagdorj said that there was a prison there.

Lamas were so humble, obedient as sheep. They thought that soon all the monasteries would move to the north. Some of them actually wanted to be arrested.

Because they did not know how to move up north, they did not understand. They understood it to mean to move spiritually to the north.

At the time that the Dotood Yaam appeared, all they had on was army clothes.

In 1929, I went to Moscow as a reward for doing such a good job confiscating rich people's property. Some people came with me.

At that time there were many false accusations. I did not understand that at that time, some of the charges seemed to me to be true, but sometimes they were false. For example, there was one person called Damdin, whose title was *qobilgaan* [a person believed to be a reincarnated lama]. People said that he was a Japanese spy. Many rich and upper-class people were labeled as Japanese spies back then. Some people reported that they were arrested as a result of whom they served.

In September 1937 many black cars gathered in front of the Agriculture Ministry and a great many people came out of this building. All these people were from the army and all of them were arrested. I think that many directors were arrested that day. At that time I just interrogated lamas. I had not arrested any lamas yet.

In 1939, in the middle of the war, the Seventeenth Division representatives of the Buriat and Russians needed a scout, so they asked the *süm* director if they could recruit some people. They brought in some Mongolian soldiers to make them spies. They accompanied them as they got out of the car.

Some lamas said that I was a member of a group that was against the party. For example, one lama said his Qamba Lama believed that soon we would destroy the Revolutionary Party and the Japanese would help us. His name was Cholgoi. Secret department director, Sanduijav, usually made me instigate fighting between the lamas.

I was to go to the places where many lamas gathered, and there I would create a disturbance. Because of this, they would start to beat each other up. After this, the police would come and take them away. We used this kind of strategy or method to arrest lamas. I would write things up with ten other people. Usually I would choose the place, which would be close to the police [station].

This interview was translated by Michael Jerryson and Narangerel from field notes of an interview conducted by Ölziibaatar.

NARRATIVE 16

NAME: Luvsanchültem Sodov   DATE: December 1989
SEX: Male   LOCATION: Övörqangai, Bürd *süm*
OCCUPATION: Policeman
BACKGROUND: MPRP and Dotood Yaam member during the socialist period

---

I am a citizen of Tüsheet Qan *aimag*. Nowadays, it is Övörqangai, Bürd *süm*. My father is Sodov. My mother died at an early age. She sent me to Erdenedalai Qüree to become a monk. Until I was thirteen years old I stayed with my older brother, who was a lama. After that I came here.[25]

Until the spring I worked as a servant in one family. Then I went to another family. While I was there an official man visited. He suggested that I should study Mongolian, because at that time I was studying Tibetan.

A few days later I was sent to another person, a writer named Baldantseren. He made me a student of Gombodoo at Zuun Qüree. He became my tutor. He was living with his mother. There I studied Mongolian and the classical form for three months. After that I joined a school. There were twenty-two other students. I made friends with Shagdar's son Luvsanbaldan. I was there until 1926. Then I went back to my home. Later, I returned back to Bogdqan *aimag*. I stayed in Doctor Jadamba's *ger*. He suggested that I work there as a writer. The salary was eighteen tögrögs.

In the fall I went to the city to study. Luvsanbaldan said that there was an opportunity to study in the Soviet Union and that we should try to qualify for this. We did. We waited for the final decision for a while, but they decided that we could not go. They gave us a message and sent us to the Ministry of Religious Affairs.

We became secretaries of the representatives of the government official Losol. One day he called us in and said that we must follow Gombodoo. He said to us, "You should calculate all the livestock in thirty *aimag*s of Qüree for 1926 and 1927 and make only two copies. This is a secret job and do not let anyone know about it. You need to work with this old man, Bari."

We started our job. We were done in 1928. Then a representative of the Dotood Yaam person came and said we should not reveal the information. We had the two copies of the calculations. I gave one copy to the Dotood Yaam official.

And then we went to Dugarjav. In 1929 we got permission to study in Russia without taking the examination. Dugarjav said that we should meet with the minister of justice, Dendev. We met with him. He asked us about the things we had done.

In 1929, twenty-two people went to Russia to study at the Oriental University. Among them were a government official Tserenjav, Baljinnuyam from the Ministry of Transportation, Gonchig, Yanzan, Galsan, and others. In the spring of 1931 we were called back to the city. We held a meeting of the League of Revolutionary Youth. There were some rumors about me. At that time the financial college was established. There I started to work as a translator for a teacher by the name of Ozovskil. I translated for an accounting class about for six months. I was rewarded with a job for the Central Federation of Cooperatives for a while.

In 1934, I was called in and appointed to Arqangai *aimag* with Baldan. My mission was to find out how many shops and business branches had disappeared during the counter-revolution. About ten people were working on this together. At the end of 1934, we finished our mission and came back to UB.

In September 1937 I was appointed to another job at Tsagaannuur's transfer base. It was to check all the livestock accounts of Russia and Mongolia. I was also to verify that 17,700 camels had been transferred from Mongolia to Russia. At that time some herders of Ömnögov and Dornogov *aimag*s did not get their salaries and they were always very tired.

Also, they did not know what to do about 710 camels. I reported about this to the Center, but no answer came back.

I told the *aimag*'s leader, Lamazav, who was the vice prime minister, about the salary of the herders, but it did not work out. Therefore, I established one committee with five people including Jagdaljav, Tsend-Ayush, and Ocorbal, and sold those camels for about 150 to 400 tögrög a piece.

Since everything was getting political, I conducted all the decisions as flawlessly as possible. I did this job for about three months. When I returned in December there was a rumor that I had been arrested, so my brother-in-law moved our *ger* to another place. The Cooperative Union established a rule that allowed them to buy extra spare parts for fourteen thousand tögrögs and asked me to stay on as an accountant. In addition to this, selling camels was added to the list. In this way, I became a saboteur. One copy of the camel-related account documents was given to the Revolutionary Party's audit, and another copy was given to the Ministry of the Department of Politics for inspection. One day, an accountant for the garage, Badamtör, met me and said, "The Russians took those spare parts. All the related documents were kept in the middle drawer of the cabinet placed in the north east of the Cooperative Union's archive." I went there. Badrah was the guard. I explained the situation, and he let me in. The meeting was documented in the ledger and I submitted it.

My case was transferred to the prosecutor's office. The director of the prosecutor's office was Ölziibat. I was expelled from the party. Since everyone was against me, I did not contest this. Sainjargal interrogated me. Soon after, I was imprisoned. After seven to eight days, two men came with a truck with a tarpaulin and took me to director Jamiyandonoi's office. His Russian teacher was there, too. I drank some tea and smoked a cigarette. It was Friday. They said to each other that they would let me go that day and [I was to] come back on Monday at 9:00 AM. I could not believe this. Then they asked, "Would you work in the ministry?" I could not believe what they had asked, but I said I would. They said to come back Monday morning. Until I left the ministry building, I did not believe this [was true] since I thought they would arrest me even after saying these words. I was freed. I was told that my task would be to do all accounting work for the years 1936, 1937, and 1938.

I had no idea what position I was holding, but I finished all the work. In May 1938, I started wearing the "green cap" and joined the military.

Let me tell you one fact: the German spy, Derinburg, was arrested and all his possessions were confiscated, too. Later on, I was appointed to the committee to search his house again; Sharhuu, Dorj, and I completed that task. We found seventy-six pieces of gold. We told the minister about it and decided to transfer the gold to the Ministry of Finance. While the minister was counting all gold pieces, he noticed that only seventy-two pieces were written down on the transferred account.

The administration had its own store and provided its staff with groceries. The minister's wife used to buy meat on credit. Mostly, she chose the tenderloin cuts. She was a very picky lady, and Shagdarjav would require services and supplies on a par with what Choibalsan demanded.

Dugerjav Arslan, the director of the party's committee, reported to his superiors about this situation, and Shagdarjav was fired on May Celebration Day, and he had to settle accounts with the financial department. The only meat that he had bought on credit weighed more than four hundred kilograms.

I did not know Jambaldorj very well. Malikov came and participated in checking the delegates who were involved in the affair. After that, many people were freed. Skokov was not Russian, and he was hot tempered. Tsyimbyilistov worked for a long [time?], and he drank quite a lot.

As the person who would decide the size of prisoners' meals, I would report about the condition of the prisoners every morning. Sometimes, the size [of the meal] changed a little bit. The prisoners were beaten, and they would cry out endlessly. Many prisoners were trampled in the crowded trucks, which were covered by tarpaulin. Four soldiers stood at the four sides and hit anyone who moved with their guns.

I remember that Naidanjav, who was the vehicle inspector, shouting and groaning through the fence. Also, Demberel, a son of Sumiya Beis, the director of the metal factory, came to see Choibalsan, but Demberel wasn't allowed to and was dragged out shouting, "You are killers and butchers!" The ministry's investigators locked those detainees in topless wooden wardrobes with the people standing up.

In order to impose the stiffest penalty possible, most often Dashjav, a colonel, was sent. The two-storey wooden house, which was located in front of the ministry, was used as a prison. Also, there was [another] one in Amgalan.

Kichkov is a Kalmak, the first adviser and he had a bad temper. Chuluun was his driver. When Dorjpalam, the director of the base, was transferred to the countryside, I substituted for him. The secretary of the Marshal called me and asked if Kichkov's car was there. I was ordered to lock the car in the garage, so I sent Gendenjamts and found Chuluun hanging around outside the store. In the afternoon, Kichkov came and complained about his car not being ready; then he left. That same night, some Soviet officers arrested Kichkov and some of us did not see him again until he was released at age seventy-two.

Malikov was the marshal's advisor, and Skokov was Jambaldorj's as well.

About Losol. I married Losol's sister-in-law, so Losol and I sometimes met and talked about different things. Once Losol said, "Choibalsan wants to marry but he was unable to marry the one he loved as he has spent his life married to Bortolgoi." Then I asked [him to tell me] about the story. Losol said, "One day, I came to Choibalsan's home with Suqbaatar. Choibalsan was afraid of Suqbaatar. Choibalsan came home with us. Then Suqbaatar told Choibalsan, "We have found a pretty wife for you, and you should marry her. She is the oldest daughter of Senior Attendant Tseveen Jalba." Choibalsan did not say anything. Suqbaatar asked, "Do you understand?" and then added, "This is a party assignment. You must find out what information you can about the Saj lama's affair, the rumor of which is going on around Bogd. You should be able to manage it." By the time Suqbaatar was ready to leave, Choibalsan had agreed.

Senior Attendant Tseveen Jalba was the Bogd's close advisor and a close friend, so Choibalsan needed to use this relationship to his advantage. Losol told this story to Chuluunbat, the deputy director of the Cooperative Union, to Luvsanbaldan, the secretary, and to me.

The arrests were made on July 9, 1939. At that time, I was a member of the Naadam commission. We projected seventeen thousand tögrögs for the Naadam's expenses, and in order to be approved by Khas-Ochir, the deputy minister of the Ministry of Internal Security, we went to his office. There, three Russian preceptors seized us. I did not understand what had happened. Then the fifth sector preceptor told me, "You should contact the Marshal about this." When I went there [to the marshal], the director of supplement[?], Rentsen, was standing outside with a gun, and there was somebody else with a gun inside the room. The marshal was sitting with his preceptor. I showed the budget to the marshal. He changed the budget to five thousand tögrögs and signed it. Also, the Marshal said he wouldn't organize the reception for this Naadam. On the same evening, I went to the Naadam's yurt in Yarmag. Tsend and Galsan-Ochir were drinking cognac in the corner of the yurt. At that period of time, every sector director would set up a yurt during Naadam, but that night, most of the yurts' roof flaps were closed, with women and children carrying and moving things around. It turned out that everyone was arrested except Dorjpalam, the base director, and the director of the foreign relations sector, Jadamba. Later on, the fourth sector's director was released from prison because of ill health. I do not know what happened to the rest or where they were jailed. Choibalsan visited the jail. At that time, Luvsant-seren, whose nickname was "Runny Nose," was the prison guard.

He [the guard] was very tired, and he slept during the entire visit of Choibalsan, so he gave an order to the higher-rank officer to check the guard's clothes. The officer found lice, so the guard was asked to change his clothes and take seven days off.

I knew that the minister Amar would be arrested soon because he had livestock in the countryside, but his commissar brought me the account of his livestock.

I heard the following about Losol. It was during Naadam. Choibalsan invited Losol and his wife to his home [Iq Tenger].

The two wives talked together, and Choibalsan and Losol talked together until late at night. When Losol's wife entered the room, both of them were crying, holding glasses of [whiskey, vodka?]. Choibalsan told Losol's wife, " Losol is leaving for the countryside," and gave Losol red decanter filled with alcohol.

Losol had to leave. When his wife started to prepare his baggage as usual, three suits and fifteen packets of cigarettes, Losol said, "Do not pack so many things. Only one suit and two packets of cigarettes is enough. I have to go to Dornod *aimag* and have the people, who are living close to the border, move closer. It is getting to be rough times."

Before his departure, he saw his mother-in-law and then left the city. TQ's Damba saw him off at the airport. I was told that the airplane that he boarded did not look official because it was a commercial transport plane. Losol's brother-in-law, Nanzad, was the director of a department in Dornod *aimag*. Losol's daughter was called Nanzad and told him about Losol's trip to Dornod *aimag*. But Nanzad responded to her that Losol had not come to Dornod. Later, when I saw Nanzad, I asked him about it and he told me that Losol had not come. And this is how I found out that Losol had disappeared.

Will you tell us about how private property was confiscated by the government?[26]

I found out that the confiscation commission was first established in the ministry's administration. Shar Damba, an accountant, was managing it. For the most part, confiscated properties were appropriated in a strange and disorderly fashion. Then, later, in 1940, another confiscation commission was reestablished when I came to the Office of Affairs, and I was appointed as the director.

Also Sholga Dorj, who was the director of the Department of Treasury, and Ovgor Demchig, from the same department, participated in the commission.

Aquiline Natsag, from the Department of Economic Support, was responsible for the accounting. By the order of Minister Shagdarjav, the confiscated goods would be sold after their value had been determined, but I did not see the actual orders. I only received oral instructions. Before we started to sell the goods, Minister Dordog and others came to see the things. They said that foreigners needed the Chinese wares and took some of the goods.

Commissar Namjil came and took two light chests that looked like bundles of textiles, a big Bulgarian suitcase, and some other things to feed Choibalsan's need to be in style.

Three of us took the account of the collected goods and checked it out with the records at the Special Department. I remember that there were 126 persons, and some minor dissimilarities were found by thorough checking.

Then we went to some stores and markets to determine the value and price the confiscated goods accordingly. We priced and labeled every single item, then appointed Maam, an agent of the Ministry of the Treasure, to store them and then handed over all the goods to him.

When we valued the goods, Palam, from the ministry's control office, participated (later, this person worked as the director of Geology Base).

After they were priced, we sold the goods at the west side of the treasury building. Everything sold in one night. Only our ministry's employees were allowed to purchase them.

These goods had been confiscated during 1938. After this, Dugarjav and Logi Dendev's properties were confiscated. Navaanyunden's property was searched twice. I remember that more of Beard Tsedendamba's things were taken. Amar's possession were not very very valuable, such as his coat, a *del,* and so forth.

Gold and silver were not among the confiscated goods. Only a golden cigarette box with Voroshilov's signature on it was in the goods belonging to Dovchin, the minister of the treasury. We submitted it under act number 83 by the Ministry of the Treasury and handed it over to the ministry. The items sold were estimated to be more than 637,000 tögrögs, and we handed it over to the Ministry of the Treasury. After we sold everything, we made an accounting, and four thousand tögrögs, which were Maam's responsibility, was missing. This is how our commission worked.

When we checked the documents of confiscated things, we discovered that Losol, the deputy minister, had given permission for people to take out gold on several occasions. For instance, Dendev, from the third department, was given permission twice, and Bandan was given permission as well. I saw the document that showed how much gold was given out.

Confiscated gold and silver goods were first sent to the ministry building. I do not know where they were sent to later.

Our commission confirmed all the accounts and registrations on how the goods were sold and checked out, then placed these accounts in a wooden box, and sealed it with wax. Then we handed it over to Dorj, the director of the Department of Central Treasure. I would recognize that box, even today. The account list is very specific because I knew that people, who were acquitted, would demand their goods. Once, Renchin

Byambayev came to me and demanded his property. I was tired of him. When he left, he told me "OK, I understood the situation. You cannot give me my things. However, please, look for my two pairs of glasses that were made in Germany, and give them to me. They are my life." He gave all his animals to the state to be butchered. About seventy-two of them were *qainag* [a cross between a cow and a yak].[27]

Later, Dogsom's wife said that "When Choibalsan came to Dogsom's house and said, 'We have business to do tonight. Be ready,' Dogsom responded, 'I will not participate in your slaughter,' and they quarreled." She is now living in Arqangai and I heard that she is writing a book.

Her son is Mahbol, who built a sculpture of Chinggis Qaan. I do not know anything else except I heard that fourteen people were shot behind the Songino ravine.

Marshal Choibalsan's budget for one year was 120,000 tögrögs. Animals were cheap, so the budget was sufficient. Tsedendambe was his cook, Galdanbuu was the laboratory assistant, and there was also a Russian cook. Every single day, one sheep was killed for the meals. The sheep's neck was given first to the dogs to check to see if the meat was poisoned. I heard from his commissar that the fat was thrown out, so I went to put a stop to it. Commissar Namjad was held accountable for that. I reported this to Minister Shagdarjav; he politely advised me "Do not go there again." Once Öndör Galsanjamts told me about how the marshal's assistants fabricated accounts for the alcohol in the marshal's budget and took it. The marshal used to smoke only one cigarette "with an airplane."

This interview was translated by Michael Jerryson and Erdenebaatar Erdene-Ochir from field notes of an interview conducted by Ölziibaatar.

NOTES

CHAPTER 1

1. Harjot Oberoi, *The Construction of Religious Boundaries: Culture, Identity and Diversity in the Sikh Tradition* (Delhi: Oxford University Press, 1997), 18.

2. In Mahayana scholarship the Theravada school is often referred to as Hinayana, a term that is highly derogatory. Although Hinayana is defined as the "Lesser Vehicle," a further examination reveals a greater degree of discrimination. The point is illustrated in the plethora of definitions found in the Monier-Williams dictionary, where the prefix *hina-* can mean: deficient, faulty, insufficient, incomplete, poor, vile, bad. Sir Monier Monier-Williams, *A Sanskrit-English Dictionary* (Delhi: Motilal Banarsidass Publishers, 1999), 1296.

3. This claim could be further explored, but that is beyond the scope of this volume. While most Buddhologists would accept the claim that Vajrayana Buddhism is distinctly different from Mahayana Buddhism, the difference would not be considered substantial enough to warrant a tripartite division into Theravada, Mahayana, and Vajrayana Buddhism.

4. Donald Lopez, *Prisoners of Shangri-La: Tibetan Buddhism and the West* (Chicago: University of Chicago Press, 1998), 20–21.

5. Ibid., 41.

6. Bulcsu Siklos directly confronts the issue over lamaism and Mongolian Buddhism in "Mongolian Buddhism: A Defensive Account," in *Mongolia Today*, edited by Shirin Akiner (London: Kegan Paul International, 1991).

7. Trevor Ling uses the term "Buddhisms" to underscore the importance history, politics, and society have on a transnational religion such as Buddhism. For more information on this issue, see Trevor Ling, "Introduction," in *Buddhist Trends in Southeast Asia*, ed. Trevor Ling (Singapore: Institute of Southeast Asian Studies, 1993), 1.

8. Monier, *Sanskrit-English Dictionary*, 1129.

9. There are terms other than Sangha that could be used to refer to the Mongolian Buddhist institution, such as *church*, which derives from a Judeo-Christian

template of religion. Although *church* is a more familiar term to the Western eye, it is disharmonious with the subject at hand.

10. Lonely Planet, *Mongolia*, Lonely Planet World Guide. Available online at http://www.lonelyplanet.com/destinations/north_east_asia/mongolia/ [accessed September 1, 2004]

11. Italics inserted for emphasis. Lopez, *Prisoners of Shangri-La*, 2.

12. Rudiger Busto, "A 'Living Buddha' in Asian America: Looking for the Dilowa Gegen Khutukhtu," Drawing Outside the Lines: Extending the Boundaries of Asian North American Religions Panel (American Academy of Religion conference, Toronto, November 25, 2002), 1.

13. Examples of these estimates can be seen in death statistics and taxes on Mongolian lamas among Western scholars. For more information, see Robert Rupen, *How Mongolia is Really Ruled* (Stanford, Calif.: Hoover Institution Press, 1979); Larry William Moses, *The Political Role of Mongol Buddhism* (Bloomington, Ind.: Indiana University Publications, 1977); and D. Dashpurev and S. K. Soni, *Reign of Terror in Mongolia* (New Delhi: South Asian Publishers, 1992).

14. One example of this is Moses's claim that the most intense period of terror in Mongolia existed prior to 1935. However, on the basis of new interviews and research, this claim must be revised. The evidence indicates Choibalsan's attack on the Mongolian Sangha was at its greatest intensity between 1937 and 1939. Moses, *Political Role of Mongol Buddhism*, 175.

15. Baabar has promised a second volume that will address the period 1947 to the present.

16. "It is quite wrong to see narratives as constricting and essentially reactionary myths that have little to do with historical truth or to argue, as some postmodernists do, that narrative is essentially conservative or even fascist." See Richard Evans, *In Defense of History* (New York: W. W. Norton & Company, 1999), 128.

17. The less obvious effort behind the television series is to offset the impact of the local Christian television network, Eagle TV. This network has the clearest reception of any public Mongolian station; its program is replete with Christian propaganda, both subtle and blatant. An unfortunate and insidious aspect of Eagle TV is its attempt to link Christianity with the material success of the West. The Preservation of Mahayana Buddhism is hoping to demonstrate that the success of the West is not inextricably linked to Christianity. They propose to introduce famous and successful Buddhist entertainers from the US to demonstrate that success can also be achieved through Buddhism.

18. William A. Brown and Urgunge Onon, trans., *History of the Mongolian*

People's Republic (Cambridge, MA: Harvard University East Asian Research Center, 1976), 644.

19. Research for these interviews was supported through a grant from the International Exchange and Research Board (IREX), with funds provided by the Henry Luce Foundation.

20. Brown and Onon, *History of the Mongolian People's Republic*, 644.

21. Ancient past, in this sense, refers to the period that includes Chinggis Qaan and his empire's later accomplishments, including those of the Golden Horde.

22. Research for these interviews was supported through a grant from the International Exchange and Research Board (IREX), with funds provided by the Henry Luce Foundation.

CHAPTER 2

1. In the study of Mongolia's indigenous religions, *shamanism* is generally used as a term of designation. Shamanism, a term applicable to the religious practices within Outer Mongolia, is still regarded as problematic when referring to Mongol religions. While employing the term themselves, Humphrey and Onon reflect that "shamanism may not be an 'it' at all. Among practitioners there was no name for the various activities that outsiders have called 'shamanism' and these practices were not thought of as all one thing." See Caroline Humphrey and Urgunge Onon, *Shamans and Elders: Experience, Knowledge, and Power Among the Daur Mongols* (Oxford: Clarendon Press, 1996), 4.

2. Caroline Humphrey, "Shamanic Practices and the State in Northern Asia: Views from the Center and Periphery," in *Shamanism, History, and the State*, ed. Caroline Humphrey and Nicholas Thomas (Ann Arbor: University of Michigan Press, 1994), 193.

3. Christopher Atwood, "Buddhism and Popular Ritual in Mongolian Religion: A Reexamination of the Fire Cult," *History of Religions* 36, no. 2 (November 1996): 132.

4. Samuel admits to the cultural relativity of his work, stating: "Shamanic Buddhism is a more specifically Tibetan modality. . . ." Geoffrey Samuel, *Civilized Shamans: Buddhism in Tibetan Societies* (Washington, DC: Smithsonian Institution Press, 1993), 7.

5. Examples of this can be found within the Tibetan religious system where philosophies distinguish the individual schools, such as the Sa-skya-pa's *lamdré* ("stages of the path") and the dGe-lugs-pa's *lamrim* ("fruits of the path").

6. Atwood, "Buddhism and Popular Ritual," 121.

7. J. Z. Smith, *To Take Place: Towards Theory in Ritual* (Chicago: University of Chicago Press, 1987), 103.

8. Kevin Trainor, *Relics, Ritual and Representation in Buddhism: Rematerializing the Sri Lankan Theravada Traditions* (Cambridge: Cambridge University Press, 1997), 137.

9. Lamas have been known to perform shamanistic rituals, but this ambiguity is addressed by following their claim of authority, which would derive from the Mongolian Sangha, whereas a shaman's authority would not.

10. For an analysis of the "White Old Man," see Walther Heissig and Geoffrey Samuel, trans., *The Religions of Mongolia* (Berkeley: University of California Press, 1980), 76–81.

11. For additional information, see Patricia Berger and Terese Tse Bartholomew, *Mongolia, The Legacy of Chinggis Khan* (San Francisco, Calif.: Thames and Hudson, 1995), 150.

12. Sechin Jagchid and Paul Hyer, *Mongolia's Cultur and Society* (Boulder, CO: Westview Press, 1979), 101.

13. Atwood, "Buddhism and Popular Ritual," 136, 137.

14. Ibid., 124.

15. "Buddhism does not appear in the political or religious affairs of the Mongol Qagans [Qaans] until after the first wave of conquest under Chinggis. Nor does any religion other than Shamanism." See Moses, *Political Role of Mongol Buddhism*, 48.

16. The current Qamba Lama [abbot] at Gandan Monastery in Ulaanbaatar, Mongolia, said, "Like [around] 2000 or more than 2000 years ago there was Buddhism in Mongolia in the ancient [areas of] Hunyun and the area of Tyron [and] in the state of Nyron. Two thousand years ago, Mongolian State, then Buddhism, was the state religion and [there were] several ancient Mongolian states [that historically had] Buddhism as their state religion in their history." Qamba Lama [abbot] interviewed by Christina Lundberg, "Tape [recording] 172 Ganden Abbot" for Dharma Vision, funded by the Preservation of Mahayana Buddhism, Ulaanbaatar, Mongolia, summer of 1999.

17. "Uighur, [eighth century AD] was the most Buddhist of all states and a prosperous one at that, which existed in the territory of Mongolia. During the excavations conducted by a Mongolian-Soviet expedition in 1946–7, pieces from part of Buddhist temples with fragments of wall-murals on them were removed from Ögedei *Qaan*'s palace 'A Thousand Tranquilities.' Scientists attribute these murals to a number of schools of the Uighur and Central Asian

painting of the 9th–10th centuries AD." N. Tsultem, *Mongol Zurag* [Mongolian Pictures] (Ulaanbaatar: State Publishing House, 1986).

18. "Outside the grassy mound which marks the circumvallation rise two stupas, one half fallen into ruins, the other more or less intact, vestiges of Buddhist life in Mongolia two centuries or more before the rise of Genghis Khan." C. R Bawden, *The Modern History of Mongolia* (London: Kegan Paul International Limited, 1989), 26.

19. Buddhism's assimilation of shamanistic beliefs has not put an end to shamanism in Outer Mongolia. Caroline Humphrey states: "However, it is observable that over the longer term (since the thirteenth century) some peripheral regions of Mongolia have never developed strong chieftainship and are renowned for their shamanism." See Caroline Humphrey, "Chiefly and Shamanist Landscapes in Mongolia," in *The Anthropology of Landscape: Perspectives on Place and Space*, ed. Eric Hirsch and Michael O'Hanlon (Oxford: Clarendon Press, 1995), 139.

20. Humphrey documents three phases of religious advance by Buddhism prior to the twentieth century, the last phase being the most successful in assimilating shamanism in Mongolia. Ibid., 140.

Mongolian historiography has addressed this form of periodization. Earlier scholarship has taken note of the first two waves placing the rebirth of the second wave at the end of the sixteenth century. Shagdaryn Bira and John R. Krueger, trans., *Mongolian Historical Writing from 1200 to 1700* (Bellingham: Center for East Asian Studies, Western Washington University, 2002), xxi.

21. Heissig claims that "from an intellectual and religious point of view, the first conversion of the Mongols to Lamaism did not go very deep." Heissig and Samuel, *Religions of Mongolia*, 24.

22. Jiunn Chang posits that Gödan foresaw in Sakya Pandita a relatively easy way to control Tibet. "Since the Mongols had a hard time conquering that society, due to terrain, it would be much easier for them to set up a puppet regime there until they could figure out a better way [to rule it]. The selection of *Sa-Skya* was due to its unique *Gdan-sa* succession system, which indeed helped to build the Mongols' authority in Tibet at the beginning. . . ." "A Study of the Relationship between the Mongol Yuan Dynasty and the Tibetan Sa-Skya Sect," (Ph.D. diss., Indiana University, 1984), 38.

23. Samuel proposes that Tibetan lamas saw political and religious activity as interrelated from the very inception of their religion. See *Civilized Shamans*, 489.

24. The political move to use Buddhism in Mongolia might have occurred even earlier than this. Bira writes that: ". . . it was necessary for the rulers of

the Mongolian Empire to resort to the aid of Buddhism, to the so-called law of the doctrine, hoping thereby to strengthen their dominance both over Mongols and conquered nations." Bira and Krueger, *Mongolian Historical Writing,* 59.

25. Rerikh, Yu. N., "Mongol-Tibetan Relations in the 13th and 14th Centuries," trans., Jan Nattier, *The Tibet Society Bulletin* 6 (1973): 51, 40–55.

26. Siklos, "Mongolian Buddhism: A Defensive Account," 160.

27. Turrell V. Wylie, "The First Mongol Conquest of Tibet Reinterpreted," *Harvard Journal of Asiatic Studies* 37, no. 1 (June 1977): 116, 103–33.

28. Baabar argues that Sorgagtani Beki, the mother of both Möngke and Qubilai, passed on Christian sympathies to her children. See Baabar and Christopher Kapolonski, *Twentieth Century Mongolia* (Cambridge: White Horse Press, 1999), 42.

29. This point is found in Christopher Dawson, *The Mongol Mission* (New York: Sheed and Ward, 1955), 184, quoted by Larry Moses in *Political Role of Mongol Buddhism,* 56.

30. See Moses, *Political Role of Mongol Buddhism,* 59–64. Jagchid and Hyer also document this religious clash, noting the key roles that Phags-pa and a Kashmiri monk Namo play in the Buddhist advocacy: "During the rule of Mongke (1251–[12]59), a great clash occurred at court in China between the Taoists and Buddhists. The Buddhists were able to gain the support of Namo and Phags-pa, and the Taoists were eventually suppressed." Jagchid and Hyer, *Mongolia's Culture and Society,* 179.

For an in-depth look at the political decisions and policies under Mongke, see Thomas T. Allsen, *Mongolia Inperialism: The Policies of the Grand Qan Mongke in China, Russia, and the Islamic Islands, 1251–1259* (Berkeley: University of California Press, 1987).

31. Turrell V. Wylie's description of Qubilai's rise to power lends a great deal of weight to the role of the Mongol-Tibetan power-dynamic: "Presumably to prove that he was no master of Prince Köden's domain, Khubilai sent cavalry to Köden's camp to bring the *Sa-Skya* lama—symbol of Tibet's surrender—to his own camp . . . but the venerable Pandita was already dead, so the cavalry took his nephew, 'Phags-pa Lama instead. Once the *Sa-Skya* lama was transferred to a prince of the Tolui lineage, Prince Köden seems to disappear from the historical scene." Wylie, "The First Mongol Conquest of Tibet Reinterpreted," 117.

32. Baabar and Kaplonski, *Twentieth Century Mongolia,* 46. Hai-yün had had contact with Qubilai, having been appointed to the Mongol court as a superintendent of Buddhist affairs by Möngke *Qaan.* See Jagchid and Hyer, *Mongolia's Culture and Society,* 178.

33. Social elevation through the role of the *cakravartin* can be found throughout the history of South and Southeast Asia. For additional information, see Stanley Tambiah, *The Buddhist Conception of Universal King and Its Manifestations in South and Southeast Asia* (Kuala Lumpur: University of Malaya, 1987). Bira and Krueger also offer Mongolian literary references for the *cakravartin* in *Mongolian Historical Writing*, 130.

34. Moses, *Political Role of Mongol Buddhism*, 67. Some scholars, such as J. Isamu Yamamoto, view 'Phags-pa's visit as an official diplomatic venture and have said that 'Phags-pa's visit "was to devise a writing system for the Mongols." J. Isamu Yamamoto, "Tibetan Buddhists: Exiled from Their Homeland, Extolled in the West" [online]. Christian Research Institute, 1994. Available from http://www.summit.org/Resources/BuddhismFour.html (accessed April 10, 2003)

Regardless of the true purpose of the meeting, 'Phags-pa did, in fact, teach the first Mongolian lama the Tibetan language. Larry Moses avoids the Tibetan/Mongol interpretations and simply states, "How Godan became an adherent of the Sa-skya-pa is, of course, lost in history." Moses, *Political Role of Mongol Buddhism*, 77.

35. In his writings, 'Phags-pa addresses the religious influence on Mongolian polity in his outline of history, where he elevates Mongolian qaans to the rank of a *cakravartin*. Bira and Krueger, *Mongolian Historical Writing*, 51. Warren W. Smith Jr. notes the longevity of 'Phags-pa's influence in the posthumous recognition of Qubilai: "'Phagspa's theory [of monastic rule of spiritual and temporal realms] provided religious legitimation for Khubilai and subsequent Mongol rulers, as *chakravartins*, or universal Buddhist kings. Khubilai was glorified as an incarnation of the Buddhist deity Manjushri." Warren W. Smith Jr., *Tibetan Nation: History of Tibetan Nationalism and Sino-Tibetan Relations* (Boulder, CO: Westview Press, 1996), 95.

36. This Buddhist decline does not pertain to the geographic region of China proper, where Buddhism remained a political force, but rather the Mongolian frontier, which later was labeled *Outer* Mongolia.

37. Siklos states that, during this period in Mongolia, "the worship of tantric deities in their wrathful forms was much more prominent than any other aspect of Tibetan Buddhism in the religious life of upper echelon Mongols." Siklos, "Mongolian Buddhism: A Defensive Account," in *Mongolia Today*, 161. The Manchus and the Tibetans found much later that in order to preserve the Mongolian Sangha, it was essential to convert the nomads, who clung tenaciously to shamanism.

38. Ibid., 84–85.

39. Bira and Krueger, *Mongolian Historical Writing*, 113.

40. Although Mongolian Buddhism experienced a decline, it was still present according to Bira and Krueger. Henry Serruys adds that as early as the 1400s, Mongolian nobility requested Buddhist sutras and other Buddhist articles from the Ming court. Henry Serruys, *The Mongols and Ming China: Customs and History* (London: Variorum Reprints, 1987), 215.

41. Jagchid and Hyer, *Mongolia's Culture and Society*, 251.

42. For additional information on Mongolian Buddhist medicine, see Urtnasangiin Ligaa and Danzanhuugiin Tsembel, "Medicinal Plants of Mongolia and Their Use in Traditional Medicine," *Mongolia Today: Science, Culture, Environment and Development* (London: RoutledgeCurzon, 2003).

43. As with other qaans before him, the title Altan Qaan, meaning Golden Ruler, is an honorific.

44. Altan Qaan has been widely recognized among scholars for his contribution to Mongolian Buddhism. The Mongolian historian Shagdaryn Bira stresses Altan's contribution and by extension, the second wave's influence, when he says: "It is indisputably and commonly recognized that never earlier had Buddhism in Mongolia had such meaning for the whole nation as it took on with uncommon speed after its adoption by Altan Khan. Bira and Krueger, *Mongolian Historical Writing*, 121.

45. Bira and Krueger give special credit to the Tibetan lama and translator, Sakya Dondub, for "popularizing" Tibetan religious-historical literature to the Mongols during this period. Ibid., 151.

46. See George Cheney, "The Pre-Revolutionary Culture of Outer Mongolia," The Mongolia Society Occasional Papers, no. 5 (Bloomington, Ind.: The Mongolia Society, 1968), 53.

47. "Lamaist academics or schools modeled after those in Tibet were developed, and, eventually, the study of the Tibetan language gained greater prestige among the Mongols than the study of the Mongolian language." Jagchid and Hyer, *Mongolia's Culture and Society*, 227.

48. The earliest contributions of Chorji are from 1587, the latest being 1618. Bira and Krueger, *Mongolian Historical Writing,* 141.

49. Ibid., 147.

50. Jagchid and Hyer, *Mongolia's Culture and Society*, 98.

51. "The flora of Mongolia furnishes a wide range of herbs used by lama doctors, who very readily borrowed directly from the abundance of Chinese medicine." Ibid., 99.

52. "It was not by design, however, that the Lamas became the *de facto* centralized state institution; it was much more the result of the lack of such

an indigenous institution. There was no supra-national ruler, after the Yüan Dynasty, who possessed both the personal prestige and military power sufficient to override tribal animosities and re-unite the tribes into a unified state." See Moses, *Political Role of Mongol Buddhism*, 108.

53. C. R. Bawden explains this period in more detail: "With the reality of independent power the newly-arrived petty monarchs began to make use of the title of Khan. . . . Each new khan would allot fiefs to his relatives, who in turn did the same, so that by the end of the sixteenth century Mongolia had ceased in all but name to be an empire, and was a mere collection of more or less independent petty princedoms." See Bawden, *Modern History of Mongolia*, 25.

54. Even though Qubilai moved his capital to Peking, he remained in control of Qaraqorum.

55. "After decades of warfare, the Chinese had changed their policy toward Altan from military defense to diplomacy. . . . Altan, by accepting the title *Shun-iwang* (Rightful Prince), agreed to the pretense of being listed as a tributary prince." See Moses, *Political Role of Mongol Buddhism*, 92.

56. Baabar and Kaplonski, *Twentieth Century Mongolia*, 69.

57. Siklos, "Mongolian Buddhism," 162.

58. Zahiruddin Ahmad, *Sino-Tibetan Relations in the Seventeenth Century* (Rome: Istituto Italiano Per il Medio ed Estremo Oriente, 1970), Serie orientale Roma 40, 89–91, cited by Larry Moses, *Political Role of Mongol Buddhism*, 96.

59. See Bawden, *Modern History of Mongolia*, 32–33. "The newly converted Altan Khan allowed the Dalai Lama to burn up all his ongons [small felt idols] in a ritual fire, and he also published decrees ordering his people to refrain from slaughtering their beasts, to reverence the Lama, to burn their ongons and in their place to make a meatless sacrifice to the Buddhist deity Mahākāla. If they did not give up their old customs they would be executed or have their property confiscated or be banished from their pastures."

60. According to Shagdaryn Bira, special laws were enforced during this period, among them one that equated high-ranking lamas with the "corresponding ranks for secular parties of the Mongolian aristocracy." See Bira and Krueger, *Mongolian Historical Writing*, 134. Noting that in 1579 Altan Qaan requested Mongolian translations, such as the *Golden Beam Sutra*, Bira and Krueger state, "At that time [Altan] was vigorously working to reintroduce Lamaism from Tibet." Ibid., 127.

61. Urunge Onon and Derrick Pritchatt, *Asia's First Modern Revolution* (Leiden: E. J. Brill, 1989), 111.

62. Donald Lopez claims that the role of the Dalai Lama altered the Tibetan perspective of China, leading Tibetans to see Tibet's relationship with China as one of patron and priest. Lopez, *Prisoners of Shangri-La*, 206.

63. See Moses, *Political Role of Mongol Buddhism*, 103.

64. Ibid.

65. Sain Noyon Qaan can be translated as "Great Noble King". The Sain Noyon Qaan's reincarnations continued to influence Mongol leaders into the twentieth century.

66. Baabar and Kaplonski, *Twentieth Century Mongolia*, 71.

67. "In order to begin the spread of the Buddha's doctrine . . . the Tushiyetu Khan of the Khorchin lets it be publicly known that he will give a horse to whoever learns by heart the summary of the Doctrine, and a cow to whoever can recite the Yamantakadharani by heart." Heissig and Samuel, *Religions of Mongolia*, 36.

68. Urga was the title given by Russians and other Europeans to Mongolia's capital. The Mongols called their capital Iq Qüree. For more information on the names Iq Khuree and Urga, see A. Pozdneev, *Mongolia and the Mongols* (Bloomington, Ind.: Indiana University Publications, 1971). See also Bawden, *Modern History of Mongolia*, 12.

69. Christopher Kaplonski, *Truth, History and Politics in Mongolia: The Memory of Heroes* (London: RoutledgeCurzon, 2004), 158.

70. Ibid., 146.

71. Many depict Zanabazar as a living god. When reading this myth, one cannot avoid seeing the comparative elements it shares with the Christian accounts of the baby Jesus.

72. "One of the Tüshiyetü Khans of Khalkha, Gombodorji (1594–1655), managed to get his son accepted at an assembly of all Khalkha tribes as the supreme head of Buddhism in Khalkha." Siklos, "Mongolian Buddhism," 165.

73. Qotagt is defined as "the title of the highest clergy which is granted to eminent reincarnations." Gombojab Hangin, *The Mongolian-English Dictionary* (Bloomington, Ind.: Research Institute for Inner Asian Studies, 1986), 694. The title, Jabzandamba Qotagt, is rarely used in Mongolia. There is a museum in Ulaanbaatar dedicated to the Bogd Gegeen and many Ulaanbaatar newspapers refer to the current Bogd Gegeen, who is planning to return to Mongolia. Western historians of Mongolia, such as Larry Moses, C. R. Bawden, and Robert Rupen more commonly refer to the Jabzandamba by the title, Qotagt, rather than using the Bogd Gegeen title.

74. "It is not by chance that [Zanabazar] was the founder of the Mongolian school in Buddhist art. . . . Nonetheless, the Mongolian school of iconography

founded by G. Zanabazar, which regarded these canons as means to depict and convey human beauty, is distinctive for its profoundly realistic portrayal of a human being." Tsultem *Mongol Zurag*, 13.

75. N. Tsultem, *Mongolian Sculpture* (Ulaanbaatar: State Publishing House, 1989), 13. It is important to note that Tsultem's work was written during the socialist period.

76. The weekly Mongol English newspaper, the *Mongol Messenger*, ranked the most influential Mongols of the last century, with Altan Qaan, the leader of the third wave, ranked eighth, Zanabazar fourth, and Ögedei seventh. "The Millenium's Most Influential Mongols," *Mongol Messenger* (Ulaanbaatar, November 17, 1999), no. 46 (436).

77. "The foundations for the Great Shabi were laid in 1639 when the first donations of subjects were made to the child Khutukhtu [Zanabazar], but although soon afterwards he acquired experienced lamas from Tibet to make up administrative establishment . . ." Bawden, *Modern History of Mongolia*, 106.

78. The word *shabi* is the singular form of *shabinar*, which means "disciples, serfs of a *qotagt*." Gombojab Hangin, *The Mongolian-English Dictionary* (Bloomington, IN: Indiana University, Research Institute for Inner Asian Studies, 1988), 798.

79. Baabar and Kaplonski, *Twentieth Century Mongolia*, 94.

80. See Akademiia Nauk SSSR , *History of the Mongolian People's Republic* (Moscow: Nauka Publishing House, 1973), 182.

CHAPTER 3

1. Baabar and Kaplonski, *Twentieth Century Mongolia*, 93. Rolf Gilberg and Jans-Olof Svantesson also note that this tactic was a way for the Manchus to implement a feudal administration system. "The Mongols, Their Land and History," in *Mongolia in Transition: Old Patterns, New Challenges,* ed. Ole Bruun and Ole Odgaard (Surrey: Curzon, 1996), 12.

2. Jagchid and Hyer, *Mongolia's Culture and Society*, 319.

3. Cheney, "Pre-Revolutionary Culture," 24.

4. Science is used here in reference to the intellectual endeavors oriented toward development. Robert Rupen refers to the Sangha's monopoly of medical practitioners in *How Mongolia Is Really Ruled*, 37. In addition to being astrologists, Mongolian lamas were also scientists and inventors. The Eguzer Qotagt, Ja. Galsandash, was an inventor and an advocate for science. He introduced

the production of paper from plant roots and made household items out of stone. The *UB* [Ulaanbaatar] *Post*, August 5, 2000, no. 30 (219),

6. Education was the domain of the Mongolian Sangha until the establishment of the Mongolian People's Republic. According to Kaplonski, education remained exclusively under the aegis of the Mongolian Sangha until 1902. See his *Truth, History and Politics in Mongolia*, 96.

5. Fred W. Bergholz, *The Partition of the Steppe: The Struggle of the Russians, Manchus, and the Zunghar Mongols for Empire in Central Asia, 1619–1758* (New York: Peter Lang Publishers, 1993), 186.

6. See Bawden, *Modern History of Mongolia*, 82.

7. "Under the terms of the Convention of Dolonnor of 1691, Mongolia ceased to exist as a political entity and became a frontier of China." Elizabeth Milne, et al, *The Mongolian People's Republic: Toward a Market Economy* (Washington DC: International Monetary Fund, 1991), 1.

8. See Bawden, *Modern History of Mongolia*, 23. Although the translations were completed under the Manchus, as Bira and Krueger point out, the translation of the Kanjur began before Ligdan Qaan's reign, well over a century before the Manchu occupation of Mongolia. See Bira and Krueger, *Mongolian Historical Writing*, 123.

9. Bat-Ochir Bold, *Mongolian Nomadic Society: A Reconstruction of the 'Medieval' History of Mongolia* (New York: St. Martin's Press, 2001), 171, n. 10.

10. See Bold, *Mongolian Nomadic Society*, 142.

11. Hangin, *Modern Mongolian-English Dictionary*, 210.

12. See Bold, *Mongolian Nomadic Society*, 138.

13. Bawden offers some descriptions of the original Gadan monastery in *Modern History of Mongolia*, 11.

14. S. Púrevjav and D. Dashjamts, *BNAU-d Süm Qiid*, Lama*syn Asuudlyg Shiidverlesen N', 1921–1940* [How the Question of the Lamas and Monasteries was Resolved in the mpr, 1921–1940] (Ulaanbaatar: State Publishing House, 1965), 30. For a more detailed account of the *shabi*'s duties, see Bold, *Mongolian Nomadic Society*, 140–44.

15. Many Soviet and Mongol socialist writers needed to provide evidence of a religious system that was an oppressive feudal system in order to promote the freedoms that communism represented. For a socialist account of this period, see Brown and Onon, *History of the Mongolian People's Republic*, 255.

16. See Bawden, *Modern History of Mongolia*, 85.

17. See Moses, *Political Role of Mongol Buddhism*, 47.

18. "The Mongol prince, or chief, was by origin a *leader*, whose power depended

primarily on his ability to lead successfully. Under the Manchus, he became a petty sovereign, at once restrained and supported by an overlord." Owen Lattimore, *The Mongols of Manchuria* (London: Kimble and Branford, 1935), 78.

19. It is difficult to discern the actual role of the Mongolian Sangha during the Manchu period. This is partly due to the fact that the Manchus were behind the scenes in many of the Mongol religious activities, such as the building of monasteries and the incarnations of the Bogd Gegeen. Western observers, such as Przheval'skiy, Carruthers, and Kent, contend that the Sangha became an integral part of the feudal system. See also Alan K. Sanders, *The People's Republic of Mongolia* (London: Kegan Paul International Ltd., 1968), 66.

Larry Moses goes so far as to say that, "Instead, the Church also decayed, lapsing into the same style of that parasitic existence as had the nobility, each living on the produce of the commoners." Moses, *Political Role of Mongol Buddhism*, 121.

It is easy for us to view the Mongolian Sangha as parasitical. Any religious monastic system can be judged in this way. However, it should be noted that, as with other monastic systems, the Mongols considered themselves as recipients of merit when they made donations. To have a monastery in the community was seen as a benefit to the community, not an economic hardship. If a family member became a lama, good merit was received and spread throughout the whole family. To presume that the Mongolian Sangha was feeding parasitically upon the laity overlooks the value of merit which the Mongols received in return. There is no record of rebellion against the Mongolian Sangha, nor any evidence that would imply harsh or unfair conditions imposed by the Sangha on the laity. In fact, another crucial factor must be weighed. Soviet historians, who were in the position to interpret Mongolian history for over three generations, were motivated to paint a primitive and malevolent feudal system prior to the Mongolian socialist revolution of 1921. Any information contrary to that depiction easily could have been buried or erased.

20. "The Jabzandamba Khutukhtu emerges comparatively early as a figure of international political significance . . . But, from other sources, particularly Russian diplomatic archives and Chinese historical works, we get the impression of a busy statesman, a personage whom both neighboring great powers had to take into regard." See Bawden, *Modern History of Mongolia*, 69.

21. "In the lower ranges of society discontent expressed itself through round robins of complaint against the local nobility, addressed to the local administration, through banditry and through occasional riots or attacks on Chinese property." Ibid., 6.

22. Ibid., 133.

23. See Moses, *Political Role of Mongol Buddhism*, 139.

24. They even went so far as to influence Tibetan figures, such as the Panchen and Dalai Lama. See Robert Lee, *The Manchurian Frontier in Ch'ing History* (Cambridge: Harvard University Press, 1935), 52.

25. Bawden, *Modern History of Mongolia*, 127.

26. "Persons of spiritual calling (*lamas*) formally were obliged to observed celibacy, but in fact this rule was violated: Lamas who lived outside the monastery (and these were at least two-thirds of their number) usually married." See W. E. Butler, trans., *The Mongolian Legal System: Contemporary Legislation and Documentation* (London: A. J. Nathanson Marinus Nijhoff Publishers, 1982), 11. Bawden also gives the example of the lama, Sambuu, who was fined one *angiu* (a unit of nine animals) for drawing a knife on a *shabi*. See Bawden, *Modern History of Mongolia*, 167.

27. "The fourth Khutukhtu, the only one apparently who had a real sense of clerical discipline, and who was known in consequence as the 'terrible incarnation', tried to curb this un-Buddhistic activity as early as 1797, when he issued a encyclic letter condemning excessive trading and money-lending along with brawling and rowdyism, singing and archery, chess-playing and smoking, but this had no effect at all." See Bawden, *Modern History of Mongolia*, 164.

28. Pritchatt, "The Development of Education in Mongolia," in Akiner, *Mongolia Today*, 206.

29. Zondon Altangerel, and D. Tsagaan, *Ih Gobiin Dogshin Noyon Hutugtu* [The Ferocious Noyon Qotagt of the Great Desert] (Ulaanbaatar: uuls Publishers, 1996), 10.

30. "Lamas saw shamanic 'ruler-spirit' sites as power points, to be controlled, obliterated, or converted." See Humphrey, "Chiefly and Shamanist Landscapes," 157.

31. Jagchid and Hyer, *Mongolia's Culture and Society*, 280.

32. Ibid., 168.

33. The Eighth Bogd Gegeen, who was born in Tibet, proved to be an adversary when the Mongols sought autonomy in 1911.

34. Heissig and Samuel, *Religions of Mongolia,* 7, quoted in Kaplonski, *Truth, History and Politics in Mongolia*, 98.

35. See Moses, *Political Role of Mongol Buddhism*, 125.

36. Onon and Pritchatt, *Asia's First Modern Revolution*, 117.

37. See Rupen, *How Mongolia Is Really Ruled*, 12.

38. "In 1899, under the pressures of the *arats* and the ordinary *lamas*, a comprehensive petition was drawn up by a group of princes and addressed to the Manchu Emperor. It was signed by the most important princes and *lamas*. . . .

The petition wound up as a threat: 'If matters continue to go on in this way, there will be nothing left for the Mongols but to take up arms.' " See the *History of the Mongolian People's Republic*, 212. Although current scholars are weary of using Soviet records and contend that they could obscure the true roles of Mongol feudal lords, the depiction here is not an aspersion. In fact, it is quite the opposite. For examples of Soviet and socialist slander against the Mongolian Sangha in prerevolutionary Mongolia, see Tsedenbal's *Great October and the Peoples of the East*. In this book Prime Minister Tsedenbal clearly articulates that Buddhist activities involved: "The reactionary clergy, who led parasitic lives, shamelessly exploited the working people both from the economic and spiritual points of view." Yumjagiin Tsedenbal, *Great October and the Peoples of the East* (Ulaanbaatar: State Publishing House, 1981), 23.

39. See Akademiia Nauk SSSR, *History of the Mongolian People's Party*, 217.

40. See Rupen, *How Mongolia Is Really Ruled*, 6.

41. "However, when the Dalai Lama fled to Urga in 1904, the Jebtsun Damba Khutukhtu of Urga, who very obviously regarded the Dalai Lama as a potential temporal rival as well as a religious one, isolated him as much as possible." Robert Rupen, *The Mongolian People's Republic* (Stanford, California: Hoover Institution Studies, 1966), 21. Rupen also writes that more than ten thousand Mongols journeyed several miles to meet and prostrate before the Dalai Lama in his *How Mongolia Is Really Ruled*, 13.

42. As previously mentioned, Bawden described the Manchu influence as an "antithesis of colonial policy" in *Modern History of Mongolia*, 82.

CHAPTER 4

1. See Baabar, *Twentieth Century Mongolia*, 99. The White Guard (AKA the White Army) were those who fought for monarchial control and were opposed to the Bolsheviks. The Red Army, opposed by the White Guard, supported the Soviets and communist ideology.

2. See Rupen, *How Mongolia Is Really Ruled*, 12.

3. Ibid., 16.

4. Kaplonski states that many were "exposed to the ideas of Sun Yat-Sen and other Chinese leaders, as well as Japanese, who were showing an increased interest in Mongolia during this period." See his *Truth, History, and Politics in Mongolia*, 94.

5. See Cheney, "Pre-Revolutionary Culture," 41, 42.

6. Ibid., 41.

7. See Moses, *Political Role of Mongol Buddhism*, 127, 131.

8. See Rupen, *How Mongolia Is Really Ruled*, 18.

9. See chapter 2, n. 76. The Eighth Bogd Gegeen was ranked ninth on this list of the most influential Mongols of the last century, before Mongolia's first astronaut, J. Gurragch, and right behind Altan Qaan.

10. Baabar and Kaplonski, *Twentieth Century Mongolia*, 135.

11. Ibid., 136. Baabar claims: "The Mongols had been waiting two hundred years for the overthrow of the Manchu and the revival of the country's independence." This sentiment is also reflected in the Mongolian popular press: "In the early 1900's Chinese were flooding into Mongolia after the New Administration policy was formed by the Chinese Empress Zixi. The Mongols, who respected the earth, resented the Chinese for tilling the land and digging mines. A new movement of opposition against the Chinese was formed." See "Free At Last, 1911: New Independence," *The Mongolia Messenger* (Ulaanbaatar, January 12, 2000), no. 2 (444).

Although these may have been some of the official reasons for the Mongolian government's discontent with the Chinese, they may not reflect the true motivations for the Mongol rebellion. Nakami Tatsuo claims that the Chinese reforms "directly threatened Mongolia, and prompted the Mongols to reconsider their long-time relationship with the Qing dynasty." See Tatsuo Nakami, "Russian Diplomats and Mongol Independence, 1911–1915," in *Mongolia in the Twentieth Century: Landlocked Cosmopolitan*, ed. Stephen Kotkin and Bruce A. Elleman (Armonk, NY: M. E. Sharpe, 1999), 70.

12. See Rupen, *How Mongolia Is Really Ruled*, 6.

13. There is a discrepancy concerning the exact date of the Bogd Gegeen's inauguration. There was an enthronement ceremony at the *Udzun-qure* monastery for the Bogd Gegeen on December 16, 1911, according to Akademiia Nauk SSSR, *History of the Mongolian People's Republic*, 238.

Contemporary Mongol scholars cite a different date that was noted in the the *Mongol Messenger* newspaper. The article, "Free At Last, 1911: New Independence," tells us that "The Eighth Jebzundamba directed the Mongols into independence. The Manchu-installed governor Sanduo was escorted to the Chinese territory. Independence was declared on December 1. Troops were mobilized to defend the borders and liberate the western towns. On December 29, 1911, an auspicious day, Jebzundamba was installed on the throne as the Bogd Khan of Mongolia—establishing a new Mongol state."

14. See Akademiia Nauk SSSR, *History of the Mongolian People's Republic*, 237.

15. Onon and Pritchatt, *Asia's First Modern Revolution*, 22.

16. His prestige carried into Inner Mongolia. Mei-Hua Lan claims that: "During the post-1911 period of Outer Mongolian independence, many princes of Inner Mongolia sent letters to Urga expressing their willingness to join the new Mongolian state . . ." Mei-Hua Lan, "China's 'New Administration' in Mongolia," in *Mongolia in the Twentieth Century: Landlocked Cosmopolitan,* ed. Stephen Kotkin and Bruce A. Elleman (Armonk, NY: M. E. Sharpe, 1999), 52.

17. See Moses, *Political Role of Mongol Buddhism*, 166. For an account of the Bogd *Qaan's* homosexual relations with Legtseg, see C. R. Bawden, trans., *Tales of An Old Lama* (Tring, England: The Institute of Buddhist Studies, 1997), 26.

18. Onon and Pritchatt, trans., *Asia's First Modern Revolution: Mongolia Proclaims Its Independence in 1911*, 63, 64.

19. Ibid., 30.

20. "In 1911, after the Chinese revolution of that year, the Urga Khutukhtu, head of the Lamaist church in Mongolia, became head of an autonomous government, an action resulting almost entirely from the prompting of tsarist diplomatic agents in the area." George G. S. Murphy, *Soviet Mongolia* (Berkeley and Los Angeles: University of California Press, 1966), 4. Akademiia Nauk SSSR gives an example of this intervention: "December 1911 the Russian Ambassador in Peking proposed to the government of China the conclusion of a formal treaty with Khalkha giving the latter extensive internal autonomy within the limits of the Chinese State" in Akademiia Nauk SSSR, *History of the Mongolian People's Republic*, 240.

21. Trade was the only political avenue for the Russians during the nineteenth century. C. R. Bawden notes the nominal role Russia played in Mongol trade and the Chinese domination of the Mongol economy: "The economic strength of the Chinese shops in Mongolia, protected against Russian competition and never worried by the few Mongol merchant houses which grew up in the nineteenth century, rested on a double foundation and was well able to survive the half-hearted restrictions imposed from Peking." See Bawden, *Modern History of Mongolia*, 97.

22. See Baabar and Kaplonski, *Twentieth Century Mongolia*, 138.

23. The Sain Noyon Qaan was a very influential figure in foreign affairs as well, being among the first group of Mongols to meet with the Russians at a conference on October 12, 1912. Onon and Pritchatt, *Asia's First Modern Revolution*, 41

24. See Moses, *Political Role of Mongol Buddhism*, 152.

25. The Sain Noyon Qaan was Mongolia's second official prime minister.

Soviet sources state that "In the struggle against political opponents, the *Bogdo-gegen's* clique did not hesitate to make use of poison. This was how they removed Prime Minister Sain-noyon-khan, and Foreign Minister Khangda-Dordji, who were following the policy of strengthening links with Russia." See the *History of the Mongolia People's Party*, 253. Two political figures, Foreign Minister Qangda-Dorj and Tseren Chimid, were sent to Russia to request assistance. See Rupen, *How Mongolia Is Really Ruled*, 6. It is important to note that Tseren Chimid, whose title, Da Lama, was an official sent by the Dalai Lama and was functioning, in effect, as a Chinese. See Akademiia Nauk sssr, *History of the Mongolia People's Party*, 242. There is also no definitive evidence implicating the Bogd *Gegeen* in Namnonsuren or Qangda's death. Ibid., 36.

26. See Bawden, *Modern History of Mongolia*, 14.

27. Tatsuo Nakami refers to this Inner-Outer Mongolia unity of the Bogd Qaan as, "*Yeke Monggol ulus.*" Nakami, "Russian Diplomats," 74. Russian help was sought partly due to political and military backing, but also due to the financial backing that Russia had provided after the Mongols proclaimed autonomy. "During the years of the *Bogdo-gegen* Monarchy's existence Russia on three occasions advanced to the government of the *Bogdo-gegen*. . . . Tsarist loans were of the 'string attached' type and were always accompanied by fresh concessions on the part of the *Bogdo-gegen* government." See Akademiia Nauk sssr, *History of the Mongolian People's Republic*, 256.

28. Ibid., 240.

29. "The failure of Inner and Outer Mongolia to unite in 1911–12 had serious consequences. The Jebtsun Damba Khotokhto, or Urga Living Buddha, was then so commanding a figure that he could easily be made a kind of sovereign . . . by adding temporal authority to his religious primacy it was possible to create a personal sovereign, replacing the Manchu Emperor . . ." See Lattimore, *Mongols of Manchuria*, 122.

30. Rupen, *How Mongolia Is Really Ruled*, 11.

31. See Bawden, *Modern History of Mongolia*, 157.

32. Uradyn E. Bulag states that the Mongolian Sangha was divided into three different categories: the high-ranking lamas, middle-ranking lamas, and lower-ranking lamas. It should be noted that a lama's rank refers not only to religious status but also to economic status. However, this division is not easily discerned in the time before the autonomous period. See Uradyn E. Bulag, *Nationalism and Hybridity in Mongolia* (Oxford: Clarendon Press, 1998), 40.

33. See Bawden, *Modern History of Mongolia*, 166.

34. See Cheney, "Pre-Revolutionary Culture," 53.

35. See Akademiia Nauk SSSR, *History of the Mongolian People's Republic*, 167–68.

36. "The system of Buddhism brought a whole series of very important consequences for practical life . . . foremost among these is respect for the human being . . . At no time did Buddhism impose national, class, or caste barriers on its adherents. . . . Thus Buddhism becomes a kind of declaration of human rights and of citizens' rights in the East." See Siklos, "Mongolian Buddhism," 168.

37. One clear example of this is the *dekwat*, the Thai Buddhist temple boy, who serves Thai monks at a temple.

38. Bawden followed the history of Losol, who was one of the seven famous revolutionaries, the others being: Choibalsan, Bodoo, Losol, Danzan, Suqbaatar, Dogsom, and Chakdorjav. "Losol . . . who went to the Soviet Union in 1920 to enlist communist support, had a very varied career. Born in 1890 as an imperial subject, he had been transferred to the *shabi* estate, and from 1899 onwards was a lama." See Bawden, *Modern History of Mongolia*, 159. Here was a lama, who importantly remained a lama, and was an intellectual leader against the Bogd Qaan administration. One of the most important persons to join the revolutionary party was Puntsagdorj, to whom Moses gives credit: "Lamas were found as members of the Mongolian People's Revolutionary Party, and the Minister of Internal Affairs was the Da Lama [Puntsagdorj] until his execution in the Bodo plot of 1922. Bodo himself, prime minister and foreign minister after 1921, was also a lama." See Moses, *Political Role of Mongol Buddhism*, 165. Qasbaatar was commemorated by the Soviets and given the title of "regimental lama." See Brown and Onon, *History of the Mongolian People's Republic*, 100. Jamtsarano, who in the early 1900s ran a newspaper, later said of the socialist government: "Seeing that the basic aims of our Party and of Buddhism are both the welfare of the people, there is no conflict between the two of them." See Siklos, "Mongolian Buddhism," 172. Finally, both Damba Dorji and Dja-Damba tried to switch the Mongolian People's Revolutionary Party to a capitalistic path, calling for a "purer form of Buddhism." See Murphy, *Soviet Mongolia*, 95.

39. Bawden states that Jamtsarano was in favor of a Buddhism harmonious with socialism and supports this with a quote from Jamtsarano: "Seeing that the basic aims of our Party and of Buddhism are both the welfare of the people, there is no conflict between the two of them. . . . Our Party wants to see the Buddhist Faith flourishing in a pure form, and approves of lamas who stay in their lamaseries, reciting the scriptures and faithfully observing their vows." See Bawden, *Modern History of Mongolia*, 286.

40. Stephen Kotkin, "Introduction. In Search of the Mongols and Mongolia: A Multinational Odyssey," *Mongolia in the Twentieth Century: Landlocked Cosmopolitan,* ed. Stephen Kotkin and Bruce A. Elleman (Armonk, NY: M. E. Sharpe, 1999), 6.

41. For more information on the Buddhists' contribution to the new socialist government, see chapter 4, n. 25.

42. See Baabar, *Twentieth Century Mongolia*, 168.

43. See Murphy, *Soviet Mongolia*, 11.

44. Soviet sources indicate that contact between the revolutionaries and Russians began here: "In the years of Autonomous Mongolia . . . Sukhe Bator, the organizer and leader of the Mongolian revolution, worked for some time in a printing shop, where he not only became a skilled compositor but also established relations with Russian workers. . . . A major event was the opening of the first secular school attached to the Ministry of Foreign Affairs. It was in this school that Kh. Choibalsan began his education. It should be mentioned that Danchinov, a political émigré from Russia, who was working as a teacher in this school, helped Choibalsan to enter the school." See Akademiia Nauk SSSR, *History of the Mongolian People's Republic*, 260.

45. See Dashpurev and Soni, *Reign of Terror in Mongolia*, 8. In some accounts, it should also be noted that Choibalsan was the younger brother of Bodoo. See Murphy, *Soviet Mongolia*, 23

46. For a discussion of how Choibalsan's significance in Mongol society compares with Stalin's role in the USSR see Rupen, *How Mongolia Is Really Ruled*, 59.

47. Moses, *Political Role of Mongol Buddhism*, 159.

48. Murphy suggests that the Bogd Gegeen was in no position to make a choice: "In 1919 a Chinese warlord, Hsu Shu-Ch'eng, gifted with more energy and capacity for action than diplomatic skill, forced the Mongols by threat of arms to the status they had held in 1911." Murphy, *Soviet Mongolia*, 5. Lattimore infers that autonomy was defrauded from the Mongols by threatening the life of the Bogd Gegeen: "It was also the year [1919] in which General Hsü Shu-tseng, 'Little' Hsu, took advantage of the fall of the Russian Empire to invade Outer Mongolia. The expedition . . . was allowed to reach Urga without opposition. It then seized the person of the Jebtsun Damba Khotokhto and coerced the Mongols into signing away the degree of autonomy which they had won in 1911–12." See Lattimore, *Mongols of Manchuria*, 125. The Soviets depict the loss of autonomy as a collusion between the Chinese and the high-ranking lamas and princes: "Chen Yi, the Chinese viceroy in Urga [the summer of 1919], persuaded the Bogdo-gegen and his government that the princes would

retain all their advantages and privileges. . . . The result was the appearance of a shameful document, known under the title '64 Paragraphs Concerning the Improvements of the Future Situation of Mongolia.' Under these 'paragraphs' the government of Autonomous Mongolia was abolished." See Akademiia Nauk SSSR, *History of the Mongolian People's Republic*, 275. Whether or not the Bogd Qaan remained firm in his stance on Mongolia's autonomy or immediately bent to Chinese pressure, his initial break from the Chinese in 1911 was a clear indication that his acquiescence in this situation came by force.

49. See Akademiia Nauk SSSR, *History of the Mongolian People's Republic*, 273.

50. "Ungern's units, which were in such places as Niislel Khuree, areas near the northern Mongolian frontier, Uliastai, Khovd, and Ulaangom, conscripted troops everywhere, strengthened their forces, and requisitioned from the *ard* masses livestock, *gers* . . ." See Brown and Onon, *History of the Mongolian People's Republic*, 91.

51. Ibid., 59. Baabar claims that the Ungern-Sternberg's legion under Semenov was actually working for the Japanese, who, since the independence of Mongolia, had also taken an interest in Mongolia. Baabar and Kaplonski, *Twentieth Century Mongolia*, 185.

52. See Brown and Onon, *History of the Mongolian People's Republic*, 92.

53. See Murphy, *Soviet Mongolia*, 6.

54. See Moses, *Political Role of Mongol Buddhism*, 159.

55. Murphy, *Soviet Mongolia*, 2, n. 5.

CHAPTER 5

1. Kaplonski cites Shagdaryn Bira for "dividing the socialist Mongolian historiography into two stages," the first stage being from 1921 to 1940 and the second stage from 1940 to 1991. Whereas this is useful for political analysis, the deconstruction of the Mongolian Sangha merits a special emphasis on the preliminary stage (1921–1929). See Kaplonski, *Truth, History and Politics*, 103.

2. Mongols use the acronym, MAQN (Mongolyn Ardyn Qu'vgalt Nam), which refers to the MPRP or the Mongolian People's Revolutionary Party.

3. Christopher Kaplonski states that the motivated killings by the MPRP began as early as the 1920s. Christopher Kaplonski, "Thirty Thousand Bullets: Remembering Political Repression in Mongolia," conference paper on Remember and Forgetting—The Political and Social Aftermath of Intense Conflict in Eastern Asia and Northern Europe, Lund University (Lund, Sweden, April 15–17, 1999), 214.

4. Contemporary Mongol scholars are beginning to investigate the archives, which, in the future, could provide more definitive evidence. In 1999, Ölziibaatar and Todbaatar used records from the State Historical Archives in their dissertations. Ölziibaatar's dissertation traced political repression during this period, and Todbaatar's addressed the history of the Ministry of Internal Affairs. Since the 2000 elections, MAQN has regained power, but access to such archival information may continue to be difficult to obtain.

5. George Murphy and Robert Rupen are criticized by socialist scholars for their views. Murphy states: "Military force made possible the establishments of the first enduring political satellite of the Soviet Union. Years later, modern Soviet historians would invent a 'revolutionary situation' in the Mongolia of 1921; they would manufacture 'revolutionary heroes'; they would minimize the role played by Soviet troops and agents, and would portray the events of 1921 as a genuine national uprising." See Murphy, *Soviet Mongolia*, 2.

Soviet scholars holding this same position attack Rupen. "Failing to appreciate the successful historical mission of the Mongolian people, Rupen attempts to prove that, since the Mongols are situated between two major powers of Russia and China, it is as if their fate merely shifts continuously and successively in the hands of these two major nations; his attempt to demonstrate that the Mongolian people themselves could not create even the 1921 People's Revolution shows the extreme shortsightedness of [this] American historian." Brown and Onon, *History of the Mongolian People's Republic*, 41.

6. There are consistent occurrences of socialist propaganda concerning Mongol involvement in the revolution. An example of this is found in Soviet records: "News of the revolutionary happenings in the north spread all over the country. The Party slogans summoning people to fight for the expulsion of the occupation authorities and their troops and the establishment of popular rule met with an eager response from the masses." See Akademiia Nauk SSSR, *History of the Mongolian People's Republic*, 295.

7. Murphy cites Choibalsan as stating that there were around four hundred Mongols involved in the actual revolution (*Soviet Mongolia*, 1). Rupen gives different statistics that still show disproportional participation: "When ten thousand Red Army troops entered Mongolia alongside seven hundred Mongolian ones, it was hard to avoid the interpretation that Russia was directing events." See Rupen, *How Mongolia is Really Ruled*, 29.

8. These are, in fact, nicknamed the "Qalqa Seven" by Rupen, in *How Mongolia Is Really Ruled*, 30. Puntsagdorj was also a key figure but was not includedin Rupen's expression.

9. Shagdariin Sandag states that Suqbaatar was "falsely represented as the founder of the MPR and the MPRP." Shagdariin Sandag and Harry H. Kendall, *Poisoned Arrows: The Stalin-Choibalsan Mongolian Massacres, 1921–1941* (Boulder, CO: Westview Press, 2000), 39.

10. Suqbaatar's face can be found everywhere in Mongolia. His picture is at the beginning of children's Mongolian textbooks—see *Tsagaan Tolgoi* [Alphabet] (Ulaanbaatar: Ministry of Education, 1994), a children's book on the Mongolian language published through the Ministry of Education—and he is commemorated with a statue at the landmark area of Suqbaatar's Square in the capital of Mongolia. Suqbaatar often is compared to Lenin in the Soviet Union. Coincidentally, they died around the same time: Suqbaatar died on February 20, 1923, and Lenin died eleven months later on January 21, 1924.

With regard to the exaggeration of Suqbaatar's role in Mongol history, Bawden writes: "The demands of the cult of personality, which exalted Choibalsan and, to a lesser extent, the dead Suqbaatar, meant that for a long time all supposedly serious accounts of the events of these times were subjected to grotesque distortions, though these have not been corrected to a certain extent." See his *Modern History of Mongolia*, 214.

With regard to Choibalsan's significance to Mongolia, Rupen says: "Choibalsan has often been referred to as 'Mongolia's Stalin' and there was indeed a parallel. Both men led their countries practically single-handed [*sic*] for many years, having gained power through internecine struggle and the elimination of many rivals. . . . Both also built up what came to be called a 'cult of personality,' and both were posthumously attacked for having done so." See Rupen, *How Mongolia Is Really Ruled*, 59.

Although not as much as Suqbaatar, Choibalsan still is highly regarded by the Mongols. Prof. Namjil from the *Bagshyn Iq Surguul'* (Pedagogical University) in Mongolia credits Choibalsan for Mongolia's current independence. Choibalsan's statue can be found in front of the Mongol Ulsyn Iq Surguul' (Mongol National University) in Ulaanbaatar, Mongolia. Both Choibalsan's and Suqbaatar's statues were erected in 1946. For short biographies on Choibalsan and Suqbaatar and accounts of their heroism, see Urgunge Onon, *Mongolian Heroes of the Twentieth Century* (New York: AMS Press, Inc., 1976).

11. The work of Dashpurev and Soni, *Reign of Terror in Mongolia*, is evidence of their separation from other socialist scholars. In this book they agree with socialist claims regarding the initial presence of the two parties: "In the initial stage, two small underground revolutionary groups were established in Urga, the capital of Mongolia." The two parties receive considerable attention by

socialist scholars because they represent the birth of future socialist heroes. "The first revolutionary group, which was called the Urga Group, sprang up in the centre of the city." See Akademiia Nauk SSSR, *History of the Mongolian People's Republic*, 277. The second group, the Consul, is said to be a later formation: "Somewhat later a second revolutionary group was formed; it was called the 'Consul Group,' as if sprang up in the consular quarter of the city." Ibid., 278.

12. Dashpurev and Soni, *Reign of Terror in Mongolia*, 8.

13. For a more detailed account of Dogsomiin Bodoo and Dambiin Chagdarjav, see Sandag and Kendall, *Poisoned Arrows*.

14. See Akademiia Nauk SSSR, *History of the Mongolian People's Republic*, 277. Dashpurev and Soni suggest that they formed as early as 1918. *Reign of Terror in Mongolia*, 24, n. 1.

15. Dashpurev and Soni, *Reign of Terror in Mongolia*, 8.

16. See Rupen, *How Mongolia Is Really Ruled*, 28. This is also testament to the fact that earlier MPRP advocates still respected and acknowledged Buddhism. Like some of his contemporaries, Jamtsarano is said to have been a Buddhist as well as a socialist. "Jamtsarano maintained that it was the Buddha and the Bodhisattvas who would protect humanity and cited as trustworthy authorities for his opinions not Marx and Lenin but the theologians Nagarjuna, Jobo Atisha, and Tsongkhapa. . . . 'What a good thing it would be if the members of our Party and League were to acquire a proper understanding, to the best of their ability, of the qualities and teachings of the Buddhist Faith, and, in their criticism of matters of religion, were able to distinguish right and wrong, without groping about as if blind.'" Bawden in *Modern History of Mongolia*, 286, quotes from S. Pürevjav and D. Dashjamts *BNMAU-d Süm Qiid Lamasyn Asuudlyg Shiidverlesen N', 1921–1940* [How the Question of the Lamas and Monasteries was Resolved in the MPR, 1921–1940] (Ulaanbaatar: State Publishing House, 1965), 112.

17. See Baabar and Kaplonski, *Twentieth Century Mongolia*, 205.

18. Owen Lattimore, trans., *Nationalism and Revolution in Mongolia* (New York: Oxford University Press, 1955), 139, quoted by George Murphy in *Soviet Mongolia*, 15.

19. See Murphy, *Soviet Mongolia*, 15.

20. "There are two things important in [regard to the activities of the Mongolian revolutionaries]. Firstly, Mongolian revolutionaries, in all their activities, had received guidelines from Russian and Buryatian communist advisors. Secondly, the Mongolian People's Party (MPR) was formed under the tutelage of the Russian Communist (Bolshevik) Party. This fact can be

verified from the materials of the first Congress of the Mongolian People's Party (MPP)." Dashpurev and Soni, *Reign of Terror in Mongolia*, 10. A Buriat named Rinchino and the Consul group member, Choibalsan, were considered to be integral parts of this earlier collusion. Dashpurev, Soni, and Rupen give credence to Choibalsan's and Rinchino's relationship with the Soviets and their proficiency in Russian.

21. See Murphy, *Soviet Mongolia*, 8.

22. Ibid.

23. The American diplomat, Sokobin, investigated Russian influence in Mongolia in the 1920s. According to Alicia J. Campi, "In general, Sokobin did not have a high opinion of the members of the Mongolian People's Revolutionary Government. . . . He felt that the main aim of the Bolsheviks was to use Mongolia as a bargaining chip with the Chinese government in negotiations over recognition, commercial relations, and the returning of certain White Russian counter-revolutionaries." Alicia J. Campi, "United States Government Perceptions of the Mongols, as Reflected in the US Kalgan Consular Records, 1920–1927," The International Conference on China Border Area Studies: National Chengchi University (Taipei, Taiwan, April 23–30, 1984), 11.

24. "Realizing the important part played in Mongolian life by the religious authority of the Bogdo-gegen, Ungern decided to bring the latter into his service. He managed to make contact secretly with the Bogdo-gegen, who was in Urga. At the end of January 1921, Ungern, with the full complicity of the Bogdo-gegen removed him from Urga and settled him at his own headquarters, thus gaining all possibility of posing as the executant of the 'divine' will of the head of the church." See Akademiia Nauk SSSR, *History of the Mongolian People's Republic*, 284.

25. Brown and Onon, *History of the Mongolian People's Republic*, 153. A *gamin* (in Mongolian) comes from the Chinese *ko-ming* (revolution) and means that the Chinese forces were still present in Mongolia at this time. Gombojab Hangin on page 110 of his *Modern Mongolian-English Dictionary* states that "In Mongolian *gamin* is always used in a hostile or derogatory sense."

26. This was made legal in Mongolian administrative law on July 10, 1921. On this date it was legally declared that the ministries of the Bogd Qaan were not accepted and that chief ministers were to be appointed in accordance with the Mongolian People's Republic. Butler, *The Mongolian Legal System,* 255.

27. Aside from the lamas present in the initial MPRP ranks, the MPRP was supported by former princes, lamas, and wealthy commoners who were later removed from office in order to weaken Danzan's political leverage. See Murphy, *Soviet*

Mongolia, 99. Jamtsarano's endorsement of a neo-Buddhism and Danzan's efforts for autonomy had held appeal for many of the bourgeoisie. Bawden writes that Jamtsarano's new Buddhist ideology won support even from the high-ranking lamas, "Many high lamas were anxious to reform and strip down Buddhism to its pure essentials . . ." See Bawden, *Modern History of Mongolia*, 287. Rupen writes that Jamtsarano's demand for modification of religious practice, instead of a suppression of it, continued as late as 1926, with circulated pamphlets that ascribed their views to Jamtsarano. See Rupen, *How Mongolia Is Really Ruled*, 37.

28. See Murphy, *Soviet Mongolia*, 41.

29. See Moses, *Political Role of Mongol Buddhism*, 169.

30. Bulag, *Nationalism and Hybridity in Mongolia*, 41.

31. See Murphy, *Soviet Mongolia*, 76.

32. Todbaatar, D. "Mongol ulsyn ayuulgui baidlyg hangah baiguullagyn uil ajillagaany ehen ueiin tuuhiin asuudald 1922–1930" [The Early Historical Functions of the Institution in Order to Insure the Safety of Mongolia, 1922–1930]. PhD diss., Academy of Sciences, the Institute of History, Ulaanbaatar, Mongolia, 1999, cited from notes taken at Todbaatar's defense of his dissertation on June 18, 1999. According to the same source, there were fourteen "workers" for the revolution—six were Russian. At present there is insufficient information to substantiate any claims concerning their identities or the degree of influence they had on the revolution. It can be assumed, however, that these six had a significant impact on the revolution and on the future foreign relationship with the Soviet Union. The Ministry of Internal Affairs later evolved into an operation similar to the Soviet's KGB. See Dashpurev and Soni, *Reign of Terror*, 3.

33. "The Oath-Taking Treaty of November 1, 1921, imposed strict limits on exercise of any secular power, but it could not destroy the Jebtsun Damba's legitimacy and authority, which did not rest on the authorization of the Russian-influenced government." See Rupen, *How Mongolia Is Really Ruled*, 37.

34. This revolt is referenced in both Rupen and Soviet records. According to the Soviet account, which differs little from Rupen's: "In December 1921 there was exposed the conspiracy of the Saj Lama, and 48 men who had participated in it were arrested." For the Soviet version of this revolt, see Brown, *History of the Mongolian People's Republic*, 172.

35. Ibid.

36. See chapter 3, n. 4. See also Jagchid and Hyer, *Mongolia's Culture and Society*, 319.

37. Moses, *Political Role of Mongol Buddhism*, 166. Contrary to Moses' statement, there were lamas such as the lama Bodoo who introduced change, but

they were the third-party lamas who had split from the Sangha during the autonomous period.

38. Bawden writes that the low-ranking lamas were "an impoverished mass of lowly lamas who could never hope to rise to be anything else and who, to a great extent, were mere temple-servants." See Bawden, *Modern History of Mongolia*, 157.

39. See Murphy, *Soviet Mongolia*, 64.

40. For specific examples see chapter 4, n. 7, and the source for n. 38 above.

41. Borin Jambal recalls giving a rough estimate of 14,850 among the thirty different states for the revolutionaries. However, these only account for the registered lamas who were present at the time. See Bawden, *Tales of An Old Lama*, 76.

42. Brown and Onon, *History of the Mongolian People's Republic*, 180. The initial Mongol form of socialism never directly impeded the inertia of Buddhism. After the revolution the *shabinar* continued to gain strength. The sheer numbers of *shabinar* and lamas, however, created a powerful political threat to the MPRP.

43. See Moses, *Political Role of Mongol Buddhism*, 155. These numbers indicate that the Sangha was still growing during the autonomous period. In 1919 there were forty thousand lamas living within monasteries, with an additional sixty thousand living outside the monastery walls. See Murphy, *Soviet Mongolia*, 41, 42.

44. See Bawden, *Modern History of Mongolia*, 254.

45. See Akademiia Nauk SSSR, *History of the Mongolian People's Republic*, 309. Baabar and Kaplonski implicate Danzan in the fall of Bodoo, claiming that Danzan "engineered various plans to remove Bodoo from office by convincing and persuading influential figures." See *Twentieth Century Mongolia*, 230.

46. See Murphy, *Soviet Mongolia*, 76.

47. See Rupen, *How Mongolia Is Really Ruled*, 30.

48. Dashpurev and Soni, *Reign of Terror in Mongolia*, 15.

49. According to Borin Jambal, Choibalsan demanded that Borin inform him of "who holds the Holy One's [Bogd Qaan's] seal and impresses it on incoming documents." See Bawden, *Tales of An Old Lama*, 77.

50. See Bawden, *Modern History of Mongolia*, 253.

51. See Murphy, *Soviet Mongolia*, 102.

52. Sandag and Kendall, *Poisoned Arrows*, 49.

53. "[Rinchino, Borisov and Iudin] must have been impressed by how few Mongolian troops had rallied to support Sukhe Bator. Perhaps they also knew that Outer Mongolia had been virtually without uprising against the status quo—a tribute to the success of Chinese policy." See Bawden, *Modern History of Mongolia*, 35. Russian analysis indicated that the Mongols would not

collectively rise up against an imposed government. So far, history has supported this claim.

54. "It is open to suspicion why Sukhe Baatar and the Bogdo Khan died so close in time, February 26, 1923 and May 20, 1924, respectively. Maybe the political scenario was orchestrated by the Soviet leaders so the Bogdo Khan could be accused of poisoning Sukhe Baatar and removed from his supreme post as head of Mongolia." Sandag and Kendall, *Poisoned Arrows*, 41.

55. The Dara Eq monastery in Ulaanbaatar was turned into a primary school after the revolution.

56. See Murphy, *Soviet Mongolia*, 77–78.

57. Often, Danzan would engage in heated debates with the Soviet-advocate El'bekdor Rinchino over economic issues. In *Soviet Mongolia*, 80, Murphy cites J. Attree's translation of the minutes of the Third Congress of the Mongolian People's Republic, which reads, "When Rinchino demanded laws to restrain capitalism, Danzan replied with telling accuracy: 'But we have not capitalists in Mongolia; that question is not today's but tomorrow's.' Next, with considerable bravery—or was it foolhardiness?—he remarked: 'I think a heedless repeating of our friendship for the USSR without a leading point is useless.'" Attree's translation is located at the Hoover Library in Stanford, California.

58. Sandag and Kendall, *Poisoned Arrows*, 52.

59. See Bawden, *Modern History of Mongolia*, 277.

60. At this time Rinchino had the backing of the Soviets. For a time, he was chief adviser to the comintern and had close contact with the Soviet minister, Vasiliev. Murphy, *Soviet Mongolia*, 80. Dashpurev has linked Rinchino directly with the Dotood Yaam: "The Chairman of the Dotoodiig Hamgaalah Gazar was a Mongolian, but the Russian communist, Buryat E. Rinchino had controlled its activities." Daspurev and Soni, *Reign of Terror in Mongolia*, 13.

61. Sandag and Kendall, *Poisoned Arrows*, 55.

62. See Rupen, *How Mongolia Is Really Ruled*, 30. Danzan reportedly said: "Rinchino is the secret representative from Soviet Russia to our government. He will kill me at first and then all others." Dashpurev and Soni, *Reign of Terror in Mongolia*, 18.

63. Dembereliin Ölziibaatar, interview with Luvsanchültem Sodov, 1989, trans. Michael Jerryson and Narangerel (narrative 16 in appendix).

64. Later, in 1966, Sambuu was elected chairman of the Presidium of the People's Great Qural. Brown and Onon, *History of the Mongolian People's Republic*, 641–42.

65. See Bawden, *Modern History of Mongolia*, 309.

66. This information comes from another interview with a Dotood Yaam worker, Tsogt: "When I went to Moscow (because I did a good job during the collecting of rich people's property) in 1929, some people came with me." Dembereliin Ölziibaatar, interview with Tsogt Luvsansamdan, 1988, trans. Michael Jerryson and Narangerel (narrative 15 in appendix).

67. See Moses, *Political Role of Mongol Buddhism*, 183.

68. Milne, *Mongolian People's Republic*, 5.

69. Brown and Onon, *History of the Mongolian People's Republic*, 233.

70. "At the same time, atheistic propaganda was disseminated as far as the primitive methods of publicity available permitted—by means of the press, pamphlets, and crude theatrical sketches. On the side of the Sangha there was a steady stream of anti-Communist propaganda flowing out from the lamasery chanceries and printing presses, carried throughout the countryside by wandering mendicant lamas." See Bawden, *Modern History of Mongolia*, 260. Although Bawden's use of the word *primitive* is inappropriate here, the point is still valid. Technological advances had yet to transform Mongolia, so earlier forms of disseminating propaganda were used.

71. See Rupen, *How Mongolia Is Really Ruled*, 38.

72. Akiner, "Introduction," xiv.

73. Like any other law, it took more than a year for this to become fully implemented: "In 1929, when 5,773 children were enrolled in government schools, there were 18,955 attending monastery schools. Of this number 9,668 were children from eight to thirteen years of age and 9,287 from thirteen to seventeen." See Rupen, *Mongolian People's Republic*, 28.

74. Bulag offers the MPRP's account: "The separation of religion from the state was also justified by the Party and Government's vision of Mongolian national policy and its role of 'defending and protecting the territory. . . . They argued that religion was detrimental to the national interest, and indeed the very survival of the Mongols." Bulag, *Nationalism and Hybridity in Mongolia*, 39.

75. See Moses, *Political Role of Mongol Buddhism*, 184. Part of the reason for the separation of Sangha and state for the Mongols was the socialist accusation that the Mongolian Sangha unjustly held a monopoly on literacy, an accusation that bore substantial merit. Bulag, *Nationalism and Hybridity*, 39.

76. For examples of literature in the Tibetan language, see chapter 3, n. 2.

77. While Zanabazar serves as an exemplar for this, other lamas have been known for their aesthetic talents. Another example can be found at the Ravjaa museum in Dornogov *aimag*, dedicated to the nineteenth century artist and lama, D. Ravjaa. Academician Ts. Damdinsüren is credited as saying: "D. Ravjaa was a

writer, who left behind an unextinguished and everlasting lamp of belles-lettres." See Altangerel and Tsagaan, *Ih Gobiin Dogshin Noyon Hutuqtu* [The Ferocious Noyon Qotagt of the Great Desert] (Ulaanbaatar: UULS Studio), 19.

78. Since the democratization of Mongolia, these views have reverted to their traditional views prior to socialism. Ole Bruun offers an example of this Buddhist rhetoric on the accumulation of wealth: "A conventional viewpoint—supported by Buddhist clergy—holds that wealthy lamas, who contribute to the construction of temples, monasteries, and stupas, provide a greater blessing for their region than, for example, people who donate money to the poor, since poverty only exists on the material plane." Ole Bruun, *Precious Steppe: Mongolian Nomadic Pastoralists in the Age of the Market* (Lanham, Md.: Lexington Books, 2005), 163.

79. This group was organized in August 1921 with the help of Russians and the Consul group members. The formation of such a group was deemed necessary in order for the youth of Mongolia to realize the Marxist-Leninists principles of the revolution. Dashpurev and Soni, *Reign of Terror*, 11. Choibalsan was an active member, keeping himself involved in the growing political moments during this time period. Baabar, calling the Revolutionary Youth Union (Boshgig Qalaq Zaluuchuudin Evlel) a Soviet-styled terrorist organization, points to Choibalsan's involvement in this group as well, stating that he was, "one of the most stable, polite and calculating of the Mongolian revolutionaries." Baabar and Kaplonski, *Twentieth Century Mongolia*, 227.

80. See Akiner, "Introduction."

81. See Rupen, *How Mongolia Is Really Ruled*, 37.

82. See Akademiia Nauk SSSR, *History of the Mongolian People's Republic*, 326. Murphy records Dambadorj's slogan during these times as, "for a pure Buddhism." See Murphy, *Soviet Mongolia*, 95.

83. See Rupen, *How Mongolia Is Really Ruled*, 30.

84. Murphy closes this period by stating: "The purge of the late 1920s had another significant result. . . . The idea of obedience to a Comintern interest[,] rather, to the Mongolia national interest[,] was now accepted; it no longer had to be enforced, but was a spontaneous attitude." See Murphy, *Soviet Mongolia*, 105.

CHAPTER 6

1. The first Mongol attempt at a Soviet-style policy was the New Economic Policy and later the First Five-Year Plan, which is also referred to as the New

Plan. Raymond E. Zickel, ed., *Soviet Union: A Country Study* (Washington, D.C.: Federal Research Division, 1989), 473. For a discussion of the New Plan, see Bawden, *Modern History of Mongolia*, 310–15. For references to The New Turn, see Siklos, "Mongolian Buddhism," 174; and Dashpurev and Soni, *Reign of Terror*, 28–35; see also R. Nansal, *MAKb Namaas Namyn Shine Ergeltiin Bodlogyg Bielüülekhin Tölöö Temtsen N' (1932–1934 on)* [The Struggle of the MPRP to Implement the Party's New Turn Policy, 1932–1934] (*Ulaanbaatar: State Publishing House, 1958*). For a more recent account of the collectivization of Mongolia, see Baabar, *Twentieth Century Mongolia*, 292–94.

2. "Backward concepts of the Yellow Faith, which had totally dominated the *ard* masses' knowledge, minds, and all cultural matters during a period of several hundred years, were the main obstacles to developing a new culture and to spreading new concepts among the masses." Brown and Onon, *History of the Mongolian People's Republic*, 369.

3. Known to Mongol historians as the "reign of terror," this period's parameters have been inconsistently identified. For instance, Dashpurev and Soni's work, *Reign of Terror in Mongolia,* covers the time frame of 1920 to 1990, whereas Moses cites the period from 1928 to 1940. A clear delineation between Moses and Dashpurev and Soni's work is that their period includes the political purges in addition to the religious purges that lasted until 1990. Political terror may have progressed even later. An indication of this was the 1998 assassination of democratic leader, Sanjaasurengiin Zorig. The accomplices to Zorig's murder were still unaccounted for in October 2006. See "Flowers for Zorig," *UB Post*, October 5, 2006.

4. Sandag and Kendall*, Poisoned Arrows*, 70.

5. The *Mongolyn Ünen* [The Mongolian Truth], which was originally published in the Soviet Union, attacked feudalism. *Zaluuchuudyn* [The Youth's Truth], was focused on the younger generation, and the *Ardyn Tsereg* [The People's Army], was published for the military and police. Brown, *History of the Mongolian People's Republic*, 380.

6. In place of Mongolian Buddhist medicine, Russian medicine and practice became the adoptive and only prescribed method. Baabar and Kaplonski, *Twentieth Century Mongolia*, 300.

7. Bawden, *Modern History of Mongolia*, 352. This ban was effective in the urban areas, but not wholly successful in the countryside. There has been mention of Buddhist medicine surviving the 1930s under the umbrella of the hospitals. This would justify a reassessment of Choibalsan's influence on Mongolian Buddhism and a closer examination of the role hospitals played in the

propagation and maintenance of Mongolian Buddhism. As of now, Buddhist medicinal practices are seen as largely confined to pastoral and individualized occurrences, suffering the same institutionalized deconstruction as the Buddhist pedagogy.

8. See Dashpurev and Soni, *Reign of Terror in Mongolia*, 11.

9. Erdembileg Gompil stated that he retained his membership at this time because of his involvement with the Soviet Union. Dembereliin Ölziibaatar, interview with Erdembileg Gompil, 1992, trans. Michael Jerryson and Narangerel (narrative 10 in appendix).

10. R. Nansal, *MAKb Namaas Namyn Shine Ergeltiin Bodlogyg Bielüülekhin Tölöö Temtsen N'*, 22.

11. Bawden, *Modern History of Mongolia*, 313.

12. Dembereliin Ölziibaatar, interview with Rentsendavaa Danzanshagdariin, 1992(?), trans. Michael Jerryson and Narangerel (narrative 11 in appendix).

13. Bawden, *Modern History of Mongolia*, 313. From the 1920s to the 1930s, this league denounced all religious believers in the Soviet Union. See also Zickel, *Soviet Union*, 198.

14. The prominent theory at this time involved merging Marxism with Buddhism. See Rupen, *Mongolian People's Republic*, 29. This was also shown through the Eighth Congress and the Sixth Great Qural. "The VI MPR Great Khural which met in April 1930 issued decisions to bring justice agencies close to the workers, to spread simplicity and legality to their work, to purge justice agencies of elements with the viewpoint and the old feudal law, to select loyal people in the field with a truly working-class revolutionary viewpoint, to organize the training of legal cadres, and to organize widely the work of educating the working people with a revolutionary legal viewpoint." See Butler, *The Mongolian Legal System*, 93.

15. "He [Eguzer] was killed in 1930 together with seven others, all were accused of being part of a political case, 'Counter-revolutionary case of 38.' Thirty-eight people were sentenced according to this case and seven people received the death penalty. Only in 1990 did the Supreme Court consider the case again, at the request of the State prosecutor, and found that the court's decision in 1930's was a purge." Namsrai Oyunbayar, "Commemorating Those Who Died in the Purges," *The UB Post*, August 5, 2000, no. 30 (219), 6.

16. Brown and Onon, *History of the Mongolian People's Republic*, 201.

17. Ibid., 265.

18. Murphy, *Soviet Mongolia*, 124.

19. "Sokobin also investigated Russian influence in Mongolia. He believed

that because the Mongols were sheep and cattle herders or lamas, Bolshevik theory of 'liberation of the toiling masses' was not applicable to Mongolia." Campi, "United States Government Perceptions," 11.

20. For an example, see Michael Jerryson and Christopher Kaplonski, anonymous interview, 1999 (narrative 8 in appendix).

21. Charles A. Bell, "The Struggle for Mongolia," *Journal of the Royal Central Asian Society* 24 (London: Royal Central Asian Society, January 1937), 60. Quoted in Moses, *Political Role of Mongol Buddhism*, 202. A "Red Mongol" was a member of the MPRP.

22. In *The Political Role of Mongolian Buddhism* (page 210), Moses cites a letter written to the Panchen Lama by dissident lamas in Pürevjav and Dashjamts, *BNMAU-d Süm Qiid* Lama*syn Asuudlyg Shiidverlesen N', 1921–1940* [How the Question of the Lamas and Monasteries was Resolved in the MPR, 1921–1940], 41. For a discussion of the plight of the Panchen Lama and his inability to help the Inner Mongols, much less the Outer Mongols, see Baabar and Kaplonski, *Twentieth Century Mongolia*, 313.

23. Rentsendavaa mentions that there had been a revolt in his hometown, in Qövsgöl *aimag*. D. Ölziibaatar, interview with Rentsendavaa Danzanshagdariin, 1992(?), trans. Michael Jerryson and Narangerel (narrative 11 in appendix). For an account of tanks moving against lamas in Arqangai *aimag*, see Michael Jerryson, interview with Süqbat, 1999, trans. Narangerel (narrative 3 in appendix). This episode is depicted in paintings at the Political Repression Museum in Ulaanbaatar, Mongolia as well. Lamas at Erdene Zuu allegedly staged an uprising in Övörqangai *aimag*. This is quite possible inasmuch as Erdene Zuu was the most holy refuge for Mongolian Buddhists; any sacrilege here would be taken more seriously than in other places. The extent of the uprising in Bulgan was not as substantial as in Üvs. Monasteries in Üvs *aimag* backed an uprising by seven hundred lamas; reports of this incident also indicate that the lamas were armed. See Moses, *Political Role of Mongol Buddhism*, 207.

24. Baabar and Kaplonski, *Twentieth Century Mongolia*, 311.

25. Moses, *Political Role of Mongol Buddhism*, 209.

26. Siklos, *Mongolia Today*, 173.

27. Marko Milivojevic, "The Mongolian People's Army: Military Auxiliary and Political Guardian," in *Mongolia Today*, ed. Shirin Akiner (London: Kegan Paul International Ltd., 1991), 149.

28. Moses, *Political Role of Mongol Buddhism*, 181.

29. Michael Jerryson, interview with Süqbat, 1999, trans. Narangerel (narrative 3 in appendix).

30. "This Little Qural also dealt with the leaders of the rebellion who had been captured in September, 1932. Sixteen of them . . . were tried, and then executed in November, 1933." Moses, *Political Role of Mongol Buddhism*, 229.

31. Brown and Onon, *History of the Mongolian People's Republic*, 284.

32. Bawden, *Modern History of Mongolia*, 352.

33. Brown and Onon, *History of the Mongolian People's Republic*, 326.

34. Moses, *Political Role of Mongol Buddhism*, 238.

35. Brown and Onon, *History of the Mongolian People's Republic*, 316.

36. Milivojevic, *Mongolia Today*, 142.

37. Rupen, *How Mongolia Is Really Ruled*, 40.

38. Murphy, *Soviet Mongolia*, 3.

39. "By the end of 1930 Genden said at the Party First Little Khural that 'within the city there has emerged the view that Leftist Deviation is more harmful than the Rightist threat. I personally do not agree." Brown and Onon, *History of the Mongolian People's Republic*, 278.

40. Cited by Brown and Onon, *History of the Mongolian People's Republic*, 297, from P. Genden, *Namyn Baiguulaguudyn Chuqal Zoriltuud* [Important Goals of Party Organization] (Ulaanbaatar: State Publishing House, 1933), 33.

41. Genden's relationship with Stalin appears to have been tenuous at best. Rumors revolve around an exchange between the two in which on one occasion Genden harassed Stalin and smashed his pipe, thereby sealing his fate. Sandag, *Poisoned Arrows*, 77.

42. The penal code was altered in 1934. "For example, there was ordered punishment ranging from fines to several years in prison for elements who committed such things as putting children under the age of 18 in monasteries." Brown and Onon, *History of the Mongolian People's Republic*, 326.

43. Sandag, *Poisoned Arrows*, 72.

44. Baabar and Kaplonski, *Twentieth Century Mongolia*, 332.

45. Dashpurev and Soni also write, "Genden's refusal to support Stalin's policy of political gains in Mongolia irked the latter much and now he along with his representatives began to search for someone else in Mongolia who could help the Soviet Union in achieving its political aims," *Reign of Terror in Mongolia*, 31–32.

46. She also commented in her interview that the Russians confiscated all photos and materials that they owned before they were sent back to Mongolia. D. Ölziibaatar, interview with Tserendulama and Peljee, 1988, trans. Michael Jerryson and Narangerel (narrative 12 in appendix). Their father and father-in-law, Genden, resigned in 1936. The following year, he was accused of conspiring

with the lamas and Japanese spies. See Brown and Onon, *History of the Mongolian People's Republic*, 813, n. 94.

47. Genden has become a hero to the democratic Mongols: "The founder of the museum [The Political Repression Museum] is G. Tserendulam, a retired school teacher and the daughter of Minister Genden. Genden refused to carry out Stalin's purge policy and accused him of 'Red Imperialism'. After Genden was gone and Choibalsan recruited, the path was clear for the mass execution of thousands." "Lest We Forget: The Genden House is a Quiet Reminder of Mongolia's Quiet Purge," *Mongol Messenger*, November 10, 1999, no.45 (435).

48. See Dashupurev and Soni, *Reign of Terror in Mongolia*, 32, and Murphy, *Soviet Mongolia*, 134.

49. From an interview and a brief biography, there are claims that Choibalsan's father was a fully ordained lama, a *gelen*. D. Ölziibaatar, interview with Tseren Tserendorj, 1988, trans. Michael Jerryson and Narangerel (narrative 13 in appendix).

50. See Akademiia Nauk SSSR, *History of the Mongolian People's Republic*, 522. One might theorize that the lack of further contact with his family and the Mongolian Sangha was an indication of an extremely negative experience that might have caused Choibalsan's later animosity towards Buddhism.

51. Sandag states, "On the eve of the revolution Bodoo was an erudite lama, a teacher in the Russian consulate's translation school in Urga. Choibalsan had studied there, living at times in Bodoo's *ger* (yurt)." *Poisoned Arrows*, 21. See also chapter 4, n. 38 of this volume.

52. There are numerous accounts of Choibalsan's proficiency in the Russian language. However, an interview of Choibalsan's reader, Tsedev Dash, states that: "Choibalsan couldn't write [Russian], but could speak Russian without an interpreter, he could convey his ideas adequately." D. Ölziibaatar, interview with Tsedev Dash, 1988, trans. Michael Jerryson and Narangerel (narrative 14 in appendix).

53. Murphy, *Soviet Mongolia*, 23.

54. Bawden, *Modern History of Mongolia*, 301.

55. Dashpurev and Soni, *Reign of Terror*, 32.

56. D. Ölziibaatar, interview with Erdembileg Gompil, 1992, trans. Michael Jerryson and Narangerel (narrative 10 in appendix).

57. Choibalsan's reader, Tsedev Dash, gave credence to the idea that Choibalsan was drinking from 1928 to 1935. D. Ölziibaatar, interview with Tsedev Dash, 1988, trans. Michael Jerryson and Narangerel (narrative 14 in appendix).

58. D. Ölziibaatar, interview with Tseren Tserendorj, 1988, trans. Michael Jerryson and Narangerel (narrative 13 in appendix).

59. Although the Internal Ministry was arresting lamas prior to this, the height of the Dotood Yaam's notoriety occurs during this period.

60. D. Ölziibaatar, interview with Tseren Tserendorj, 1988, trans. Michael Jerryson and Narangerel (narrative 13 in appendix).

61. Kaplonski, "Thirty Thousand Bullets: Remembering Political Repression in Mongolia," 218.

62. Baabar and Kaplonski, *Twentieth Century Mongolia*, 354.

63. L. Moses, *Political Role of Mongol Buddhism*, 249.

64. D. Ölziibaatar, interview with Tsogt Luvsansamdan, 1988, trans. Michael Jerryson and Narangerel (narrative 15 in appendix).

65. D. Ölziibaatar, interview with Tseren Tserendorj, 1988, trans. Michael Jerryson and Narangerel (narrative 13 in appendix).

66. According to Tsogt Luvsansamdan, this ploy was also used for the lamas at the Gandan monastery and to arrest wealthy high-ranking Mongols. D. Ölziibaatar, interview with Tsogt Luvsansamdan, 1988, trans. Michael Jerryson and Narangerel (narrative 15 in appendix).

67. Bulag writes in detail on the ethno-politics involved in the formations of Mongolian government and argues that "[I]n the discourse of socialist ethnicity, the Halh have an advantageous position, indeed, all other groups in Mongolia have to be defined *via-a-vis* the Halh. This has given rise to, or strengthened, a notion that Halh are the quintessential Mongolia." Bulag, *Nationalism and Hybridity in Mongolia*, 70.

68. Kaplonski, *Truth, History and Politics in Mongolia*, 147.

69. Bulag, *Nationalism and Hybridity in Mongolia*, 84. Bulag does note that religion was the cause for ethnic conflicts. "Ultimately, we shall see the Communists relentlessly destroying some communities like the Buryats and Barga who were tempted by these movements dominated by religious leaders." Ibid., 40.

70. For references to particular accusations, see Rupen, *How Mongolia Is Really Ruled*, 57. Moses states that there is no validity to these charges in *Political Role of Mongol Buddhism*, 214. There are specific examples of this propaganda in Ölziibaatar, Interviews from his dissertation and collection of interviews conducted by Mongols during the rehabilitations in the 1960s, plus visual examples at the Political Repression Museum in Ulaanbaatar.

71. D. Ölziibaatar, interview with Tseren Tserendorj, 1988, trans. Michael Jerryson and Narangerel (narrative 13 in appendix).

72. "Then Choibalsan came along—he was our godfather. He was as honored and respected as the Eighth Bogd Khan had been. We believed and trusted every word he uttered. Songs were written to praise him. We really had no idea

what was going on. Choibalsan announced that there were enemies in Mongolia that were trying to tear down the revolution. He said society should be purged of all counter-revolutionaries, and we believed everything. "My Century . . . Take a Step Back in Time As One of the Mongolia's Most Well Known Writers, Dr. P. Khorloo, Recounts the Twentieth Century Through His Own Eyes," *Mongol Messenger*, November 17, 1999, no. 46 (436).

73. PR-2 [pseud.], interview by Christopher Kaplonski, tape recording, Ulaanbaatar, Mongolia, August 24, 1999.

74. Dashpurev and Soni, *Reign of Terror in Mongolia*, 38.

75. Brown and Onon, *History of the Mongolian People's Republic*, 345.

76. "By the end of 1934 when Genden and Stalin had an official meeting in Moscow, Choibalsan was made the Deputy Prime Minister of Mongolia for which Stalin himself took the initiative. . . . Further, the fatal consequences of the failure of Genden's . . . refusal to support the Soviet policies, brought Choibalsan class to Stalin who discovered on [*sic*] him an alternative to Genden for the fulfillment of his future aims in Mongolia." Dashpurev and Soni, *Reign of Terror in Mongolia*, 33.

77. Milne et. al., *Mongolian People's Republic*, 5.

78. Brown and Onon, *History of the Mongolian People's Republic*, 329.

79. Baabar, writing on the purges of 1937 and 1938, states "But in 1937 through 1938 alone, with Soviet help, 16,631 lamas were persecuted, mostly shot." Baabar and Kaplonski, *Twentieth Century Mongolia*, 363.

80. During this time the Dotood Yaam was known as the Dotoodiik Qamgaalaq Yaam.

81. Butler, *Mongolian Legal System*, 566.

82. For Genden's plot against the radicals, see Dashpurev and Soni, *Reign of Terror*, 28–35. During this period, Mongolian socialists regarded Genden's involvement in the MPRP and his use of the Dotood Yaam as licentious to the party's cause. "Genden separated the Office of Internal Security from the control of the Party and Government, harmfully used it for his own personal interests, and crudely violated revolutionary law." Ibid., 338.

83. Ibid., 42.

84. D. Ölziibaatar, interview with Luvsanchültem Sodov, 1989, trans. Michael Jerryson and Narangerel (narrative 16 in appendix).

85. D. Ölziibaatar, interview with Tsogt Luvsansamdan, 1988, trans. Michael Jerryson and Narangerel (narrative 15 in appendix). A *gavj* is "the rank of a lama who has passed all the *tsanid* examinations." Hangin, *Modern Mongolian-English Dictionary*. A *zurqaich choijin* is an astrologer who goes into trance in

order to predict the future. The *gürtem* are Mongols who are able to connect directly to deities. This class is applicable to both shamans and lamas.

86. Baabar and Kaplonski, *Twentieth Century Mongolia*, 363.

87. The *Mongol Messenger* reports that sometimes the Mongolian guards would take lamas behind the mountain and execute them. "One hundred lamas were taken at a time. If one escaped, the commander in charge could have been arrested or even killed. So, when a lama did manage to get away, the commanders casually picked up any random herder or passerby to substitute for their escaped prisoner." "Lest We Forget: The Genden House is a Quiet Reminder of Mongolia's Quiet Purges," no. 45 (435).

88. Christopher Kaplonski, untitled paper, Ulaanbaatar, Mongolia, September 1999. Unpublished.

89. D. Ölziibaatar, interview with Tsogt Luvsansamdan, 1988, trans. Michael Jerryson and Narangerel (narrative 15 in appendix).

90. Ölziibaatar on August 11, 1999, informed the author that he was in the process of completing his dissertation on the political repression of Mongolia during the end of the socialist era.

91. Michael Jerryson, interview with Zondon Altangerel, 1999, trans. Michael Jerryson and Narangerel (narrative 5 in appendix).

92. D. Ölziibaatar, interview with Rentsendavaa Danzanshagdariin, 1992(?), trans. Michael Jerryson and Narangerel (narrative 11 in appendix).

93. "In September 1937, many black cars gathered in front of the Agricultural Ministry and a great many people came out from this building. All these people were from the army and all them were arrested." D. Ölziibaatar, interview with Tsogt Luvsansamdan, 1988, trans. Michael Jerryson and Narangerel (narrative 15 in appendix). It is important to note that, at this time, Choibalsan was in charge of the Agricultural Ministry.

94. Michael Jerryson, interview with Namuubudaa, 1999, trans. Narangerel (narrative 2 in appendix).

95. Michael Jerryson and Christopher Kaplonski, anonymous interview, 1999 (narrative 8 in appendix).

96. Sandag and Kendall, *Poisoned Arrows*, 121. After the socialist period ended in 1991, rehabilitation hearings were held for the families of those accused of being counter-revolutionaries.

Ginsberg and Ganzorig state that "In 1993 the government enacted a decree authorizing general assistance to families of those who suffered repression. So far this assistance program has provided about 649,200 tugrik to about 150 relatives of victims." Tom Ginsberg and Gombosuren Ganzorig ,"Constitutional

Reform and Human Rights," in *Mongolia in Transition: Old Patterns, New Challenges* ed. Ole Bruun and Ole Odgard (Surrey: Curzon, 1996), 155.

According to an interview conducted by Michael Jerryson and Christopher Kaplonski, one subject reported receiving one million tögrög in 1995. Anonymous interview, 1999 (narrative 8 in appendix). Although the tögrög inflation increased by over 100 percent between 1995 and 2000, this would still not account for the discrepancy.

97. Sandag and Kendall, *Poisoned Arrows*, 121.

98. For more information on Erdembileg's process of his testimony, see D. Ölziibaatar, interview with Erdembileg Gompil, 1992, trans. Michael Jerryson and Narangerel (narrative 10 in appendix).

99. PR-2 [pseud.], interviewed by Christopher Kaplonski, tape recording, Ulaanbaatar, Mongolia, August 24, 1999.

100. Dashpurev and Soni, *Reign of Terror*, 39.

101. Michael Jerryson, interview with Zondon Altangerel, 1999 (narrative 5 in appendix).

102. Translated by Michael Jerryson, June 4, 1999. These numbers differ for each source. The border guard in Kaplonski's interview states that about twenty thousand lamas were killed during the reign of terror. Dashpurev believes that there were many more and states that these inaccuracies are due to inaccessible information. "Although some people have written that 'over 30,800 people fell victim to the arbitrariness and reprisal in 1930's and 1940's.' . . . But O. Zerendorj criticized this figure saying that it is merely an eyewash, because the Mongolian Secret Police [*Dotood Yaam*] till today does not want to unmask the truth and give right figures of those killed to the people. I also agree with him that this figure is not correct." See Dashpurev and Soni, *Reign of Terror*, 44.

103. Jerryson, interview with Yasanjav, 1999, trans. Narangerel (narrative 1 in appendix). Non-Buddhist intellectuals were also targeted by the Green Hats. Shagdariin Sandag recounts his father's and most of his families' arrests by the Green Hats. Sandag's father, like so many other victims of the reign of terror, never returned. Sandag and Kendall, *Poisoned Arrows*, 157–58.

104. This was an effort to limit the influence of Buddhism. The labor camp was a method of removing potential advocates of Buddhism and instilling obedience in them.

105. A Mongol's memories exemplify this preferential treatment: "My mother's brother lived at the Gandan monastery. He was a Gants Lam, the highest rank for a *lam*. When he was arrested, he was about seventy years old. It was 1937. I was with my family, so I did not see him get arrested. At that

time, one of my older brothers lived with him. He was twenty-three years old. My brother was also arrested and spent ten years in a labor camp, and was released." Michael Jerryson and Christopher Kaplonski, anonymous interview, 1999 (narrative 8 in appendix).

106. Murphy, *Soviet Mongolia*, 138.

107. Tsedenbal states that "Lamas who exchanged their monk's robes for a job received material assistance and support. Thanks to this host of measures and the agitation organized by the Party among the masses, the organization of Lamaist clergy ceases to exist in the thirties; the same applies to the monasteries which were abandoned by the lamas . . . it was one of the major victories of the people's revolution." Tsedenbal, *Great October*, 25.

108. Elena Boikova, "Soviet-Mongolian Relations," in *Mongolia in the Twentieth Century: Landlocked Cosmopolitan* (Armonk, NY: M. E. Sharpe, 1999) 118.

109. Baabar notes that the initial difficulty of conscripting Mongols into the army was one of the causes for the religious purges. Baabar and Kaplonski, *Twentieth Century Mongolia*, 383.

110. Ölziibaatar, personal conversation with the author, Ulaanbaatar, August 11, 1999. Ölziibaatar was in the process of completing his dissertation on the political repression of Mongolia during the socialist era. According to Moses, there were thirty-five thousand low-class lamas who were of eligible age for the military by 1938. His estimate that 251 low-ranking lamas remained in 1940 might be optimistic. The only operating monastery by 1940 was Ulaanbaatar's Gandan. See Moses, *Political Role of Mongol Buddhism*, 254.

111. A thousand tögrög in 1999 was equal to one US dollar. Jerryson, interview with Namuubudaa, trans. by Narangerel (narrative 2 in appendix).

112. "There are unconfirmed reports that 233,847 tögrög in cash, 5,916 kilograms of gold, silver and gems, 336,734 livestock and 556 truckloads of copper and bronze wares were confiscated in 1937 alone." Baabar and Kaplonski, *Twentieth Century Mongolia*, 370.

113. The bell and the *damar*, a hand drum, are used in Tibetan and Mongolian Buddhist rituals. D. Ölziibaatar, interview with Rentsendavaa Danzanshagdariin, 1992(?), trans. Michael Jerryson and Narangerel (narrative 11 in appendix).

114. "Setsen Khan Navaanneren," *The Mongol Messenger*, November 17, 1999, no. 8 (450).

115. Brown and Onon, *History of the Mongolian People's Republic*, 335.

116. Siklos, "Mongolian Buddhism," 175.

117. "Lest We Forget: The Genden House Is a Quiet Reminder of Mongolia's Quiet Purge," *The Mongol Messenger*, no. 45 (435).

118. Baabar and Kaplonski, *Twentieth Century Mongolia*, 370.

119. Bawden, *Modern History of Mongolia*, 383.

120. Rupen, *How Mongolia Is Really Ruled*, 67. It is rumored among Mongols that Stalin was worried America might sense the decimation and accuse the MPRP of crimes against humanity.

121. Jerryson, interview with Badan-Qand, 1999, trans. Oyunt (narrative 9 in appendix).

122. Moses, *Political Role of Mongol Buddhism*, 263.

CHAPTER 7

1. The observation that Mongolian religion is now being confined solely to the strictly religious sphere, in contrast to its previous all-pervasive position throughout Mongolian society, was first noted by Ole Bruun and Ole Odgaard in "A Society and Economy in Transition," *Mongolia in Transition: Old Patterns, New Challenges*, ed. Ole Bruun and Ole Odgaard (Surrey: Curzon, 1996), 35.

2. Communism had to fill the void in Mongolian culture that was left by Buddhism. Uradyn Bulag writes, "By destroying this link between religion and Mongol social groups, and by exploiting the differences between groups and separating them, the Communists helped create not only 'class' but also ethnicity." Bulag, *Nationalism and Hybridity in Mongolia*, 40.

3. See chapters 2 and 3 of this volume for a description of the first, second, and third waves.

4. Akademiia Nauk SSSR from the *History of the Mongolian People's Republic*, 510. Concerning the conversion to Cyrillic, Sandag and Kendall criticize the Mongolian intellectual Damdinsuren for assisting in this changeover: "I think Damdinsuren made the biggest mistake of his life when, under pressure from the Communist Party of Mongolia, he actively participated in introducing the Cyrillic alphabet into Mongolia rather than continuing with our old but fine letters, a great legacy from the times of Genghis Khan." Sandag and Kendall, *Poisoned Arrows*, 152.

5. Yeshen-Khorlo Dugarova-Montgomery and Robert Montgomery, "The Buriat Alphabet of Agvan Dorzhiev," *Mongolia in the Twentieth Century: Landlocked Cosmopolitan*, ed. Stephen Kotkin and Bruce A. Elleman (Armonk, NY: M. E. Sharpe, 1999), 79.

6. D. Ölziibaatar, interview with Tsedev Dash, 1988, (narrative 14 in appendix).

7. Dashpurev, *Reign of Terror in Mongolia*, 48.

8. For additional information, see Christopher Atwood, "Sino-Soviet Diplomacy and the Second Partition of Mongolia, 1945–1946," in *Mongolia in the Twentieth Century: Landlocked Cosmopolitan,* ed. Stephen Kotkin and Bruce A. Elleman (Armonk, NY: M. E. Sharpe, 1999).

The weekly Mongol English newspaper, the *Mongol Messenger*, ranked the most influential Mongols of the last century on November 17, 1999, no. 46:436. Also ranked was the Mongol who was most influential during the twentieth century. "Kh. Choibalsan, the Mongolian leader that carried out Stalin's policy of religious and intellectual purge in the 1930s, has been voted 'The Most Historic Figure of the Century.'"

9. D. Ölziibaatar, interview with Tsedev Dash, 1988, trans. Michael Jerryson and Narangerel (narrative 14 in appendix).

10. Kaplonski, "Thirty Thousand Bullets: Remembering Political Repression in Mongolia," 218.

11. Heissig and Samuel, *Religions of Mongolia*, 113.

12. After the coming of democracy, Christopher Atwood's inability to find a shaman or even a Mongol who had met with a shaman, led him to postulate: "Thus, throughout the largest part of Mongolia, shamanism, if it exists, is practiced by a miniscule number of furtive shamans and shamanesses." See Atwood, "Buddhism and Popular Ritual," 122.

13. Humphrey and Onon, *Shamans and Elders*, 338.

14. Bulag, *Nationalism and Hybridity in Mongolia*, 21.

15. By 1960, the major cities in Mongolia were Ulaanbaatar, Darqan, and Erdenet. Dendeviin Badarch, Naidangiin Batsukh, and Sereeteriin Batmunkh, "The Impacts of Industrialization in Mongolia," in *Mongolia Today: Science, Culture, Environment and Development*, ed. Devdeviin Badarch, Naidangiin Batsukh, and Sereeteriin Batmunkh (London: RoutledgeCurzon, 2003), 10.

16. Michael Taussig, *Defacement* (Stanford: Stanford University Press, 1999).

17. Michael Jerryson, interview with Tsendgiin Düsh, 1999, (narrative 6 in appendix).

18. Christopher Kaplonski, trans., "N-214," *Mongol Ulsyn Tov Tuuhin Archiv* 2: 1–7.

19. Humphrey, "Chiefly and Shamanist Landscapes," 158.

20. Bruun, *Precious Steppe*, 150.

21. Humphrey, "Shamanic Practices," 217.

22. Ibid., 159. Christopher Atwood also comments on the limitations of the Mongol nomad in such a situation, stating: "What I do dispute is the view that nomadism as such has any determining influence on the Mongol's

ability or interest in understanding a world religion. Atwood, "Buddhism and Popular Ritual," 123.

23. Michael Jerryson and Christopher Kaplonski, interview with Yasanjav, 1999, (narrative 1 in appendix).

24. David Sneath, "Mobility, Technology and Decollectivization of Pastoralism in Mongolia in *Mongolia in the Twentieth Century: Landlocked Cosmopolitan*, ed. Stephen Kotkin and Bruce A. Elleman (Armonk, NY: M. E. Sharpe, 1999), 233.

25. Michael Jerryson and Christopher Kaplonski, anonymous interview, 1999, (narrative 8 in appendix).

26. Dashpurev, *Reign of Terror in Mongolia*, 54.

27. Ölziibaatar, interview with Tsedev Dash, 1988 (narrative 14 in appendix) and interview with Erdembileg Gompil, 1992 (narrative 10 in appendix).

28. R. Narangerel, "Political Repression During Tsedenbal Period in Mongolia: Broken Ideals and Careers," Conference on Remember and Forgetting: The Political and Social Aftermath of Intense Conflict in Eastern Asia and Northern Europe at Lund University in Lund, Sweden, April 15–17, 1999, 226.

Bulag considers Tsedenbal to be a "de-nationalized man," in the sense that he was not interested in Mongolian nationalism, but instead advocated closer integration with the Soviet Union." Bulag, *Nationalism and Hybridity*, 46.

29. Jerryson, interview with Zondon Altangerel, 1999 (narrative 5 in appendix).

30. Jerryson, interview with Badan-Qand, 1999 (narrative 9 in appendix).

31. Jerryson, interview with Namuubudaa, 1999 (narrative 2 in appendix).

32. Jerryson and Kaponski, interview with Yasanjav, 1999 (narrative 1 in appendix).

33. Secularism offered some form of Buddhist pedagogy. Scholars were able to study Buddhism at an academic level, but this was fairly limiting and restrictive. In his interviews, Mark Juergensmeyer notes that "Bayantsagaan . . . became a research scholar in Buddhist Philosophy for the Institute of Oriental Studies in the state's Academy of Sciences." See Juergensmeyer, *The New Cold War? Religious Nationalism Confronts the Secular State* (Berkeley: University of California Press, 1993), 123.

34. Sneath claims that many elements of the Mongolian pastoral *habitus* pervaded during this period, but he makes no mention of a surviving religious *praxis*. "Pastoralism in Mongolia," 231. However, pastoralism, rather than urban society, may have created an opportunity for nominal Buddhist practices to survive. Bulag notes that urban workers became the ideal models in the Mongolian socialist society, whereas the herdsmen were seen as backward. See Bulag, *Nationalism and Hybridity*, 50.

35. Ölziibaatar personal conversation with the author, August 11, 1999.

36. Jerryson, interview with Zondon Altangerel, 1999 (narrative 5 in appendix).

37. See Rupen, *How Mongolia Is Really Ruled*, 87.

38. "Tsedenbal and his supporters in the MPRP had pursued the Soviet policy of expansionism into the guise of Marxism-Leninism against Tömör-Ochir and his band of 'anti-party group' till the middle of the 1980s. At last, some Tsedenbalist leaders of the MPRP had killed Tömör-Ochir in 1985 with the help of the Mongolian Secret Police—Dotood Yaam." Dashpurev, *Reign of Terror in Mongolia*, 63.

39. Jerryson, interview with Tsendgiin Düsh, 1999 (narrative 6 in appendix).

40. Batbold Baast is a lama at Gandan monastery in Ulaanbaatar, Mongolia. This information was taken from an interview that was conducted by Dharmavision for a series of television programs on Mongolian Buddhism. See Christina Lundberg, "Batbold Baast 174," for Dharma Vision, funded by the Preservation of Mahayana Buddhism, Ulaanbaatar, Mongolia, Summer, 1999.

41. Jagchid and Hyer, *Mongolia's Culture and Society*, 221.

42. Milivojevic, "Mongolian People's Army," 151. One factor for this could be the economic changes taking place. During this time industrialization grew, giving rise to new jobs and new opportunities for Mongol officials. Alicia J. Campi, "Nomadic Cultural Values and Their Influence on Modernization," in *Mongolia in Transition: Old Patterns, New Challenges*, ed. Ole Bruun and Ole Odgaard (Surrey: Curzon, 1996), 100.

43. Ölziibaatar, personal conversation with the author, August 11, 1999.

44. Dashpurev, *Reign of Terror in Mongolia*, 1.

45. Murphy, *Soviet Mongolia*, 204.

46. This was 99 percent of Mongolia's debt, all owed to the Soviet Union. See Bhanuphol Horayangura et al., *Mongolia: A Centrally Planned Economy*, Asian Development Bank (New York: Oxford University Press, 1992), 75.

47. Ram Rahul, *Mongolia between China and the USSR* (New Delhi: Munshiram Manoharial Publishers Pvt. Ltd., 1989), 50.

48. Sneath, "Pastoralism in Mongolia," 229.

49. Morris Rossabi, "Mongolia in the 1990s: from Commissars to Capitalists?" Project on Open Society in Central Eurasia. http://www.eurasianet.org/resource/mongolia/links/rossabi.html (accessed September 10, 2004).

50. Tom Ginsberg, "Nationalism, Elites, and Transformation," in *Mongolia in the Twentieth Century: Landlocked Cosmopolitan*, ed. Stephen Kotkin and Bruce Bruce A. Elleman (Armonk, N.Y.: M. E. Sharpe, 1999), 263.

51. "Undoubtedly, it was Mikhail Gorbachev's drive for 'perestroika' or restruc-

turing of management of the national economy in the Soviet Union and his evident dissatisfaction with the inefficiency of Soviet aid which gave impetus to a similar drive in Mongolia, where restructuring (Öörchön Bayguulalt) had a late start." See Alan K. Sanders, "Restructuring and Openness," in *Mongolia Today*, ed. Shirin Akiner (London: Kegan Paul International), 60.

52. Bulag, *Nationalism and Hybridity in Mongolia*, 16.

53. Christina Lundberg, "Purebat Interview Tape 202," for Dharma Vision, funded by the Preservation of Mahayana Buddhism, Ulaanbaatar, Mongolia, Summer, 1999.

54. "Mongolian Social Democratic Party," *The UB Post*, March 29, 2000, no. 13, 202.

55. No longer under the umbrella of socialism, the Mongolian tögrög has inflated from 40:1 to a 1000:1 ratio to the US dollar. Although Mongols are beginning to understand capitalist ventures, they are still experiencing economic pressures. Elizabeth Endicott explains that one of the causes for the decreasing rate of trade between Mongolia and Russia is Mongolia's difficulty transitioning to a market economy. See Elizabeth Endicott, "Russian Merchants in Mongolia," in *Mongolia in the Twentieth Century: Landlocked Cosmopolitan*, ed. Stephen Kotkin and Bruce Elleman (Armonk: M. E. Sharpe, 1999), 67.

56. Ginsburg, "Nationalism, Elites, and Transformation," 263.

57. Tom Ginsburg and Gombosuren Ganzorig, "Constitutional Reform and Human Rights," in *Mongolia in Transition: Old Patterns, New Challenges* ed. Ole Bruun and Ole Gdgaard (Surrey: Curzon, 1996), 152.

58. Jerryson, interview with Namjil, 1999 (narrative 4 in appendix).

59. Bulag, *Nationalism and Hybridity*, 64.

60. Kaplonski, *Truth, History and Politics in Mongolia*, 67.

61. Juergensmeyer, *New Cold War*, 120–21.

62. Ibid., 123.

63. Bruun, *Precious Steppe*, 152. During the rule of the Ninth Bogd Qaan, at his stop in Qotont Arqangai in 1999, he addressed this issue in a speech which Ole Bruun cites: "After blessing the local area in eloquent wording and expressing wishes for its economic development, he turned to the questions of morality and lifestyle. 'It is wrong to kill animals', he told the herders. 'You should eat less meat'. Some people raised their eyebrows. When he turned to alcohol and stated that 'Mongolian men should drink less and work harder for their country', a surly murmur spread among the men; the women giggled." Ibid.,152–153.

64. In July 1999, a Mongol approached me in Arqangai and tried to sell

me a Tibetan *sutra* that he had kept in his family for generations. He wanted only twenty US dollars.

65. Jerryson, interview with Badan-Qand, 1999 (narrative 9 in appendix).

66. Mongolian law acknowledges the important role of Buddhism, yet respects individual religious preferences. Ginsburg and Ganzorig, "Constitutional Reform and Human Rights," 159.

67. Jerryson, interview with Zondon Altangerel, 1999 (narrative 5 in appendix).

68. Gunjima, a young Buddhist Mongol, is a twenty-two-year-old assistant editor of a Mongolian electronic newspaper. Christina Lundberg, "Gunjima tape No. 173," for Dharma Vision, funded by the Preservation of Mahayana Buddhism, Ulaanbaatar, Mongolia, Summer, 1999.

69. Lundberg, "Batbold Baast 174."

70. "A Religious Renaissance," *The Mongol Messenger,* January 12, 2000, no. 12: 44).

71. On numerous occasions in 1997 and later in 1999 I found that while Mongols do conduct these rituals, they are unaware of any significance they hold.

72. For instance, by jumping lines in the airport or asking for special favors or services in public offices. Some examples are given in chapter 7.

73. Bruun, *Precious Steppe: Mongolian Nomadic Pastoralists in the Age of the Market,* 149.

74. On August 29, 2000, the Dalai Lama announced that he was planning a five-day trip to Mongolia starting September 12, 2000. Unfortunately, this trip was postponed due to strained Chinese-Mongol relations that returned in 2002.

75. "Mongolia: the last frontier Buddhists are battling Christians for market share in post-communist Mongolia," *World Tibet Network News*, December 4, 1999.

76. Ibid.

77. Gandan ex-lama, personal conversation with the author, April, 2003.

78. Jerryson, interview with Namuubudaa, 1999 (narrative 2 in appendix).

79. Bruun, *Precious Steppe*, 166.

80. On July 22, 1999, Bakula Rinpoche and eighteen lamas arrived in Tsetserlig, Arqangai to inaugurate the new head Qamba Lama, a reincarnated lama.

81. Jerryson, interview with Bakula Rinpoche, 1999 (narrative 7 in appendix).

82. See Bruun, *Precious Steppe*, 149.

83. Cheney, "Pre-Revolutionary Culture," 79.

84. Christina Lundberg, "Interview Tape 202."

85. British Broadcast Corporation news, July 2, 2000.

86. Tserenpil, Dandii-Yadam, personal conversation with the author, June 19, 1999.

87. N. Enqbayar and Christopher Kaplonski, trans., "MAHN Itself was the Most Repressed Political Force," *Ünen* (The Truth), (September 12, 2000), no. 168: 1.

88. Jerryson, interview with Bakula Rinpoche, 1999 (narrative 7 in appendix).

APPENDIX

1. A thousand tögrög in 1999 was equal to one US dollar.

2. Altangerel spent fifteen years as curator of the museum and is still the curator.

3. This interview took place at the Ravjaa Museum. The Ravjaa Museum contains a collection of artifacts and belongings of Danzan Ravjaa, a Karma-pa lama who lived from 1803 to 1856. The museum was constructed in 1842 and it has published a book with photographs from the museum and its collections. Ravjaa was famous for trying to unite the two largest schools of Buddhism in Mongolia, dGe-lugs-pa and Karma-pa of the Kagyu.

4. A Red Hat was the common Mongolian designation for the Kagyu Karma-pa sect of Tibetan Buddhism.

5. These were paintings, religious artifacts, books, and other possessions belonging to Ravjaa.

6. Qamba Lama is the lama who is in charge of a monastery, and ranks just below the Bogd Qaan, who is second to the Dalai Lama in Mongolian Buddhism.

7. Dornogov is located at Qamariin Qiid.

8. Gavji in Tibetan means "Refuge Lord."

9. Bakula Rinpoche was India's ambassador to Mongolia. He is a dGe-lugs-pa and appears in the seventh interview and is referred to in the sixth interview.

10. Tibetan lamas tutored these lamas in the summer of 1999.

11. *Süm* is Mongolian for an administrative unit, similar to a county or district, within an *aimag* or province.

12. A pan-Mongolist is one who holds the view that different ethnicities within Central Asia should be consolidated.

13. The term used here is *üür*, a "nest, political party cell, a party's cell," according to Hangin's *Modern Mongolian-English Dictionary*.

14. The Torguud is a Mongolian tribal group.

15. There is a break in the translation. The references are unclear, and the text appears to be jumbled.

16. UB is the common Mongol abbreviation for the capital, Ulaanbaatar.

17. Tsagaan Sar means White Moon, which is the Mongolian New Year, one of the two most important Mongolian holidays, aside from Naadam.

It usually falls in the middle of February, starting on the first day of the full moon.

18. The title Tsorg stands for a doctor.

19. The bell and the *damar*, a hand drum, are used in Tibetan and Mongolian Buddhist rituals.

20. A *del* is a Mongolian robe, used either as a decorative coat or as a protective one.

21. This is in reference to the methods of interrogation used by the Dotood Yaam.

22. A *gelen* is a fully ordained male lama in Mongolia. *Gelenmaa* is the female counterpart, much like that of the Buddhist *bhikkhu*, and *bhikkhuni*, which refers to women who become nuns.

This revolution should not be confused with the socialist revolution. It is implied from the time frame that this was the 1911 revolution.

23. The passage here reads "Myanngan Dzul". *Myanngan* is Mongolian for "one thousand." However, Dzul's definition is "to kindle an offering candle," according to Hangin's *Modern Mongolian-English Dictionary*. However, here I believe it is used to indicate the religious candle used by Buddhists. An example of this is found in The *UB Post*, which reported on May 25, 2000, "108 *zul*, a kind of candle made from butter, were lit by Khamba lamas of major Buddhist monasteries and temples in Ulaanbaatar at the Wrestling Palace on May 18, the holy day of Buddha's birthday . . ."

24. *Gavj* means "the rank of a lama who has passed all the *tsanid* examinations." Hangin, *A Modern Mongolian-English Dictionary*. A *zurqaich choijin* is an astrologer who goes into trance in order to predict the future. The Gürtem are Mongols who are able to connect directly to deities. This class is applicable to both shamans and lamas.

25. In this case it would be the capital.

26. It is unclear from the text if this question was posed by Ölziibaatar or by someone else.

27. A *qainag* is a cross between a yak and a cow.

GLOSSARY

aimag. Province
arats. Lower class people, commoners
ard. People
argal. Dried cow dung
baatar. Hero

Bogd Gegeen. Title of the Mongolian incarnations of Taranatha, the first of whom was Zanabazar, a spiritual leader in Mongolia
Bogd Qaan. The title of the Eighth Bogd Gegeen, the religious and secular head of the state
Bön. Indigenous religion of Tibet, whose practices later assimilated into Tibetan Buddhism
böo. Mongolian shaman
Buriat. A member of an ethnic group in Mongolia, typically located in the eastern region
burkhan. Buddhist icon

cakravartin. Universal emperor
Chinggis Qaan. Ghengis Khan

damar. A hand drum
dGe-lugs-pa. A Tibetan Buddhist school, referred to by Mongols as the Yellow Hat Religion
Del. A Mongolian robe used as decorative or for warmth
Diluv Gegeen Qotagt. High lama from western Mongolia, incarnation of the Indian Bodhisattva Tilopa
Dotood Yaam. Ministry of Internal Affairs, also known as the Green Hats
dzul. Buddhist offering candle

emchi. A doctor

gamin. From the Mandarin term *ko-ming*, is a derogatory term that historically refers to the Chinese forces in Mongolia in the early twentieth century

Gandan. Full name Gandantegchilen, the most famous Buddhist monastery in Mongolia located in the capital of Ulaanbaatar

Gants Lama. The highest rank for a lama

Gavji. Lit., "Refuge Lord"; Buddhist monastic rank or degree for a lama who has passed all the *tsanid* examinations

gelen. A fully ordained Buddhist monk

gelenmaaa. A fully ordained Buddhist nun

Ger. Traditional Mongolian home, *yurt*

Greater Qural. Part of the Mongolian parliament that confirms the cabinet and elects the Prime Minister. *See* Lesser Qural

Iq Qural. Mongolian term for the Greater Qural. *See* Greater Qural

jas. Monastery's treasury or property

Kanjur. Part of the Tibetan Buddhist Canon meaning "translated words," consisting of works purportedly written by the Buddha, the monastic discipline, the *Perfection of Wisdom Sutra*, and other works. *See* Tanjur

Karma-pa. The head of the Kagyu school of Tibetan Buddhism, referred to Mongols as the Red (Hat) Religion

khutukhtu. Classical Mongolian spelling of *qotagt*.

lama jiao. An early designation for Lamaism in the Chinese court, *jiao* is the Mandarin term for "teaching"

lamdré. "Fruits of the path," a doctrine of the Sa-skya-pa school of Tibetan Buddhism derived from Aticha's *A Lamp for the Path*

lamrim. "Stages of the path," a doctrine of the dGe-lugs-pa school of Tibetan Buddhism based on the *Hevajra Tantra*

Lesser Qural. Part of the Mongolian Socialist Parliament, second to the Greater Qural and higher than local qurals. *See* Greater Qural

negdel. A collective

Nogoo Malgai. Mongolian for "Green Hats." This was a dreaded nickname for the Internal Ministry (Dotood Yaam), the Mongolian equivalent to the German Nazi Gestapo

Oirats. An ethnic group in Mongolia, typically from the western region

ongon. Small felt idols

ovoo. Rock cairn; a grouping of stones and religious artifacts used both as a landmark and a shrine

qaan. Emperor, as opposite to *khan*, a smaller king

qainag. A cross between a cow and a yak

Qalqa. The ethnic majority group in Mongolia, typically located in the central region

qamba lama. The head lama of a monastery, an abbot

Qamariin Qiid. A famous monastery in Dorngovi province

Qaraqorum. The political and religious capital of Mongolia during the time of Chinggis Khan

qavrac. Spring

qiid. Mongolian term for a monastic compound

Quuchiin Bichig. Classical Mongolian script

qobilgaan. A person believed to be a reincarnated lama

qoroo. Mongolian term for community

qotagt. A title that means saintly or holy and is reserved for clergy with the most eminent incarnations

Qubilai. Khubilai

qural. A meeting, religious service, or simply congress

qüree. Monastic settlement in the former Mongolia's capital Urga

Sain Noyon Qaan. Great Noble King

Sa-skya-pa. A Tibetan Buddhist school, sometimes referred to as the Red Hat School

shabi. Religious disciple, also referred to as serfs

shabinar. Collective term for the *shabi*

shamanism. Indigenous religious traditions of the Mongols that focuses on ritual over doctrine

süm. A district, an administrative unit within a province, like a county within a state

Tanjur. Part of the Tibetan Buddhist Canon meaning "Translated Treatises", the 224-part volume consists of commentaries and independent works dealing with various subjects. *See* Kanjur

thangka. A religious scroll painting originating in Tibetan Buddhism

tenger. Heaven
tsam. Sacred Buddhist dance
tsorg. Doctor
tsets. Court
Tsorj. "King of Dharma," a monastic title
Torguud. A Mongolian people from the west
Tümed. A Mongolian group hailing from Southern Mongolia, who settled
    in Inner Mongolia
tumet. Court

Urga. "Palace," the former name of the capital of Mongolia

vinaya. Buddhist monastic code of rules

White Guard. Sometimes referred to as the White Army, a renegade Russian
    army led by Ungern-Sternberg that opposed the Bolsheviks in and around
    the time of the Russian Revolution

BIBLIOGRAPHY

Akademiia Nauk SSSR. *History of the Mongolian People's Party*. Moscow: Nauka Publishing House, 1973.

Akiner, Shirin. "Introduction." In *Mongolia Today*, edited by Shirin Akiner. London: Kegan Paul International Ltd., 1991.

———. "Mongolia 1990." In *Mongolia Today*, edited by Shirin Akiner. London: Kegan Paul Internatonal Ltd., 1991.

Allsen, Thomas T. *Mongol Imperialism: The Policies of the Grand Qan Möngke in China, Russia, and the Islamic Islands, 1251–1259*. Berkeley: University of California Press, 1987.

Altangerel, Zondon, and D. Tsagaan. *Ih Gobiin Dogshin Noyon Hutugtu* [The Ferocious Noyon Qotagt of the Great Desert]. Ulaanbaatar: UULS Publishers, 1996.

Atwood, Christopher. "Buddhism and Popular Ritual in Mongolian Religion: A Reexamination of the Fire Cult." *History of Religions* 36, no. 2 (November 1996): 112–39.

———. "Sino-Soviet Diplomacy and the Second Partition of Mongolia, 1945–1946." In *Mongolia in the Twentieth Century: Landlocked Cosmopolitan*, edited by Stephen Kotkin and Bruce A. Elleman. Armonk, NY: M. E. Sharpe, 1999.

Baabar [Bat-Erdene Batbayer], and Christopher Kaplonski, editors. *Twentieth Century Mongolia*. Cambridge: White Horse Press, 1999.

Badarch, Dendeviin, Raymond A. Zilinskas, and Peter K. Balint, editors. *Mongolia Today: Science, Culture, Environment and Development*. London: RoutledgeCurzon, 2003.

Badarch, Dendeviin, Naidangiin Batsukh, and Sereeteriin Batmunkh, editors. "The Impacts of Industrialization in Mongolia." In *Mongolia Today: Science, Culture, Environment and Development*. London: RoutledgeCurzon, 2003.

Bawden, C. R., trans. *The Modern History of Mongolia*. London: Kegan Paul International Ltd., 1989.

———, trans. *Tales of an Old Lama*. Tring, England: The Institute of Buddhist Studies, 1997.

Berger, Patricia, and Terese Tse Bartholomew. *Mongolia, the Legacy of Chinggis Khan*. San Francisco: Thames and Hudson, 1995.

Bergholz, Fred W. *The Partition of the Steppe: The Struggle of the Russians, Manchus, and the Zunghar Mongols for Empire in Central Asia, 1619–1758*. New York: Peter Lang Publishers, 1993.

Bira, Shagdaryn, and John R. Krueger, trans. *Mongolian Historical Writing from 1200 to 1700*. Bellingham: Center for East Asian Studies, Western Washington University, 2002.

Boikova, Elena. "Soviet-Mongolian Relations." In *Mongolia in the Twentieth Century: Landlocked Cosmopolitan*, edited by Stephen Kotkin and Bruce A. Elleman. Armonk, NY: M. E. Sharpe, 1999.

Bold, Bat-Ochir. *Mongolian Nomadic Society: A Reconstruction of the 'Medieval' History of Mongolia*. New York: St. Martin's Press, 2001.

Brown, William A., and Urgunge Onon, trans. *History of the Mongolian People's Republic*. Ed. B. Shirendev and M. Sanjdorj. Cambridge, MA: Harvard University East Asian Research Center, 1976.

Bruun, Ole. *Precious Steppe: Mongolian Nomadic Pastoralists in the Age of the Market*. Lanham, MD: Lexington Books, 2006.

———, and Ole Odgaard, editors. In *Mongolia in Transition: Old Patterns, New Challenges*. Surrey: Curzon, 1996.

———, and Ole Odgaard. "A Society and Economy in Transition." In *Mongolia in Transition: Old Patterns, New Challenges*, edited by Ole Bruun and Ole Odgaard. Surrey: Curzon, 1996.

Bulag, Uradyn E. *Nationalism and Hybridity in Mongolia*. Oxford: Clarendon Press, 1998.

Busto, Rudiger. "A 'Living Buddha' in Asian America: Looking for the Dilowa Gegen Khutukhtu." Paper presented for the panel, Drawing Outside the Lines: Extending the Boundaries of Asian North American Religions at the annual meeting of the American Academy of Religion, Toronto, Canada, November 25, 2002.

Butler, W. E., trans. *The Mongolian Legal System: Contemporary Legislation and Documentation*, London: A. J. Nathanson Marinus Nijhoff Publishers, 1982.

Campi, Alica J. "Nomadic Cultural Values and Their Influence on Modernization." In *Mongolia in Transition: Old Patterns, New Challenges*, edited by Ole Bruun and Ole Odgaard. Surrey, England: Curzon, 1996.

———. "United States Government Perceptions of the Mongols, as Reflected in the US Kalgan Consular Records, 1920–1927." The International Conference on China Border Area Studies, National Chengchi University, Taipei, Taiwan, April 23–30, 1984.

Chang, Jiunn Yih. "A Study of the Relationship between the Mongol Yuan Dynasty and the Tibetan Sa-Skya Sect." PhD. dissertation, Indiana University, 1984.

Cheney, George. "The Pre-Revolutionary Culture of Outer Mongolia." *The Mongolia Society Occasional Papers*, no. 5. Bloomington, Ind.: The Mongolia Society, 1968.

Dashpurev, D., and S. K. Soni. *Reign of Terror in Mongolia: 1920–1990*. New Delhi: South Asian Publishers, 1992.

Dawson, Christopher. *The Mongol Mission*. New York: Sheed and Ward, 1955. Quoted in Larry Moses, *The Political Role of Mongol Buddhism*. Bloomington, IN: Indiana University Publications, 1977, 56.

Dugarova-Montgomery, Yeshen-Khorlo, and Robert Montgomery. "The Buriat Alphabet of Agvan Dorzhiev." In *Mongolia in the Twentieth Century: Landlocked Cosmpolitan*, edited by Stephen Kotkin and Bruce A. Elleman. Armonk, NY: M. E. Sharpe, 1999.

Endicott, Elizabeth. "Russian Merchants in Mongolia." In *Mongolia in the Twentieth Century: Landlocked Cosmopolitan*, edited by Stephen Kotkin and Bruce A. Elleman. Armonk, N.Y.: M. E. Sharpe, 1999.

Evans, Richard J. *In Defense of History*. New York: W. W. Norton & Company, 1999.

Gilberg, Rolf, and Jans-Olof Svantesson. "The Mongols, Their Land and History." In *Mongolia in Transition: Old Patterns, New Challenges*, edited by Ole Bruun and Ole Odgaard. Surrey: Curzon, 1996.

Ginsburg, Tom. "Nationalism, Elites, and Transformation." In *Mongolia in the Twentieth Century: Landlocked Cosmopolitan*, edited by Stephen Kotkin and Bruce A. Elleman. Armonk, NY: M. E. Sharpe, 1999.

———, and Gombosuren Ganzorig. "The Mongols, Their Land and History." *In Mongolia in Transition: Old Patterns, New Challenges*, edited by Ole Bruun and Ole Odgaard. Surrey: Curzon, 1996.

———. "Constitutional Reform and Human Rights," In *Mongolia in Transition: Old Patterns, New Challenges*, edited by Ole Bruun and Ole Odgaard. Surrey: Curzon, 1996.

Hangin, Gombojab. *A Mongolian-English Dictionary*. Bloomington, IN: Indiana University, Research Institute for Inner Asian Studies, 1986.

Harvey, Peter. *An Introduction to Buddhism: Teachings, History and Practices*. Cambridge: Cambridge University Press, 1990.

Heissig, Walther. "A Mongolian source to the Lamaist repression of shamanism in the 17th Century." *Anthropos* 48 (1–2): 1–29.

Heissig, Walther, and Geoffrey Samuel, trans. *The Religions of Mongolia*. Berkeley: University of California Press, 1980.

Horayangura, Bhanuphol, Khaja H. Moinuddin, Pradumna B. Rana, Graham M. Walter. Bruce Murray, Vladimir Bohun, Ivan Ruzicka, and Omar L. Shresta. *Mongolia: A Centrally Planned Economy*. Asian Development Bank. New York: Oxford University Press, 1992.

Hsi, Chen-tuo. "The Visit of Prince Te to the Mongolian People's Republic (December1949–September 1950)—Extracts from the Transcripts of Te Wang's Interrogation After His Return to China." The International Conference on China Border Area Studies, National Chengchi University, Taipei, Taiwan, April 23–30, 1984.

Humphrey, Caroline. "Chiefly and Shamanist Landscapes." In *The Anthropology of Landscape: Perspectives on Place and Space*, edited by Eric Hirsch and Michael O'Hanlon. Oxford: Clarendon Press, 1995.

———. "Shamanic Practices and the State in Northern Asia: Views from the Center and Periphery." In *Shamanism, History, and the State*, edited by Nicholas Thomas and Caroline Humphrey. Ann Arbor: University of Michigan Press, 1994.

Humphrey, Caroline, and Urgunge Onon. *Shamans and Elders*. Oxford: Clarendon Press, 1996.

Jagchid, Sechin, and Paul Hyer. *Mongolia's Culture and Society*. Boulder, CO: Westview Press, 1979.

Jerryson, Michael. Interviews conducted, taped, and translated by Michael Jerryson in Ulaanbaatar, Mongolia, 2000. (*See* appendix).

Juergensmeyer, Mark. *The New Cold War? Religious Nationalism Confronts the Secular State*. Berkeley: University of California Press, 1993.

Kaplonski, Christopher, trans., "N-214." *Mongol Ulsyn Tov Tuuhin Archiv*, 1–7.

———. "Thirty Thousand Bullets: Remembering Political Repression in Mongolia." Paper presented at a conference on Remember and Forgetting: The Political and Social Aftermath of Intense Conflict in Eastern Asia and Northern Europe, Lund, Sweden: Lund University, April 15–17, 1999.

———. *Truth, History and Politics in Mongolia: The Memory of Heroes*. London: RoutledgeCurzon, 2004.

Kotkin, Stephen. "Introduction. In Search of the Mongols and Mongolia: A Multinational Odyssey." In *Mongolia in the Twentieth Century: Landlocked Cosmopolitan*, edited by Stephen Kotkin and Bruce A. Elleman. Armonk, NY: M. E. Sharpe, 1999.

Lattimore, Owen. *The Mongols of Manchuria*. London: Kimble and Bradford, 1935.

———, trans. *Nationalism and Revolution in Mongolia*. New York: Oxford University Press, 1955.

Lee, Robert H. G. *The Manchurian Frontier in Ch'ing History*. Cambridge, Mass.: Harvard University Press, 1970.

Ligaa, Urtnasangiin, and Danzanhuugiin Tsembel. "Medicinal Plants of Mongolia and Their Use in Traditional Medicine." In *Mongolia Today: Science, Culture, Environment and Development*, edited by Dendeviin Badarch, Raymond A. Zilinskas, and Peter J. Balint. London: RoutledgeCurzon, 2003.

Ling, Trevor. "Introduction." In *Buddhist Trends in Southeast Asia*, edited by Trevor Ling. Singapore: Institute of Southeast Asian Studies, 1993.

Lopez, Donald. *Prisoners of Shangri-La: Tibetan Buddhism and the West*. Chicago: University of Chicago Press, 1998.

MAQN-YN *TÜÜ Qin Asoodal* [Questions on the History of the Mongolian People's Revolutionary Party]. Ulaanbaatar, Mongolia: The Mongolian People's Revolutionary Party's Central Committee for Party History Institute, 1971.

Mei-hua Lan. "China's 'New Administration' in Mongolia." In *Mongolia in the Twentieth Century: Landlocked Cosmopolitan* Edited by Stephen Kotkin and Bruce A. Elleman. Armonk, NY: M. E Sharpe, 1999.

Milivojevic, Marko. "The Mongolian People's Army: Military Auxiliary and Political Guardian." In *Mongolia Today*, edited by Shirin Akiner. London: Kegan Paul International Ltd., 1991.

Milne, Elizabeth, John Leimone, Franek Rizwadowski, and Padej Sukachevin. *The Mongolian People's Republic: Toward a Market Economy*. Washington DC: International Monetary Fund, 1991.

Mongolia: *A Centrally Planned Economy*. Asian Development Bank, New York: Oxford University Press, 1992.

Monier-Williams, Sir Monier. *A Sanskrit-English Dictionary*. Delhi: Motilal Banarsidass Publishers, 1999.

Moses, Larry William. *The Political Role of Mongol Buddhism*. Bloomington, IN: Indiana University Publications, 1977.

Murphy, George G. S. *Soviet Mongolia*. Berkeley: University of California Press, 1966.

Nakami, Tatsuo. "Russian Diplomats and Mongol Independence, 1911–1915." In *Mongolia in the Twentieth Century: Londlocked Cosmopolitan*, edited by Stephen Kotkin and Bruce A. Elleman. Armonk, NY: M. E. Sharpe, 1999.

Nansal, R. *MAKb Namaas Namyn Shine Ergeltiin Bodlogyg Bielüülekhin Tölöö Temtsen N' (1932–1934 on)* [The Struggle of the MPRP to Implement the Party's New Turn Policy, 1932–1934]. Ulaanbaarar: State Publishing House, 1958.

Narangerel, R. "Political Repression during Tsedenbal Period in Mongolia: Broken Ideals and Careers." Conference on Remember and Forgetting: The Political and Social Aftermath of Intense Conflict in Eastern Asia and Northern Europe. Lund, Sweden: Lund University, April 15–17, 1999.

Oberoi, Harjot. *The Construction of Religious Boundaries: Culture, Identity and Diversity in the Sikh Tradition.* Delhi: Oxford University Press, 1997.

O'Donnell, Linda. "Mongolia: The Last Frontier Buddhists Are Battling Christians for Market Share in Post-Communist Mongolia." *World Tibet Network News,* December 4, 1999.

Onon, Urgunge, ed. *Mongolian Heroes of the Twentieth Century.* New York: AMS Press Inc., 1976.

Onon, Urgunge, and Derrick Pritchatt. *Asia's First Modern Revolution: Mongolia Proclaims Its Independence in 1911.* Leiden: E. J. Brill, 1989.

Petech, Luciano. *Central Tibet and the Mongols: The Yuan–Sa-skya Period of Tibetan History.* Rome: Istituto Italiano Per Il Medio Ed Estremo Oriente, 1990.

Pozdneev, Aleksei Matveevich. *Mongolia and the Mongols.* Bloomington, IN: Indiana University, 1971.

Purevjav, S., and D. Dashjamts. *BNAU-d Sum Qiid, Lamasyn Asuudlyg Shiid-verlesenN', 1921–1940* [How the Question of the Lamas and Monasteries was Resolved in the MPR, 1921–1940]. Ulaanbaatar: State Publishing House, 1965. Quoted in Larry Moses, *The Political Role of Mongolian Buddhism.*

Rahul, Ram. *Mongolia between China and the USSR.* New Delhi: Munshiram Manoharial Publishers, 1989.

Rerikh, Yu. N. "Mongol-Tibetan Relations in the 13th and 14th Centuries." Translated by Jan Nattier. *The Tibet Society Bulletin* 6 (1973): 40–55.

Rossabi, Morris, ed. *China Among Equals.* Berkeley: University of California Press, 1983.

———. *Khubilai Khan: His Life and Times.* Berkeley: University of California Press, 1988.

Rupen, Robert. *How Mongolia is Really Ruled: A Political History of the Mongolian People's Republic 1900-1978.* Stanford, CA.: Hoover Institution Press, 1979.

———. *The Mongolian People's Republic.* Stanford, CA: Hoover Institution Studies, 1966.

Samuel, Geoffrey. *Civilized Shamans: Buddhism in Tibetan Societies.* Washington: Smithsonian Institution Press, 1993.

Sandag, Shagdariin, and Harry H. Kendall. *Poisoned Arrows: The Stalin-Choibalsan Mongolian Massacres, 1921–1941.* Boulder, CO: Westview Press, 2000.

Sanders Alan K, *The People's Republic of Mongolia*. New York: Oxford University Press, 1968.

———. "Restructuring and Openness," In *Mongolia Today*, edited by Shirin Akiner. London: Kegan Paul International Ltd., 1991.

Serruys, Henry. *The Mongols and Ming China: Customs and History*. London: Variorum Reprints, 1987.

Siklos, B. "Mongolian Buddhism: A Defensive Account." In *Mongolia Today*, edited by Shirin Akiner. London: Kegan Paul International Ltd., 1991.

Smith, Jonathan Z. *To Take Place: Towards Theory in Ritual*. Chicago: University of Chicago Press, 1987.

Smith, Warren W., Jr. *Tibetan Nation: History of Tibetan Nationalism and Sino-Tibetan Relations*. Boulder, CO: Westview Press, 1996.

Sneath, David. "Pastorialism in Mongolia." In *Mongolia in the Twentieth Century: Landlocked Cosmopolitan*, edited by Stephen Kotkin and Bruce A. Elleman. Armonk, NY: M. E. Sharpe, 1999.

Tambiah, Stanley. *The Buddhist Conception of Universal King and Its Manifestations in South and Southeast Asia*. Kuala Lumpur: University of Malaya, 1987.

Taussig, Michael. *Defacement*. Stanford: Stanford University Press, 1999.

Todbaatar, D. "Mongol ulsyn ayuulgui baidlyg hangah baiguullagyn uil ajillagaany ehen ueiin tuuhiin asuudald 1922–1930" [The Early Historical Functions of the Institution in order to Insure the Safety of Mongolia, 1922–1930]. PhD dissertation, Academy of Sciences, the Institute of History, Ulaanbaatar, Mongolia, 1999.

Trainor, Kevin. *Relics, Ritual and Representation in Buddhism: Rematerializing the Sri Lankan Theravada Traditions*. Cambridge: Cambridge University Press, 1997.

Tsedenbal, Yumjagiin. *Great October and The Peoples of the East*. Ulaanbaatar, Mongolia: State Publishing House, 1981.

Tsultem, N. *Mongolian Sculpture*. Ulaanbaatar, Mongolia: State Publishing House, 1989.

———. *Mongol Zurag* [Mongolian Pictures]. Ulaanbaatar, Mongolia: State Publishing House, 1986.

UNESCO. *Cultural Policy in the Mongolian People's Republic*. Mongolian National Commission for Paris, 1982.

Wylie, Turrell V. "The First Mongol Conquest of Tibet Reinterpreted," *Harvard Journal of Asiatic Studies,* 37, no. 1 (June 1977): 103–33.

Zickel, Raymond E., ed. *Soviet Union: A Country Study*. Washington DC: Federal Research Division Library of Congress, 1989.

OTHER SOURCES
(Interviews, Internet Essays)

Jerryson, Michael. Interviews conducted, taped, and translated by Michael Jerryson in Ulaanbaatar, Mongolia, 2000. (*See* appendix.)

Kaplonski, Christopher. "Untitled," Ulaanbaatar, Mongolia, September 1999.

Lonely Planet. *Mongolia* [online]. Lonely Planet World Guide [cited on 1 September, 2004]. Available from World Wide Web: http://www.lonelyplanet.com/destinations/north_east_asia/mongolia/

Lundberg, Christina. "Tape 172 Ganden Abbot," for Dharma Vision, funded by the Preservation of Mahayana Buddhism, Ulaanbaatar, Mongolia, summer of 1999.

———. "Batbold Baast 174," for Dharma Vision, funded by the Preservation of Mahayana Buddhism, Ulaanbaatar, Mongolia, summer of 1999.

———. "Purebat Interview Tape 202," for Dharma Vision, funded by the Preservation of Mahayana Buddhism, Ulaanbaatar, Mongolia, summer of 1999.

———. "Gunjima tape 173," for Dharma Vision, funded by the Preservation of Mahayana Buddhism, Ulaanbaatar, Mongolia, summer of 1999.

Ölziibaatar, Dembereliin. Interviews from his dissertation and collection of interviews conducted by Mongols during the rehabilitations in the 1960s. Ulaanbaatar, Mongolia, 2000. Trans. Michael Jerryson and Narangerel. (*See* appendix.)

Rossabi, Morris. *Mongolia in the 1990s: from Commissars to Capitalists?* [online]. Project on Open Society in Central Eurasia [cited on 10 September, 2004]. Available from World Wide Web: http://www.eurasianet.org/resource/mongolia/links/rossabi.html.

Yamamoto, J. Isamu. *Tibetan Buddhists: Exiled from Their Homeland, Extolled in the West* [online]. Christian Research Institute, 1994 [cited on 10 April, 2003]. Available from World Wide Web: http://www.summit.org/Resources/BuddhismFour.html.

Youso, K. *Introduction to the Mongolian Art Exhibition* [online]. Asian Art Museum, 2000 [cited on 5 September, 2003]. Available from World Wide Web: http://asianart.com/mongolia/intro.html.

INDEX

www.ingramcontent.com/pod-product-compliance
Ingram Content Group UK Ltd.
Pitfield, Milton Keynes, MK11 3LW, UK
UKHW042059250325
456722UK00002B/199